REINHOLD BOOKS IN THE BIOLOGICAL SCIENCES

Consulting Editor:
Professor Peter Gray

Department of Biological Sciences
University of Pittsburgh
Pittsburgh, Pennsylvania

Manual of INSECT MORPHOLOGY

CONSULTING EDITOR'S STATEMENT

I am happy to welcome DuPorte's Manual of Insect Morphology to the Reinhold Books in the Biological Sciences. Morphology is not so popular today as some other areas of biology, though it is difficult to see on what other basis biology could have been built or can continue to grow. Here is morphology at its best, clearly presented and logically developed from a lifetime of experience in teaching. Well-labeled diagrams and clear definitions help the student to acquire the basic vocabulary of anatomical terms so necessary to a student of entomology. This is one of those textbooks which is written to supplement, not to replace, the teacher. It may be fitted into any course since each chapter is complete in itself. There are suggestions to students as to what they might profitably draw, but these drawings are never repeated as illustrations in the book. The student, in fact, is encouraged to use the book as an aid and inspiration to learning—not as a substitute for it.

Pittsburgh, Pennsylvania   Peter Gray
January, 1961

Manual of INSECT MORPHOLOGY

E. MELVILLE DuPORTE

Professor of Entomology
Macdonald College, McGill University
Quebec, Canada

REINHOLD PUBLISHING CORPORATION
NEW YORK

Chapman & Hall, Ltd., London

Copyright 1959 by
REINHOLD PUBLISHING CORPORATION

Third Printing, 1964

Library of Congress Catalog Card Number: 59-9915

Printed in the United States of America
THE GUINN CO., INC.
New York 14, N. Y.

To my students, past and present

Preface

THIS MANUAL is the final revision of the typescript text used by the author over a period of some forty years. There have been two principal objectives in the arrangement of the text, in the selection of material to be studied and in the detail in which the directions are given. One is that the student working through the manual should acquire a reasonably balanced foundation in the elements of insect morphology. The other is to enable the student to work intelligently with a minimum of assistance from the instructor. Furthermore, the text is so arranged that an instructor can select those exercises that best fit into the length and nature of his course and still give a reasonably good cross section of the subject. My own procedure with undergraduate students is to assign certain exercises for which accurate drawings are required and some others for which semidiagrammatic drawings will be accepted. The students are advised to make the observations requested in the remaining exercises but are not required to submit drawings, though they are encouraged to make as many as their time permits.

The examples cited are those actually used in my own classes. For the most part they, or closely related species, are widely distributed and easily obtained. Most of them are also available from dealers in biological supplies. Where a different related species is used, the student will, of course, expect to find minor, but unimportant, divergencies from the descriptions given in the text. In almost every case where a specific example is given for histological study a number of other species can be substituted.

The drawings included in the manual are all schematic. They are intended as a guide to the student and none of them is an exact representation of any known insect.

The interest of the student in laboratory work is sharpened if he has some previous knowledge of the origin, development, modifications and functions of the organs he is studying. It is hoped that the summaries given at the beginning of each section will stimulate his interest and help him to work more intelligently.

Lists of questions, usually appearing in a manual of this kind, have been purposely omitted because the instructor should be in a better position than the author to frame questions which are stimulating and thought-provoking to the group with which he is working.

I wish to acknowledge gratefully the very careful attention which my secretary, Miss Bessie Robinson, has given to the typing of this and earlier revisions of the text over a number of years.

E. Melville DuPorte

April, 1959
Quebec, Canada

Table of Contents

Preface   vii

List of Illustrations   xi

INTRODUCTION   *1*

1   TAGMATA, SEGMENTS, SCLERITES AND SUTURES   *8*

2   SEGMENTATION   *11*

3   PRELIMINARY STUDY OF THE EXTERNAL STRUCTURE
OF AN INSECT   *14*

4   THE ABDOMINAL SEGMENTS   *20*
General considerations. Structure of the abdomen.
Muscles of the abdominal body wall.

5   THE THORACIC SEGMENTS   *32*
General considerations. Tergum. Pleuron.
Sternum. Thorax of a specialized insect.

6   THE WINGS   *55*
General considerations. Topography. Articulation.
Modifications in structure.

7   ABDOMINAL APPENDAGES AND THORACIC LEGS   *63*
General considerations. Abdominal appendages.
Thoracic appendages. Functional modifications
of legs. Some muscles of the leg.

8   EXTERNAL FEMALE GENITALIA   *75*
General considerations. Ovipositor.

9   EXTERNAL MALE GENITALIA   *82*
General considerations. Penis and associated structures.

10   THE HEAD   *93*
General considerations. Frontoparietal or facial region.
Occipital region. Ventral region of the prognathous head.
Tentorium. Compound eyes. Antennae.

11   MANDIBULATE MOUTHPARTS   *120*
          General considerations. Labrum and epipharynx.
          Hypopharynx. Mandibles. Maxillae. Labium.

12   SUCTORIAL MOUTHPARTS   *133*
          Structure of some common examples.

13   THE INTEGUMENT   *143*
          General considerations. Histology. Moulting.
          Tanning of the cuticle. Integumental armature.

14   THE ALIMENTARY SYSTEM AND MALPIGHIAN TUBULES   *150*
          General considerations. Cibarium and pharynx.
          Digestive tract, Malpighian tubules and labial glands.
          Histology of stomodaeum, mesenteron, proctodaeum
          and Malpighian tubules.

15   THE RESPIRATORY SYSTEM   *169*
          General considerations. Spiracles. Tracheae (and
          prothoracic gland). Tracheal and spiracular gills.
          Histology of the trachea.

16   THE CIRCULATORY SYSTEM AND ASSOCIATED ORGANS   *176*
          General considerations. Dorsal vessel and diaphragms.
          Hemocytes. Fat body. Oenocytes. Photogenic organs.

17   THE REPRODUCTIVE SYSTEM   *184*
          General considerations. Genital organs of
          the female. Genital organs of the male.

18   THE NERVOUS SYSTEM AND THE RETROCEREBRAL
      INCRETORY GLANDS   *200*
          General considerations. Generalized central nervous
          system. Concentration of the trunk ganglia. Ganglia
          and incretory glands of the head; stomatogastric
          system. Histology of the brain and optic ganglia.

19   THE SENSE ORGANS   *215*
          General considerations. A mechanical receptor.
          A chemical receptor. The compound eye.

Bibliography   *219*

Index   *221*

List of
Illustrations

FIGURE

1   Lateral view of the abdomen of a generalized insect   *21*

2   Internal aspect of the mesonotum when the forewings
     are the more powerful in flight   *33*

3   Internal aspect of the mesopleuron and mesosternum   *40*

4   Some stages in the evolution of the mesosternum   *45*

5   Hypothetical primitive wing venation   *57*

6   Lateral view of (a) hypothetical primitive head
     and (b) head of a generalized pterygote insect   *94*

7   Internal aspect of faces of (a) generalized
     and (b) specialized insects   *96*

8   Posterior aspect of the hypognathous head   *99*

9   Prognathous heads   *114, 115*

10   The positions and relationships of the
     principal internal organs   *152*

11   Female reproductive system   *186*

12   Male reproductive system   *189*

13   Neurons   *203*

14   Structure of the brain and optic ganglion   *206*

Introduction

Broadly speaking, morphology deals with the study of form and structure; but more specifically it may be defined as the zoological science concerned with the evolution of structure in the species, with the development of structure in the individual and with the causal factors underlying these phenomena. This definition is more inclusive than that usually given, but is in the author's opinion a legitimate one.

From this definition it is evident that the morphologist is concerned not merely with the study of the anatomy of an animal, but seeks also to trace the evolution of form in each organ or part from that of more generalized species, those nearer the ancestral stem of the group. This is the only aspect of morphology treated in this manual. An attempt is made first to determine the generalized structure of an organ, then to study the modified structure in more highly specialized species and to trace, where possible, the successive changes leading up to these modifications. In this way it is hoped that the student will obtain sufficient knowledge of the fundamental structure of insects to guide him in his interpretation of the structure and relationships of those insects with which he will be concerned in his later work.

LABORATORY WORK

Laboratory work in insect morphology is important, not only because of its pedagogic value, but also because it is an essential part of the professional training of the entomologist. The minute, careful and accurate, perhaps at times even tedious, observations called for in the text, and the recording of these observations by drawings, are a necessary introduction to the later

1

work of the morphologist and taxonomist and, to a considerable extent, of the physiologist and economic entomologist.

The student is therefore expected to approach his laboratory work in much the same spirit that he approaches a research problem. His observations should be as exact and his drawings as accurate and neat as if they were intended for publication.

APPARATUS

Apart from a binocular dissecting microscope and a strong microscope lamp, the apparatus required is simple and inexpensive. The student should supply himself with the instruments listed below.

Dissecting tray. This may be made from a Petri dish about 3 to 4 inches in diameter and about one inch in depth. Any other metal, glass or plastic dish of similar dimensions may be used. Melted beeswax or paraffin, or a mixture of the two, should be poured into the dish to a depth of approximately ¼ inch and the dish set to cool on a level surface.

Scissors. These must have fine points and may be angled or straight. The author prefers straight scissors manipulated by the first and second fingers. Surgeons' cataract scissors are a good type and certain kinds of spring scissors are satisfactory and easy to use. For internal dissection, the points may need to be sharpened. This should be done on a fine whetstone and checked under the dissecting microscope to make sure that the points engage perfectly.

Forceps. These also may be straight or curved. Their points should be very fine for internal dissection, and it may be necessary to sharpen them in the same way as described for scissors.

Dissecting needles. At least one pair each of fairly strong and very fine needles are necessary. The heavier needles may be purchased but both kinds can be made easily by the student from insect pins of different sizes. The heads are cut off and the pin is held either in a needle holder with an adjustable chuck or in a wooden handle whittled by the student. The tips of the needles, especially if used for internal dissection, should be bent to form a small hook.

Scalpels. Fine scalpels are sometimes necessary. Kennedy describes an efficient and inexpensive type made by breaking out conchoidal chips from the edge of a safety razor blade with a pair of pliers. One end of the chip is fastened into the end of a piece of glass rod with DeKhotinsky cement, or it may be fixed firmly by some means into a wooden handle.

Specimen holder. For study of external structures some device for orientating the specimen under the microscope is necessary. The simplest is a cork angle made by fastening two rectangular pieces of cork at right angles to each other by means of insect pins. It is often more advantageous, however, to pin the specimen in the dissecting tray and examine it under water.

Insect pins (nonrusting). These are used to pin specimens in a tray. A pair of cutting pliers should be available to cut off projecting portions of the pins which might interfere with the manipulation of the dissecting instruments.

Drawing materials. The student should supply himself with drawing paper of good quality which will take ink, hard pencils, erasers, rulers, dividers and other drawing instruments.

DRAWING

The drawing required in this course has a threefold object. (1) It assists the student in seeing many details of structure which would otherwise escape his observation. There is much truth in the statement that "the eye of the naturalist is in the point of his pencil." (2) It assists the instructor in estimating the progress being made by the student and in discovering his difficulties. (3) In all fields of entomological work the ability to make simple but accurate drawings is part of the necessary equipment of the worker. Anyone who has read descriptions of insects, whether from the standpoint of the anatomist, the taxonomist or the economic entomologist, knows the value of good illustrations. The determination of species often depends on the recognition of very small constant differences in structure, a verbal description of which needs to be supplemented by accurate figures. The making of careful and accurate drawings is, therefore, in itself, a part of the training of the entomologist.

While some knowledge of the principles of drawing is desirable, it is not essential. Accuracy in portraying detail is the chief requirement and the student without previous training will soon learn to make the kind of drawing required in this course. Simple line drawings are all that are required, each line representing some definite structural feature. The lines should be bold and definite, drawn with a moderately hard pencil and inked in with India ink after the drawings have been approved by the instructor. A student who is good at drawing is permitted to shade in order to show contours or perspective if he so desires, but the shading should never in any way obscure the structure. Shading is not required in drawings of external structures except to differentiate between sclerites, membranes and cut surfaces. Sclerites should be left unshaded, membranes should be stippled and cut surfaces, such for example as the area exposed by removal of a leg or antenna, should be shaded by fine oblique parallel lines. In drawings of internal structures, in which organs may be confused, it may be advisable to differentiate by simple shading.

Shallow depressions, grooves and eminences in a sclerite do not need to be shown unless they have some special significance and, generally speaking, it is not necessary to draw setae, unless their arrangement is especially characteristic of some organ. Sutures should be represented by a single line and internal ridges by two parallel lines.

Students are advised to study the drawings in the textbook or other writings of Snodgrass, as well as the work of other competent entomological illustrators.

The drawings should show a true outline of the insect or structure represented, all parts being drawn in their true proportions and proper spatial relations. To this end frequent use should be made of ruler, dividers or micrometer eyepiece in order to keep a uniform scale throughout the drawings.

The scale of drawing should be large enough to show all details clearly and to prevent crowding of either the structures or the lettering.

It is well to follow some uniform convention in the orientation of the drawings. Lateral views of the insect or its parts should be drawn with the dorsal side toward the top of the page and the head toward the left. Thus in drawing an external view of the thorax, the left side should be drawn, but in drawing an internal view of the lateral thoracic wall, the right side should be drawn. This makes it easier to compare the two drawings. Dorsal or ventral aspects should be drawn with the head toward the top of the page and drawings of the head should have the mouthparts pointing downward. All appendages should be drawn from the same side and the same aspect.

Labeling should be done neatly and uniformly. The student should acquaint himself with some suitable style of lettering and use this uniformly in his work. In naming parts, if the name cannot be written in full, use abbreviations in preference to key-letters or numbers. Names may be written directly on the drawings when this can be done without sacrifice of neatness or clearness. Guide lines should not be crowded together so as to obscure any part of a drawing.

In preparing drawings for reproduction, the original figures should be at least twice the size of the reproduction, preferably larger. Slight unevennesses in the original are smoothed out in the reduced figures. The lines, of course, should be correspondingly thicker and the lettering larger. Students may be required to make at least one such drawing in the course of their work.

DISSECTION

Except in very small insects most of the external features can be seen if the specimen is properly orientated with the aid of a cork angle or similar device and examined under the binocular microscope. Manipulation and dissection to expose concealed parts are of course necessary. Dry, brittle insects can be made more pliable by bringing to the boiling point in water or 5 per cent potassium hydroxide. Sometimes external structures will stand out more clearly if the specimen is pinned under water in a dissecting tray, and when it is necessary to dissect out structures this method should always be used. If the region studied is boiled for a few minutes in 10 per cent potassium hydroxide to remove soft tissues and then examined under water, sutures, sclerites and other cuticular features often stand out more clearly; it is generally desirable to use this method to supplement the study of the untreated specimen.

Except for very minute insects the internal structures are best studied by opening the insect, pinning in a dissecting tray, flooding completely with water and examining under the binocular dissecting microscope. A source of strong illumination is necessary. In dissection, cutting with scalpel or scissors should be avoided except when absolutely necessary. The most useful tools are the forceps and needles. Minute specimens are sometimes best dissected in a drop of glycerine, and occasionally clearing such specimens in cedar oil or other clearing agent will make certain structures more evident. More detailed instructions for dissecting are given in the appropriate places.

Freshly killed specimens are preferable for the study of most of the internal organs, but, since few living insects can be made available during the winter, preserved material must be used. For preservation the insect should first be fixed (in the histological sense) and then preserved in alcohol. For a fixative the author uses picroformol prepared according to the Dubosq-Brazil formula:

Picric acid, 2 gm	} 10 parts
80% alcohol, 300 cc	
Formalin	4 parts
Acetic acid	1 part

This is injected into the insect with a hypodermic needle until the specimen becomes fully distended. Care must be taken to inject the fluid into the body cavity and not into the gut. The specimens are left in picroformol for 24 to 48 hours, depending on the size, and then preserved in 70 per cent alcohol. The organs thus preserved tend to become hard and brittle, but placing the insect for a few minutes in warm water usually makes them more flexible.

5

Some Important Anatomic Terms

In order to read the directions intelligently the student should know the meanings of the following terms. Terms of direction and position do not necessarily indicate that the structure to which they are applied lies near or nearer the part suggested by the term. They mean that the structure lies *in the direction* taken by a particle moving from the center of the body toward and continuing beyond, the part in question. Thus "cephalic" relates to the *cephalon* or head but the second segment of an antenna which projects anteriorly beyond the head is cephalic to (or cephalad of) the first segment, although it is farther away from the head.

Anterior refers to the forward or head end of the animal. In some insects the anterior end of the body is formed by the mouthparts, in others by the vertex, the mouthparts being directed ventrally or even posteriorly.

Caudad, posteriorly; in the direction of the posterior or "tail" end. *Caudad of* = posterior to.

Caudal, pertaining to the posterior or "tail" end.

Cephalad, anteriorly; in the direction of the head.

Cephalic, pertaining to the head; anterior.

Distad, toward the distal end.

Distal, refers to the free end of a part or appendage, or the end furthest away from the point of attachment.

Dorsad, dorsally; toward the dorsum or back.

Dorsal, pertaining to the dorsum or back.

Dorsum, the entire back region or upper portion of an insect; may also be used for the back of a single segment.

Ectad, toward the outer surface. Used to indicate the relative position of internal structures.

Ectal, pertaining to the outer surface.

Entad, toward the inside, i.e., the long axis.

Ental, pertaining to the inside of the body.

Laterad, toward the sides (right or left).

Lateral, pertaining to the sides.

Mesad, toward the meson.

Mesal, pertaining to the meson.

Meson, the sagittal plane dividing the insect into right and left halves.

Metamere, a primary segment, which in the embryo usually contains a pair of coelomic sacs.

Notum = tergum.

Pleural region, the lateral or ventrolateral parts of the body or of a seg-

6

ment, where the legs, when present, are found.

Pleurite, a sclerotized subdivision of the pleuron; small plates in the membranous pleural region.

Pleuron, the lateral sclerotized wall of a segment (usually thoracic), formed by the incorporation of a portion of the limb base into the pleural region.

Segment, one of the linear series of rings into which the body is divided. A body segment may be *primary,* in which case the term is synonymous with *metamere,* or it may be *secondary* having its definitive limits different from those of the embryonic segment. Used also for the divisions of an appendage such as the leg or antenna.

Sternite, a sclerotized subdivision of the sternum.

Sternum, the ventral sclerotized plate or plates of a body segment.

Tergite, a sclerotized subdivision of the tergum.

Tergum, the dorsal sclerotized plate or plates of a body segment.

Venter, the entire undersurface of the body; may be also used for the lower surface of a single segment. Not to be confused with *sternum* which refers to the sclerotized plates of the venter.

Ventrad, toward the venter.

Ventral, pertaining to the venter.

1 Tagmata, Segments, Sclerites and Sutures

TAGMATA

Melanoplus sp. (or other grasshopper)

Examine the insect and note that it is made up of three distinct regions or *tagmata.* The anterior tagma is the *head,* and it bears the eyes, the antennae, the jaws and other mouthparts. The middle tagma is the *thorax* which bears three pairs of legs and two pairs of wings. The posterior tagma, the *abdomen,* bears no appendages apart from the genital apparatus and a pair of minute processes (cerci) near the free end.

SEGMENTS

Corydalis cornuta (larva)
or other soft-bodied larva

Note that the trunk is distinctly divided into a number of segments or *metameres,* separated from each other by intersegmental grooves. The three anterior segments, each with a pair of legs, constitute the thorax. The most anterior segment is the *prothorax,* the middle one the *mesothorax* and the posterior one the *metathorax.* The remaining segments constitute the abdomen. The outer covering of an insect is known as the *cuticle.* Note that the cuticle on the thoracic segments is for the most part hard with considerable rigidity. Such cuticle is said to be "sclerotized." That of the abdomen, on the other hand, is for the most part soft and flexible. It is said to be "membranous" or "unsclerotized."

Note that the lateral regions of each abdominal segment in *Corydalis,* except the last, are expanded to form large tubercles which bear a tapering filament or *stylus* laterally and *gills* ventrally. These tubercles are regarded by some authors as the vestiges of abdominal limbs. This is doubtful although they do occupy the same positions as would the limb bases if these were present. They divide the segment into four regions: (a) a *dorsal region,* bearing a spiracle on each of its lateral margins, just dorsal to the "limb base"; (b) a *ventral region* between the "limb bases" on the ventral side, (c) two *pleural regions* occupied almost completely by the "limb bases."

Melanoplus

Note that the abdominal segments are distinct, but differ from those of *Corydalis* in that they are sclerotized. Each sclerotized abdominal plate is separated from that of the next segment by an unsclerotized intersegmental membrane or *conjunctiva.*

Note that the prothorax, which bears legs but not wings, is distinct and freely movable on the mesothorax. The mesothorax and metathorax, however, are closely united with no intersegmental membrane between them. This close association is always found in insects with functional wings. Because it bears the wings the united structure is sometimes referred to as the *pterothorax.*

The head also consists of several segments but these are so completely united that their limits cannot be determined.

SCLERITES AND SUTURES

Melanoplus

Examine the lateral sides of the wing-bearing region of the thorax and note that each consists of several hardened or *sclerotized* plates separated from each other by impressed lines or grooves. These grooves mark inflections or infoldings of the integument and their position is marked on the inner surface by a corresponding ridge. The grooves are known as *sutures* and the hardened plates which they define are *sclerites.*

The term *suture* (literally, a seam) is used in entomology to designate any line which defines the limits of two united or closely adjacent sclerites, but the structures so designated may differ morphologically. Grooves such as those in the thorax of *Melanoplus* are distinguished as *sulci* (sing. *sulcus).* Occasionally sclerites are separated by a very narrow strip of unsclerotized cuticle having the appearance of a pale line. These may be called line sutures or *lineae.*

9

The cuticle of insects and all other arthropods contains a horny substance known as "chitin," and because of a mistaken idea that the hardening of the cuticle was associated with heavy deposition of chitin, the hard parts were said to be "chitinized." This term which occurs widely in the early literature is now displaced by the more accurate term "sclerotized."

Insects are very active animals and require a skeleton which is at once light and rigid. The hard exocuticle is relatively thin, light and—except in some forms such as the beetles—more or less flexible. Rigidity is provided by the development of internal struts and ridges at points where much muscular force is exerted, such as the articulations of the appendages.

The ridges are formed by inflection or infolding of the integument, therefore they are marked externally by grooves or sulci. Consequently, most of the sutures mark the positions of functional strengthening ridges and have no relation to segmentation. Nevertheless these sutures and the sclerites which they limit are fundamental features in the topographical anatomy of insects and much of external anatomy is concerned with their presence and absence. The more constant sutures and sclerites bear distinctive names.

2 Segmentation

PRIMARY SEGMENTATION
Protoparce (larva)

Examine a sphinx caterpillar or any other smooth soft-bodied larva. Note the absence of sclerites on the trunk, except for small scattered plates in some species. Each segment is separated from its neighbors by a simple annular groove. The principal longitudinal segmental muscles consist of continuous bands which are inserted on the internal surface of the intersegmental line. The muscle segmentation is therefore coincident with the body-wall segmentation. This is a primitive condition, essentially similar to that found in annelids and in the embryos of all arthropods, hence it is known as "primary segmentation." The term *metamere* is properly applied to these primary segments.

SECONDARY SEGMENTATION
Acheta assimilis (the field cricket)

Examine the abdomen of a female and note that segments one to eight are each made up of a dorsal sclerotized plate, the *tergum* or *notum,* a corresponding ventral plate, the *sternum,* and, separating these on either side, a flexible *pleural membrane*. Each tergum and sternum overlaps the one behind and is separated from it by the flexible *conjuctiva* or intersegmental membrane. The abdomen may then be said to be made up of a number of segments, sclerotized dorsally and ventrally, and separated from each other by intersegmental membranes. This condition is typical of insects with a sclerotized cuticle. The limits of the sclerotized segments are not the same as those of the primitive segments; therefore the former are known as *secondary segments*.

11

Cut longitudinally through the pleural membranes and across the anterior end of the dorsum and remove the entire dorsal wall of the abdomen. Pin this in a dissecting tray, internal surface upward, and cover with water. Examine under the binocular dissecting microscope. The surface will be found to be partly covered with irregularly arranged, opaque white tissue. This is a portion of the fat body and should be removed carefully with fine-pointed forceps. The body wall will be left, consisting of the integument and the longitudinal muscles. The latter are semitransparent and may be seen more clearly if the specimen is immersed for a few seconds in methylene blue solution, or other suitable stain.

Examine the longitudinal muscles nearest the mid-dorsal line of the anterior segments and note that they originate at the anterior edge of the segment, run posteriorly through the segment and across the intersegmental membrane to be inserted in the anterior edge of the segment behind. The lines along which the muscles are attached to the integument represent the primitive intersegmental lines such as are found in the caterpillar, but in the cricket and other sclerotized insects the intersegmental membranes lie in front of these lines. In fact, they are posterior bands of the primary segments.

This arrangement, by means of which the muscles can exert a definite pull on the sclerites, allows for a certain amount of specificity of movement as compared with the very generalized types of movement characteristic of worms and soft-bodied insects. The movements of the anterior segments of the abdomen in the cricket are, however, still relatively generalized, consisting of telescoping, bending and twisting, and there are no marked specializations in the areas to which the muscles are attached. The posterior segments, however, make more specific movements in relation to the movements of the ovipositor or of the copulatory organs of the male, and the anterior edges to which the muscles are attached are modified.

Examine the anterior edges of the apparent three last segments (8, 9 and 10) and note that they are folded in to form strong sclerotized ridges for the attachment of the muscles. These ridges are known as the *antecostae* and the corresponding groove or sulcus on the external surface is the *antecostal suture*. In front of the antecosta a very narrow sclerotic rim may be observed. This is the *acrotergite*, which in some insects forms a distinct sclerite. It is particularly well developed in certain of the thoracic segments and attention will be drawn to it later.

Note that the antecosta of the tenth segment is produced into two flattened processes or *apodemes* for the attachment of certain of the muscles of the cercus. This also is a common feature, especially in the thorax.

The *sterna* of the abdominal segments have a similar structure to that of the terga. When an anterior sclerite is developed in front of the antecosta it is known as an *acrosternite*.

DRAWINGS: Diagrams showing the relation of the muscles to the segments in primary and secondary segmentation.

3 Preliminary Study of the External Structure of an Insect

(Romalea, Melanoplus or Other Locust)

The following exercise is intended only for those students with no previous knowledge of insect structure. It is meant to give the student a comprehensive picture of the external structure of a relatively generalized insect so that in his later comparative studies of the various organs he will have a clearer conception of the relation of these parts to each other and to the insect as a whole.

THE HEAD

Observe the form and orientation of the head and the principal structures on it, such as the large *compound* eyes on the dorsolateral regions, the many-jointed *antennae* anterior to the eyes, and the *mouthparts* on the ventral edge of the head. A head like that of the locust, having the mouthparts directed ventrally, is said to be "hypognathous." When, as in most beetles, the mouthparts are directed anteriorly the head is said to be "prognathous." In relatively few insects, such as many of the Hemiptera, the head is reflexed ventrally to such an extent that the mouthparts are directed posteriorly. Such a head is said to be "opisthognathous."

Note that the antennae and mouthparts are movably attached to a strongly sclerotized "box" which forms the skeleton of the head and is comparable to (though in no sense homologous with) the skull or cranium of the vertebrates, and the same term, "cranium",* is used for it.

*A large number of terms borrowed from vertebrate anatomy are used in insect anatomy. The structures designated by these terms are, for the most part, not homologous in the two groups of animals. The names are used because of a real or fancied similarity in function, in position or in superficial appearance.

Hold the insect facing you and examine the anterior aspect of the head. The most ventral sclerite is a bilobate flap known as the *labrum*. Lift it with a needle and note that it is movably hinged to the cranium by a membranous *clypeolabral suture*. The labrum is functionally a sort of upper lip and regarded as one of the mouthparts, but morphologically it is probably an integral part of the head wall and not an appendage.

The *clypeus* lies dorsal to the labrum. It is a rectangular, transverse sclerite bounded dorsally by a sulcus, the *epistomal* or *frontoclypeal suture*.

The median area dorsal to the clypeus is known as the *frons* and the lateral areas ventral to the compound eyes as the *genae*. The top of the head, dorsal to the frons and genae is the *vertex*. The right and left halves of the vertex together with the corresponding genae constitute the *parietals*. Usage differs as to the precise limits of these regions, as will be shown later.

In some species there is a pale Y-shaped line in the vertex. This is known as the *ecdysial suture,* and is the line along which the cuticle of the nymph splits at ecdysis. It is usually absent or weakly developed in adult insects. The stem of the suture lies in the mid-dorsal line of the top of the head and is known as the *coronal suture*. The arms, which diverge and extend toward the eyes, form the V-shaped *frontal suture*.

Pull the head gently away from the thorax and note that these two tagmata are connected by the membranous *cervix (cervical membrane* or *neck)* which, because of its flexibility, allows free movement of the head.

Cut off the head and remove from it the neck membrane and any soft tissue which may come with it. Examine the posterior aspect or *occipital region* and note that the cranium here consists of an incomplete ring of sclerotized tissue forming lateral and dorsal walls surrounding a large central opening known as the *foramen magnum* or *occipital foramen*. The foramen is closed ventrally, not by the walls of the cranium, but by the base of the labium or lower lip. Most of the easily visible portion of the occipital region consists of a somewhat horseshoe-shaped sclerite. The dorsal portion of this sclerite is very narrow and is known as the *occiput*. The two ventrolateral portions expand to form triangular sclerites known as *postgenae*. The three regions are not separated by sutures.

The large *compound eyes* have already been observed. In addition find three simple eyes or *ocelli,* one in the middle of the face between the bases of the antennae, and one in the vertical ridge mesal to each compound eye, just anterior to the upper edge of the latter.

The *mouthparts* are mandibulate, i.e., adapted for chewing. They consist of two lips and two pairs of jaws. The *labrum* or upper lip has already been observed. Remove this and find a pair of strongly sclerotized unsegmented *mandibles* immediately beneath it. Posterior to the mandibles is a pair of segmented jaws, the *maxillae,* each bearing a 5-segmented, antenna-like *palpus.* The *labium* or lower lip is also segmented and bears a pair of 3-segmented *palpi.*

Remove the labium and find the blunt, tongue-like *hypopharynx* lying between the bases of the jaws. The hypopharynx, like the labrum, is formed from part of the original head wall. The mandibles, maxillae and labium are segmental appendages serially homologous with the legs.

THE THORAX

Examine the three segments of the thorax. The most anterior segment is known as the *prothorax,* the middle one as the *mesothorax* and the hindmost as the *metathorax.*

Note that the prothorax is quite large, more or less independent of the other segments, and is movable on them. The large shield which covers the dorsal and lateral sides of the prothorax is the *pronotum.* In the grasshoppers this is greatly enlarged and not only does it expand backward, covering part or all of the two succeeding terga, but it also extends laterally, almost completely covering the two pleura or lateral walls of the segment. The pleura are greatly reduced, visible externally only as minute triangular sclerites ventral to the anteroventral edges of the tergum and just in front of the bases of the forelegs. This condition is specialized and not typical.

Examine the *prosternum* which lies ventrally between the forelegs and note that it consists of an anterior *basisternite* extending laterally in front of the legs to fuse with the pleura, and a posterior *sternellum* separated from the basisternite by a suture. The basisternite bears a distinct spine, and the sternellum a longitudinal pit.

Cut carefully through that part of the pronotum which overlaps freely behind, so as to expose the intersegmental membrane. Find in the lateral parts of this membrane a pair of *mesothoracic spiracles* having the form of a small vertical slit between two minute sclerites.

Remove the prothorax so as to expose the mesothorax and metathorax. Observe that these two are closely united and not easily movable on each other. Because they form a structural wing-bearing unit these two segments are often referred to collectively as the *pterothorax.* The structure is essentially the same in both segments. Only the larger and more obvious sclerites will be referred to at this time.

Note that the terga, pleura and sterna are all conspicuously developed. Spread the wings laterally at right angles to the body and note that they are attached to the thorax by a flexible *articular membrane* between the terga and pleura.

Examine the *mesonotum* and find the following sclerites. (1) The *prescutum* is a narrow anterior sclerite with expanded lateral areas. These lateral areas are evident as triangular plates at the anterolateral angles of the tergum, immediately anterior to the wing bases. This sclerite is usually narrow and inconspicuous, but in some insects it is of considerable width. (2) The *scutum* lies posterior to the prescutum and is, in this insect, as in most others, the largest and most prominent sclerite of the tergum. (3) The *scutellum* is the posterior transverse sclerite overlapping the metatergum. The small prominence in the middle of the hinder portion of the tergum is also part of the scutellum.

Find three vertical sutures which divide the *pleura* of the pterothorax into a series of four sclerites. The middle suture, which passes just behind the second pair of legs is intersegmental, separating the anterior *mesopleuron* from the posterior *metapleuron*. The two pleura have essentially the same structure and either may be studied. Each is composed principally of two plates, the *episternum* in front and the *epimeron* behind. The former, in some species, is transversely divided into two secondary sclerites. The suture separating the episternum from the epimeron is the *pleural suture*. The *metathoracic spiracle* lies in the intersegmental area, dorsal to the base of the middle leg.

The *sternum* in the mesothorax and metathorax consists apparently of a single large bilobate sclerite in each segment. In the mesosternum, however, you will find a pair of sutures which partially separate the two lobes from the anterior transverse plate. The latter is the *basisternite* while the lobes form the *sternellum*. In the inner angles between the lobes and the hind margin of the basisternite, look for a pair of small pits. These are the *furcal pits* which mark the point of invagination of a pair of internal skeletal rods known as the *furcal arms* or *sternal apophyses*. Midway between the furcal pits is a *spinal pit,* marking the position of the *spina,* a third internal rod. The position of the furcal pits typically marks the divison between basisternite and sternellum.

Examine the *legs*. Manipulate one so as to discover the nature of the articulation with the thorax. Note that it pivots against the thorax at the ventral end of the pleural suture. This suture marks the position of a strong inflection or internal ridge known as the *pleural ridge,* and a ventral extension of this ridge provides an articulatory condyle for the leg. Identify the following leg segments: (1) the *coxa,* a short, stout, basal segment; (2) the *trochanter,* a very small segment, movable on the coxa and closely united with (3) the *femur,* the largest segment of the leg; (4) the *tibia,* a long, slender segment; (5) the *tarsus,* made up of three subsegments; (6) the *pretarsus,* consisting chiefly a pair of strong curved *claws,* and between them a somewhat concave disc, the *arolium.*

THE ABDOMEN

The male and female differ in respect to structures at the posterior end of the abdomen. The female can be distinguished by the presence of the ovipositor, consisting of two pairs of short, hard processes with sharp curved ends.

Examine the abdomen of the female and note the arrangement of the segmental *terga* and *sterna,* and the narrow *pleural membrane* which is inflected in such a way that the tergum overlaps the sternum. Note also that each segment overlaps the one behind, and by bending the abdomen dorsally and ventrally, find the *intersegmental membranes* which allow for free movements of this region.

Identify the eleven abdominal terga. The first bears the *sound-receiving* or *tympanal organs,* two lateral light-colored, somewhat bean-shaped taut membranes. The *first abdominal spiracles* are to be found at the anterior border of the tympanal membranes. The next seven segments also bear a pair of spiracles each. Look for these near the outer margins of the terga, just above the pleural membranes.

The first eight terga are essentially alike. The ninth and tenth differ in being much narrower, in the absence of spiracles, which are never found behind the eighth segment in insects, and in being partially fused with each other. The eleventh tergum has the form of a convex, diamond-shaped plate. It is known as the *epiproct* because of its position above the anus. It partly overlies laterally a pair of triangular sclerites, the *paraprocts* which are also part of the eleventh segment. Lateral to the proximal border of the epiproct there is a pair of small tapering processes. These are the *cerci* which represent appendages of the eleventh segment, serially homologous with the legs and mouthparts. Find the structures of the eleventh segment enumerated above; with the point of a needle raise the epiproct dorsally and note its relations to the paraprocts. Find the *anus* which opens mesally between the bases of the epiproct and paraprocts.

On the ventral side you will find only eight *sterna,* those of segments 9, 10 and 11 being reduced, displaced or absent. The first sternum is separated from its tergum by the leg cavity. The seven others are closely associated with their terga. The eighth sternum which is somewhat elongated is called the *subgenital* plate because it lies ventral to the genital opening and the base of the ovipositor. On its posterior border it bears a small up-curved spine, the egg guide, which passes between the ventral plates of the ovipositor. Note the *dorsal* and *ventral valves* of the *ovipositor,* two divergent pairs of stout, curved, pointed appendages near the posterior end of the abdomen.

Examine the abdomen of a male insect. You will observe that the structure is identical with that of the female except for the parts of the venter posterior to the seventh sternum. The eighth sternum is similar to those anterior to it. The ninth sternum, sometimes called the *hypandrium* because it lies beneath the male genitalia, is enlarged and divided transversely into two parts so that the venter appears to have ten visible sterna. The posterior portion of the ninth sternum probably represents the fused bases of the appendages which this segment originally bore.

4 The Abdominal Segments

GENERAL CONSIDERATIONS

Embryological studies show that in all insects except the Protura and Collembola the primitive number of abdominal segments is twelve, eleven true metameres and a small terminal telson through which the anus opens. There is, however, a general tendency toward reduction of the number of segments. In no insect is a definite telson retained during postembryonic life. The metameres also show a tendency toward reduction by coalescence or atrophy at the posterior end. In generalized insects (Figure 1) the eleventh metamere generally persists but is unsclerotized ventrally and consists of a dorsal plate, the epiproct, and two lateroventral plates, the paraprocts. The anus opens between these plates. In higher insects the eleventh metamere has disappeared as a distinct segment and the tenth also may be lost. In the generalized female the eighth segment bears the first valvifer to which the first valvula is attached, and the ninth segment bears the second valvifer to which the second and third valvulae are attached. The valvifers and valvulae constitute the ovipositor or external female genitalia. The ninth segment in the male bears the penis.

The pregenital or visceral segments have the simplest anatomic structure of any in the body, and for this reason they are selected first for study. Each segment consists of a dorsal sclerite, the tergum, a ventral sclerite, the sternum, and between them an unsclerotized pleural membrane.

The anatomical simplicity of the abdominal segments does not, however, represent a primitive condition and, from the standpoint of the morphologist, the structure of these segments is relatively complex and presents problems which are not yet certainly solved.

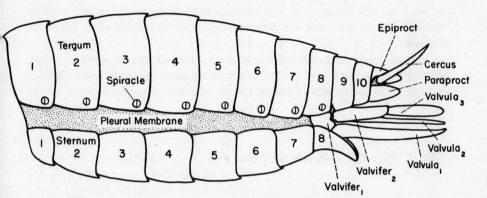

FIGURE 1. Lateral view of the abdomen of a generalized female insect.

The segmentation is secondary, the insertion of the longitudinal muscles being always behind the intersegmental membrane and at the anterior end of the definitive segment. Definite acrotergites and acrosternites are not usually developed and the antecostal suture is not always distinct. The antecosta may be a distinct ridge or a very slightly specialized marginal area to which the longitudinal muscles are attached.

It will be remembered that a segment consists primitively of a dorsal, a ventral and two pleural areas, the limb bases being inserted in the last. The tergum, sternum and the pleural membranes of a sclerotized abdominal segment are seldom, if ever, coincident with these primary areas. The spiracles are primitively dorsal in position since they originate lateral to the limb buds in the embryo, and their position has been used to determine the degree of correspondence between the primary dorsum and the definitive tergum. Actually, in adult insects, spiracles may be borne on the tergum, the pleural membrane or the sternum, and this is taken as indicating not only that the limits of the definitive tergum and sternum are different from those of the primitive dorsal and ventral areas, but also that these sclerites differ morphologically in different insects.

The ventral area, between the leg bases, becomes sclerotized to form the primitive sternum. In some primitive insects such as *Nesomachilis* (Thysanura), in which the *coxopodites,* or basal segments of the legs, persist as independent structures, this primitive ventral plate is the only sternal element, but in other Thysanura such as *Lepisma* and probably in all Pterygota it unites with portions of the two coxopodites to form the definitive sternum. Usually the three components of the sternum are indistinguishably fused but occasionally they are partly or completely separated by sutures.

In such insects the components derived from the primitive venter may be termed the *ventrosternite* and those derived from the coxopodites the *coxosternites*.

In some insects the spiracles open through the sternum. If we regard their position as fixed in the dorsal area, then the sternum in such insects includes not only the components just discussed but also the lateral parts of the dorsal area.

STRUCTURE OF THE ABDOMEN
Calosoma sycophanta, larva

Count the number of segments in the abdomen and note that there are only ten, the last being small and conical. The eleventh segment has disappeared unless it is represented by the small membranous area through which the anus opens. Note the two spine-like processes borne on the dorsal side of the ninth segment. These are the *urogomphi* and must not be confused with the cerci of other insects, which are true appendages of the eleventh segment.

The abdomen in many larval insects is wholly unsclerotized. In others, especially those which lead an active life, there are various degrees of sclerotization. In *Calosoma* there are several sclerites in each segment but the primary segmentation is not obscured. Examine a segment near the middle of the abdomen. Note the large dorsal unpaired sclerite lateral to which, on each side, is a small spiracle in the membrane. Lateroventral to each spiracle there are two small sclerites of unequal size, the larger lying anterior to the smaller. Ventral to these sclerites there is a distinct groove in the membrane which runs longitudinally along the side of the abdomen and passes forward into the thorax where its course lies dorsal to the pleura. This is the *dorsopleural line,* occasionally present in insects, which is presumably the dividing line between the dorsal and pleural regions. The area dorsal to it is therefore the primitive dorsum. The sclerites found in this area collectively constitute the *tergum* and each is a *tergite*. The large median sclerite is the *mediotergite* and the small lateral ones the *laterotergites.*

Ventral to the dorsopleural line you will find two pairs of sclerites similar in arrangement to the laterotergites, and ventral to these a second longitudinal groove, the *pleuroventral line.* The two grooves presumably mark off the primitive dorsal, pleural and ventral areas. The sclerites in the pleural area may represent the remains of the coxopodites or basal leg segments. If this is so each group of two sclerites may correctly be called the *pleuron,* a term which, in the thorax, is reserved for lateral sclerites derived from the coxopodites. The individual sclerites would therefore be *pleurites*. They may, however, be sclerotizations in the pleural area having no connection with the legs and are best referred to as *pleural sclerites*.

The ventral region of all except the three most posterior segments bears five sclerites—one large anterior one and four small posterior ones. These collectively constitute the *sternum,* which in this insect is apparently derived entirely from the ventral area. The individual sclerites are known as *sternites*.

The typical condition in the abdomen of adult insects is the presence of a single dorsal and ventral sclerotization; a true pleuron distinct from the other sclerites is rarely present.

DRAWING: A lateral view of at least two complete abdominal segments showing the structures described.

Acheta assimilis, (field cricket) female

Choose, if available, a specimen that has been injected. The membranes will be stretched, therefore the relations of the sclerites will be more readily seen.

Count the number of segments visible on the dorsal side. You should find ten distinct terga, the tenth being compound. Turning to the ventral side, however, you will find only eight distinct sterna, because the ventral parts of the segments behind the eighth are greatly modified.

THE PREGENITAL SEGMENTS. These are segments 1 to 7 and are very similar in structure. Note that in each there is a *tergum,* a *sternum* and a wide *pleural membrane*. The structure of the tergum and sternum is essentially the same. Each consists of a single undivided plate.

The pleural membrane extends from the first to the eighth segment and is not superficially segmented, except insofar as the overlap of terga and sterna extends for some distance into the pleural membrane. Find a small roundish *spiracle* in the membrane on each side of the first eight segments. This is the typical distribution of the abdominal spiracles in adult insects; that is to say, they are found in segments one to eight.

Since the spiracles lie in the pleural membrane the latter is probably derived in part from the lateral portions of the primitive dorsum.

In a specimen which has not been distended by injection you will observe a distinct *lateral groove* extending through the full length of the pleural membrane. This has been interpreted as the dorsopleural line, but is in fact a temporary fold formed by the contraction of muscles inserted in minute sclerites along its length. In the fully distended abdomen the groove has disappeared and the sclerites are visible as minute black lenticular or spindle-shaped bodies. There are two in each segment and they may be termed, for descriptive purposes, the "anterior and posterior ventral sclerites" of the pleural membrane to distinguish them from the "anterior and posterior dorsal sclerites." The latter lie one in front and one behind the spiracle and serve for the insertion of muscles to be examined later. They are extremely small, appearing like short black lines, but they are very variable and may not be seen in some specimens.

Examine a living insect, if available, under the low power of the dissecting microscope and note the alternate dorsoventral contraction and expansion of the abdomen. These are respiratory movements made possible by the flexibility of the pleural membrane and caused by the contraction of the muscles to which we have referred. Observe how with each contraction the pull of the muscles causes the "dorsopleural" groove to become deeper and narrower, while on relaxation of the muscles it becomes broader and more shallow.

THE GENITAL SEGMENTS. The eighth and ninth segments give rise to the valves of the ovipositor and are, therefore, called the *genital segments*. In insects with an ovipositor these segments are always modified, especially as regards their ventral parts. In the cricket the terga are distinct and only slightly modified in form as compared with those of the pregenital segments. Examine the last ventral sclerite in front of the ovipositor. This is known as the *subgenital plate* since the female genital opening lies above it. It forms a backward-projecting flap, free at its posterior end, and is usually regarded as the eighth sternum; but there is some evidence that the latter is reduced and that the subgenital plate is a secondary sclerite developed from a fold in the membrane between the seventh and eighth sterna.

The venter of the ninth segment is greatly reduced and modified and cannot be recognized by superficial examination.

THE POSTGENITAL SEGMENTS. The tenth and eleventh segments are modified in most insects. To study these terminal structures in the cricket, cut through the abdomen in front of the ninth segment and pin the extremity in a dissecting tray with the cut surface down. The long median spear-like process is the *ovipositor* and the two lateral filiform appendages are the *cerci*. With the aid of the dissecting needle find the *anus* which opens at the posterior end dorsal to the ovipositor and between three valve-like terminal sclerites, one dorsal and two lateroventral. Examine the dorsal sclerite and note that it forms part of a plate which extends anteriorly to the ninth tergum, but is divided by a shallow groove into an anterior transverse region and a posterior triangular region. The anterior region is the *tenth tergum*. It extends laterally to the bases of the cerci, a narrow extension of it curving around the anterior and lateral sides of the bases of these appendages. The posterior valve-like plate lying dorsal to the anus is the *epiproct* and represents the eleventh tergum or a part of it. The two lateroventral valves are the *paraprocts*. They too represent parts of the eleventh segment. Note that the *cerci* are almost surrounded by the tenth tergum, the ring being completed posteriorly by the base of the paraproct. They are, however, the segmental appendages of the eleventh segment, serially homologous with the legs and mouthparts.

Take hold of the paraprocts with the forceps and pull gently upward so as to stretch and expose the membranous fold between the paraprocts and the base of the ovipositor. This membrane represents, in part at least, the ventral region of the tenth segment which is unsclerotized except for a very small plate in front of the paraprocts.

DRAWING: A lateral view of the abdomen showing, as far as possible, the structures described.

Acheta assimilis, male

The only important differences from the female are to be found in the genital segments. The eighth is normal, i.e., it resembles the anterior segments in all essentials since it is not associated with genitalia. The sternum of the ninth is well developed and except that it is larger, resembles the subgenital plate in the female. It is sometimes referred to as the *hypandrium*. The male genitalia lie concealed in a chamber on the dorsal side of the hypandrium.

DRAWING: A dorsolateral view of the four terminal segments, with the cercus removed.

Melanoplus, Romalea, or other grasshopper

Examine the abdomen and note the following differences from *Acheta*: the *terga* and *sterna* are more extensive laterally, the spiracles being in the lateral margins of the former; the *pleural membrane* is reduced to a narrow inflected band between terga and sterna; the eleventh tergum or *epiproct* is distinctly separated from the tenth; the shape of the ovipositor is quite different. In the male there are apparently ten sterna; the apparent tenth, however, is really a subdivision or an outgrowth of the ninth, probably representing the fused bases of the segmental appendages of this segment.

DRAWING: Lateral view of the five posterior segments of male and female.

Acroneuria or other plecopteran nymph

Observe that in this insect the pleural membrane is absent except in the second segment and there is no demarcation between terga and sterna, the annuli being evenly sclerotized. The sternum of the first segment is fused with the metasternum, the tergum being free. As external genital organs are undeveloped, the eighth and ninth segments are unmodified. The tenth segment is also completely sclerotized. Rudiments of the eleventh segment are present. The *epiproct* is probably represented by the membranous fold beneath the posterior lobe of the tenth tergum. The *paraprocts* are small but distinct and sclerotized. They are closely associated with the prominent jointed *cerci*.

DRAWING: A dorsolateral view of the terminal segments.

Musca domestica, female (Diptera)

Examine a freshly killed specimen, if available, or one that has been fully relaxed. It may be necessary to boil the preserved specimen for a short time in water or potassium hydroxide to make it pliable. You will note that, on superficial examination, the abdomen appears to consist of only four segments. Examine these segments and note that the four *tergal plates* extend down the sides to the lateroventral line. The first tergal plate is a compound one consisting of the fused terga of the first and second segments. This is evidenced by the presence on it of two pairs of spiracles and by the two sterna associated with it. The last visible segment is therefore the fifth. Find the five pairs of *spiracles* near the lateral edges of the terga.

Find the five small *sterna,* the first crescent-shaped, the others elongated plates in the median area of the venter. Between terga and sterna are the broad *pleural membranes.*

In addition to the five visible segments there are four others which are slender and cylindrical and, when at rest, are telescoped into each other and retracted within the fifth, so that only the extreme tip is visible. They form a slender tube known as the *pseudovipositor*. These can best be examined by holding a living fly between the thumb and forefinger, or between the tips of blunt forceps, and exerting gentle pressure on the abdomen. When the pseudovipositor is extended, the insect should be pinned in the dissecting tray and the pseudovipositor should be grasped with a pair of fine forceps and pulled gently until fully extended, when it will be as long as the remainder of the abdomen. Note that the segments of the pseudovipositor are separated by extensive intersegmental membranes which make possible the telescoping of the segments. Each segment is largely membranous but is provided with one or two narrow tergal and sternal sclerites. The ninth segment bears a pair of minute lateral appendages.

DRAWING: Lateral view of the abdomen with the pseudovipositor extended.

Euschistus or Anasa (Hemiptera)

Examine a segment near the middle of the abdomen. Find the *tergum, pleural membranes* and *sternum.* You will observe that both the tergum and pleural membranes are restricted to the more or less flattened dorsal side of the insect, while the sternum occupies not only the whole of the convex ventral side but is bent sharply at the lateral margins of the abdomen so that it extends as a pair of lateral strips on the dorsal side also. Find the *spiracles* on the ventral side of the sternum near the lateral margins of the abdomen.

It is evident that the sclerotic material in this insect is distributed quite differently from that in the cricket or grasshopper. If we regard the position of the spiracles as fixed in the primitively dorsal region, then the definitive sternum includes the primitive venter, the pleural areas and part of the dorsum; the pleural membranes would also be part of the primitive dorsum.

DRAWING: A diagrammatic cross section of the abdominal cuticle showing the arrangement of the structures discussed.

Apis mellifera—honeybee, worker

The clistogastrous Hymenoptera, of which the honeybee is an example, show profound modifications in the anterior segments of the abdomen. The first segment or *propodaeum* is fused with, and has become a functional part of, the thorax. The second segment is greatly narrowed anteriorly (sometimes for its entire length) forming a *petiole* or narrow stalk connecting it with the propodaeum. There is thus a deep constriction between the propodaeum and the functional abdomen, or *gaster,* which allows for freer movements of the latter than is possible in other insects. It will be seen that the functional abdomen is not the same as the morphological abdomen.

Scrape the hair from the thorax of a honeybee and examine the dorsal side under the microscope. Find the deep cleft in the abdomen, at the bottom of which is the short petiole, connecting the gaster with the functional thorax. In front of this cleft, and forming the posterior portion of the dorsum of the functional thorax, find a large plate limited in front by a distinct sulcus which passes behind the attachment of the hind wings. This is the *tergum of the propodaeum,* the first segment of the morphological abdomen. The lateral edges of the plate extend from behind the bases of the hind wings to the articulation of the hind legs. Find the *spiracles* near the anterior margin.

Cut the legs off close to the body and find, in the ventral side, a very narrow transverse sclerite immediately behind the articulation of the hind legs and separated from the petiole by a distinct intersegmental membrane. This is the *sternum of the propodaeum.*

Examine the second abdominal segment (the apparent or functional first segment). Find the tergum and sternum and note how the anterior region of the former narrows and bends sharply downward in such a way that the anterior portion of the segment forms the narrow waist or *petiole.*

Behind this segment there are five visible segments, the terminal one being the morphological seventh. Each is provided with a distinct tergum and sternum, and each tergum bears the usual pair of spiracles. The eighth, ninth and tenth segments are greatly modified and retracted within the seventh, where the eighth and ninth form part of the mechanism of the sting.

> **DRAWING:** A lateral view of the thorax and abdomen showing the structures mentioned. Except for the propodaeum, details of the thorax should not be shown.

MUSCLES OF THE ABDOMINAL BODY WALL

The body-wall muscles of insects are derived from those of their annelidan ancestors. In present-day annelids there are two layers of muscle fibers, an internal longitudinal and external circular, which are not organized into distinct individual muscles. These are adequate for the generalized movements of the worms. In the insects these sheets of muscle fibers are for the most part broken up into discrete muscles whose contraction is responsible for the specific movements of the appendages and other organs. The musculature is therefore most complicated in the head, the thorax, and the genital segments where the most active movements take place. The pregenital segments, especially in adult pterygote insects, have a relatively simple musculature.

In the course of evolution many muscles have changed their direction and attachment, some have disappeared and new ones have arisen to meet new needs. It is not yet possible to trace the homologies of the muscles in all insects and only a few of the important muscles in different regions of the body will be studied in this course.

Muscles may be named according to their function, e.g., adductor of the mandible; according to their position, e.g., longitudinal ventral; or according to their attachments, e.g., tergosternal.

Acheta assimilis

Remove the head and prothorax and make a complete longitudinal incision through the body wall, passing slightly to the left of the median line. Pin the larger section in the dissecting tray and remove the digestive tract and genital organs. This will expose the heart in the mid-dorsal line, the nerve cord in the mid-ventral line, many tubular tracheae, irregular masses of white fatty tissue, and the band-like muscles. Remove carefully some of the heavier masses of fat from the middle region of the abdomen.

The muscles in the living insect are transparent and difficult to distinguish, but are more easily seen in properly preserved specimens. In either case a brief flooding of the specimen with methylene blue or other suitable stain will increase the optical differentiation of the tissues and facilitate the removal of the fat. Continue the careful removal of the fat until the muscles of the fourth, fifth and sixth segments are fully visible. Some slight variations from the description given below may be found.

The *dorsal muscles* are very simple, consisting of a thin band of longitudinal fibers, divided into two groups. The *median dorsals* lie toward the mid-dorsal line. They originate in the antecosta of one segment and are inserted in the antecosta of the next posterior segment. The *lateral dorsals* lie lateral to the medians. They are greatly shortened, having their origin in the tergum some distance behind the antecosta and their insertion in the antecosta of the segment behind. In many insects there are external and internal layers of dorsal muscles. The single layer in the cricket probably corresponds to the external dorsals of other insects.

The contraction of the longitudinal dorsals pulls the posterior tergum, in which they are inserted, forward. Acting in concert with the corresponding ventral muscles they telescope the segments; acting alone they bend the abdominal segments dorsally.

The *ventral muscles* are somewhat more complex. You will find a prominent *transverse ventral* muscle in the anterior portion of each segment, having its attachments near the lateral edges of the sternum.

Find also the relatively heavy *internal longitudinal ventral* which originates in the base of the metasternal apophysis and runs obliquely backward to the antecosta of the fifth sternum. In the second and third segments it gives off slips which are inserted on the third and fourth antecostae. External to this muscle in the fourth segment you will find a more delicate *lateral external longitudinal ventral* which originates in, or just posterior to, the antecosta of the fourth segment and is inserted in the antecosta of the fifth segment. A similar muscle is also present in the segments behind the fourth in which the internal ventral is not developed.

Near the mid-ventral line find the *median external longitudinal ventral* which originates near the middle of the sternum and is inserted in the antecosta of the succeeding segment. It will be observed that some of the longitudinal muscles, both dorsal and ventral, have changed their origin but not their insertion. This is a very common phenomenon but change in insertion is less frequent.

The *dorsoventral* group of muscles includes those which lie chiefly in the pleural area and which extend in the general direction dorsum to venter. Following the general procedure in comparative anatomy they are named according to their attachments and fall into the three subdivisions described below. The fat particles should be picked away carefully to expose the muscles which are all in the form of relatively thin, narrow fibrous bands.

An *anterior* and a *posterior tergosternal* will be found in the corresponding regions of the segment, having their attachments near the edges of the tergum and sternum. A *segmental* and *intersegmental notopleural* originate together from the notum or tergum, behind the origin of the posterior tergosternal. They diverge in their course, the segmental muscle to be inserted in the posterior ventral pleural sclerite of the same segment (described on p. 24), and the intersegmental to be inserted in the anterior ventral pleural sclerite of the segment behind.

Five *sternopleurals* originate along the lateral edge of the sternum. The *first* is inserted in the anterior ventral pleural sclerite, the *second* in the anterior dorsal pleural sclerite, the *third* in the closing apparatus of the spiracle, the *fourth* in the posterior dorsal sclerite and the *fifth* in the posterior ventral sclerite. The third sternopleural is the *dilator of the spiracle*. In contracting, it opens the spiracular orifice and allows the exit and entry of gases to the respiratory tubes. The other dorsoventrals are *compressors of the abdomen* and are concerned chiefly with the respiratory movements. They draw the dorsum and venter toward each other, compressing the abdomen and thus increasing the blood pressure. This pressure is imparted to the tracheae and air is forced out of the spiracles. When the muscles relax, the elasticity of the body wall and the increased blood pressure force the dorsum and venter apart, the body cavity expands, pressure is decreased and air is drawn into the tracheae through the spiracles. The increased hemolymph pressure caused by the contraction of the abdominal or other muscles is used by many insects in bringing about the movement or expansion of various organs by the transmission of pressure from one region to another.

DRAWING: One-half of segments four, five and six showing the arrangement of the muscles. Remove the two tergosternals from one segment to expose the muscles exernal to them.

5 The Thoracic Segments

GENERAL CONSIDERATIONS

The thorax, or second tagma, consists of three segments known as the prothorax, mesothorax and metathorax, but in many insects portions of the first abdominal segment are incorporated in the functional thorax. In the higher Hymenoptera the complete segment is incorporated and in several insects there is a partial union of this segment with the thorax. In all adult insects with functional wings the antecosta and acrotergite of the first abdominal segment form an integral part of the functional thorax.

Each thoracic segment normally bears a pair of legs and in most adult insects the second and third bear a pair of wings each. The thorax may therefore be regarded as the locomotive region of the adult insect. The evolution of its skeletal structures is correlated with the locomotive function and the locomotive muscles almost completely fill its cavity.

The prothorax is usually free from the mesothorax, i.e., separated from it by membrane. In lower insects as well as some higher insects such as the Neuroptera and Coleoptera, it is large and conspicuous, but in many of the higher groups it is reduced, inconspicuous and closely associated with the mesothorax. In larval insects and most wingless adults the mesothorax and metathorax are distinctly separated by membrane or by a conspicuous intersegmental groove, but in adult winged insects they are consolidated to form the *pterothorax*. The intersegmental line, however, remains distinct, usually in the form of a sulcus, though in some insects there may be a greatly reduced intersegmental membrane approaching a line suture. When the two pairs of wings are of equal value in flight the meso- and metathorax are approximately evenly developed, but when one pair is used exclusively or predominantly, its segment is larger and more complex in structure than the other.

32

THE TERGUM

The *pronotum* (the tergum of the prothorax) is typically a single sclerite, but may be subdivided. Any sutures or sclerites present have no relationship with those of the mesonotum and metanotum. A peculiarity of the pronotum is the loss of the antecosta and acrotergite because the anterior region is unsclerotized and forms part of the neck membrane.

The structure of the *mesonotum* (Figure 2) and *metanotum* is correlated with the development of wings. In immature insects and adult wingless insects they resemble the abdominal terga, but with the development of functional wings in the adult they undergo marked changes.

The principal flight movements are brought about, not by muscles inserted in the wing base, but by the bending and relaxation of the terga through the action of segmental muscles. To make these movements of the terga more definite and specific, the mesonotum, metanotum and the acrotergite with the antecosta of the first abdominal tergum are all consolidated, and the intersegmental membranes are eliminated or reduced to a minimum. In order to strengthen the terga, to afford attachment to muscles and to give more precise direction to the curvature of the terga during flight, a

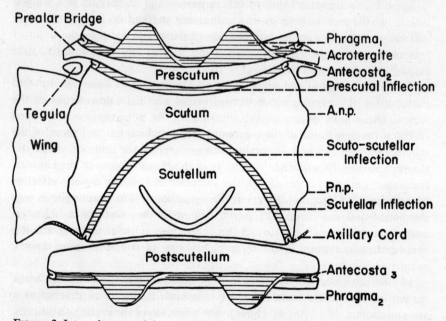

FIGURE 2. Internal aspect of the mesonotum when the forewings are the more powerful in flight. A.n.p., anterior notal wing process; P.n.p., posterior notal wing process.

number of internal ridges or inflections have developed. These are marked externally by sulci which divide the tergum into several sclerites.

The most constant of these ridges are the *antecosta* and the *scuto-scutellar inflection*. A *prescutal inflection* also is usually present but is not always strongly developed. The sulci associated with these inflections divide the tergum into four primary sclerites. The *acrotergite* lies in front of the *antecostal suture* and when it remains attached to its own segment it is usually very narrow and inconspicuous. Behind the acrotergite is the *prescutum* which also is typically very narrow though in some insects it forms a conspicuous sclerite. The *prescutal suture* which marks its posterior limit is often poorly developed, but the prescutum can be recognized by its lateral portions, the *prealar bridges,* which extend in front of the wing bases and usually meet the dorsal edges of the pleura. The third sclerite or *scutum* is always prominent and forms normally the most extensive region of the notum. Its lateral edges are parallel to the base of the wing and bear *anterior* and *posterior notal wing processes* (A.n.p. and P.n.p.) which assist in the articulation of the wing. The *scutellum* is typically triangular with the apex directed anteriorly. Its posterior edge is continuous with the axillary cords which form the posterior margin of the base of the wings.

These four sclerites are the typical components of the tergum of a winged insect, but the prescutum is often incompletely marked off from the scutum and the acrotergite may be reduced to a narrow rim forming the anterior fold of the antecosta. In many insects the scutum and scutellum are subdivided by additional sutures.

The dorsal longitudinal muscles by their contraction cause an upward curvature of the tergum, which in turn brings about the downstroke of the wings. These muscles are usually inserted on the *phragmata* or expanded plates of the antecostae of the mesonotum and metanotum and those of the metanotum and the first abdominal tergum. When the anterior wings are the principal or the sole flight organs as in the Hymenoptera or the Diptera, the antecosta and acrotergite of the metathorax become closely attached to, and form an integral sclerite of, the mesothorax. The acrotergite is well developed and now forms the *postscutellum* of the mesothorax. This arrangement increases the ability of the contracting muscles to bring about a more precise curvature of the tergum, resulting of course in more definite wing movement.

In such an insect the acrotergite may become detached from the metanotum behind the antecosta but more frequently it retains its attachment to the metanotum thus bringing about a consolidation of the entire pterothorax. When a postscutellum is present in the mesothorax there is of course no acrotergite or antecosta in the metathorax.

In a like manner the acrotergite of the first abdominal tergum forms a postscutellum to the metanotum, the original intersegmental membrane between the two segments being eliminated or greatly reduced.

Paragnetina, Acroneuria or related perlid stonefly

Remove the wings except for a short stump and examine the *pronotum*. Note that it consists of a large sclerotized plate covering the entire dorsal area of the prothorax. Apart from the division into right and left halves by a median longitudinal sulcus, there is no division into sclerites. There is an anterior submarginal groove but this must not be confused with the antecosta. Retain the specimen for further study.

DRAWING: Dorsal view of pronotum.

Romalea microptera

Examine the *pronotum* and note that it is not confined to the dorsum but grows laterally over the pleural regions also. As a result the pleuron is greatly reduced. It also grows posteriorly over most of the mesonotum and metanotum. A series of transverse sulci divide it into five sclerites. Divisions of the pronotum such as found in *Romalea* and *Paragnetina* are peculiar to the species and have no relationship to the sclerites of the mesonotum and metanotum.

DRAWING: Lateral view of the pronotum.

Acheta assimilis, nymph

Examine the *mesonotum* and *metanotum* and note that they differ in no essential detail of structure from the terga of the abdominal segments. Each consists of a very narrow acrotergite and a large undivided postcostal plate. It will be seen, from the studies which immediately follow, that the mesonotum and metanotum of winged insects are subdivided into a number of sclerites, the principal ones of which are sufficiently constant to be recognized and named. The appearance of these sclerites with their dividing inflections and sulci is coincident ontogenetically and phylogenetically with the development of wings. They are therefore absent in primitively and secondarily wingless insects and in the larvae and nymphs of winged species.

35

DRAWING: Dorsal view of mesonotum, metanotum and first abdominal segment.

Paragnetina media (Perlidae)

Remove the prothorax and examine the mesonotum. Certain areas are very lightly pigmented and might be mistaken for membrane, but testing them with a needle will show that they are hard and sclerotized.

Find the *acrotergite* which forms a narrow anterior sclerite. It is most evident in the median region where it follows the curve of the sclerite behind it, but it continues laterally in front of the prealar bridges mentioned below. The deep groove that separates it from the sclerite behind it is the *antecostal suture.*

The *prescutum* lies behind the acrotergite and consists of a median, somewhat diamond-shaped region and two lateral extensions known as the *prealar bridges* which extend to the episterna, from which they are separated by narrow membranes. This pronounced development of the prescutum is rare in insects. It is more usually a narrow, often imperfectly defined sclerite, which can be recognized most readily by the prealar bridges. The sulcus which separates the prescutum from the sclerite behind it is the *prescutal suture.*

Manipulate the stumps of the wings and note that their posterior margins are continued mesally as thickened *axillary cords.* These in turn are continuous with the free posterior edge of the mesonotum which forms a transverse fold with a deep inflection behind it. The fold forms the posterior edge of the sclerite known as the *scutellum,* and its relation to the axillary cords is characteristic of all winged insects.

Trace the suture which begins on each side at the junction of the axillary cord and the edge of the scutellum, runs straight forward to the posterior sides of two rounded shoulder-like areas, turns anteromesally along the inner edges of these two areas and comes to a point in the middle line. This is the *scuto-scutellar suture* which separates the scutum from the scutellum.

The *scutum* is that sclerite which lies anterior and lateral to the scuto-scutellar suture. It consists of the two bulging areas mentioned earlier, a narrow median bridge connecting them and two areas posterior to the bulges, one on either side of the scutellum. On the lateral side, near the anterior edge of the bulge, find a small triangular sclerite which projects laterally toward the anterior region of the wing base. This is the *anterior notal wing process.* A second lateral process, the *posterior notal wing process* is given off near the posterior end of the notum. This is long and narrow and projects obliquely forward toward the posterior region of the wing base.

Examine the *scutellum* and note that it consists of two sclerites separated by a U-shaped *scutellar suture*. The anterior sclerite may be called the *scutellar shield,* the other the *posterior scutellar plate.*

The median longitudinal sutures found in the prescutum and scutellum are characteristic of this insect and are not of general occurrence.

Behind the scutellum you will find a transverse sclerite which forms the posterior wall of the deep declivity between the mesonotum and metanotum. This is the *postscutellum* which is morphologically the acrotergite of the metanotum but functionally a part of the mesonotum. Note that it extends laterally behind the wing bases to form the *postalar bridges* which unite in part with the epimera.

Examine the *metanotum* and note that in size and structure it is essentially similar to the mesonotum except that its acrotergite is enlarged and consolidated with the mesonotum. The *postscutellum* of the metanotum is the acrotergite of the first abdominal segment.

DRAWING: A dorsal view of the mesothorax showing the sclerites and sutures mentioned.

Remove the posterior portion of the abdomen and cut lengthwise through the pleural regions of the thorax and the remaining abdominal segments. Pin the dorsal half, cut side upward, in the dissecting tray and flood with water. Remove any fat or other tissues that obscure the muscles.

You will find two sets of muscles exposed. Laterally there are several dorsoventral muscles cut across. Some of these are leg muscles, others are responsible for the upstroke of the wings in flight. Between these are the longitudinal muscles which bring about the downstroke of the wings. Note that the longitudinal muscles of the meso- and metathorax are attached anteriorly and posteriorly to inward-projecting cuticular plates or ridges.

Remove the exposed longitudinal muscles of the mesothorax and note that they are attached in front to the anterior region of the prescutum and to two flattened plates which grow inward from the antecosta. These plates are the *first phragmata*. Posteriorly the muscles are attached to the *second phragmata,* ingrowths from the antecosta between the postscutellum (metathoracic acrotergite) and the prescutum of the metathorax.

The corresponding muscles of the metathorax are attached to the second phragmata and the strongly developed antecosta of the first abdominal segment, which here lies at the posterior edge of the metathoracic postscutellum. In other insects there may be a third pair of phragmata borne by this antecosta.

37

On removing the heavy inner longitudinal muscles, other muscles will be exposed. Some of them are attached to a median longitudinal ridge in the scutellum and others to a ridge between the median region of the prescutum and the prealar bridge. The reason for the corresponding sulci in these two sclerites is now clear; they mark the positions of inflections for the attachment of muscles.

Acheta assimilis

Both pairs of wings in the stonefly are used actively in flight and the two terga are equally well developed. The acrotergite of the metanotum is well developed and forms the meso-postscutellum, but it has not lost its connection with the metanotum and the two terga are consolidated. In the Orthoptera, on the other hand, the forewings or tegmina are modified and the hindwings are the principal organs of flight; therefore, the metanotum is larger and more complex than the mesonotum. This is true of the field cricket although its hindwings are atrophied and are no longer functional in flight.

Remove the prothorax of *Acheta* and snip off the wings, leaving the stump on one side. Remove the dorsal region of the pterothorax from another specimen and boil in potassium hydroxide to remove the soft tissues. Use this to supplement your study of the untreated specimen.

Observe the difference in size between the mesonotum and metanotum. Remove the former and study the structure of the metanotum.

Anteriorly the metanotum might be likened to the human torso, the median portion representing the base of the neck and the rounded lateral portions the shoulders. To see the anterior structures it may be necessary to remove most of the abdomen and pin the specimen with the anterior end upward. At the anterior edge of the "neck" find the deep *antecostal sulcus* associated with an internal ridge, the *antecosta,* which bears two small lateral processes or *phragmata.* The *acrotergite* is very narrow, forming little more than the anterior lamina of the antecosta. It continues laterally as a narrow anterior border to the prealar bridge.

A second pronounced sulcus borders the anterior edge of each "shoulder" and joins the antecosta at the lateral edge of the "neck." These are lateral portions of the *prescutal suture* which is not continuous across the median region of the tergum. Between the prescutal suture and the lateral portions of the antecostal suture there is a forked sclerite on each side, the two constituting the *prescutum.* The anterior branch of the fork is the *prealar bridge,* which, in close association with the lateral portion of the acrotergite, extends laterally in front of the wing base. The posterior branch is triangular in form and rests on the "shoulder" of the scutum like an epaulet. In the membrane between the two branches there is a small rounded protuberance, sparsely clothed with hairs. This is the *tegula,* which in some other insects, such as the Lepidoptera, is more conspicuously developed.

Find the *scuto-scutellar suture* which forms an incomplete arch on the notum. The *scutum* lies anterior and lateral to this suture and bears the *anterior* and *posterior notal wing processes* on its lateral edges. The anterior process is just behind the prescutum and is closely associated with a fairly large, elongated sclerite which lies in the membrane between the notum and the wing. The posterior process is near the hinder end and is in contact with a smaller sclerite in the membrane. These sclerites form part of the articulatory mechanism of the wings and will be studied in detail later.

The posterior edge of the scutellum can be identified by the fact that, as in the stonefly, it is infolded and is continuous laterally with the axillary cords of the wings. Note that a *scutellar suture* divides it into an anterior *scutellar shield* and a *posterior scutellar sclerite.* The postscutellum is the narrow sclerite behind the scutellum. Note that it still retains its connection with the first abdominal tergum of which it is the acrotergite.

Examine the inner surface of the specimen treated with potassium hydroxide and note that the various sutures mark the positions of internal ridges. Weak phragmata are borne on the two antecostae.

Examine the mesonotum and observe that, apart from the absence of a postscutellum and its much smaller size, its structure is essentially similar to that of the metanotum. The male usually shows a stronger development of the scuto-scutellar ridge. This is probably correlated with the fact that the anterior wings of the female are nonfunctional, while those of the male make specific movements in producing the chirp.

> **DRAWING:** Metanotum of Acheta. Draw it as if it were flattened out to show in the one drawing the anterior and lateral structures which are partly obscured in a dorsal view.

THE PLEURON (Figure 3)

The thoracic segments of all adult insects and the more active larvae or nymphs have definite and usually extensive sclerotizations in the pleural areas. These sclerites are formed from detached portions of the basal leg segment which have become incorporated in the body wall to form the *pleuron.* They are usually termed subcoxal elements.

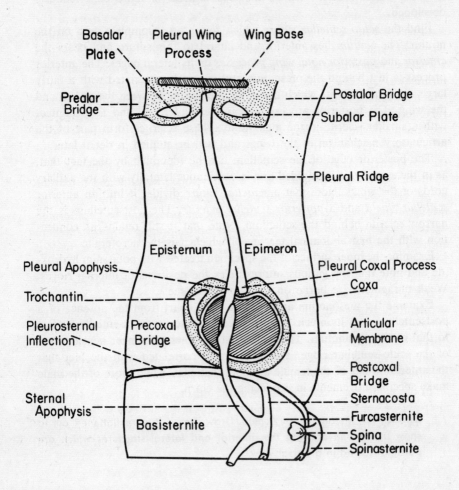

FIGURE 3. Internal aspect of the mesopleuron and mesosternum.

The fundamental structure of the pleuron is the same in the three segments, but the propleuron is usually much smaller than the pteropleura, and those structures which, in the dorsal region of the latter, are associated with the wing bases are absent in the propleura.

The *pleural sulcus* divides the pleuron into an anterior *episternum* and a posterior *epimeron*. The sulcus is typically vertical or somewhat oblique but in extreme cases may be horizontal or may follow a tortuous course. It marks the position of a strong inflection, the *pleural ridge*. This ridge terminates ventrally in an articulatory process, the *pleural coxal process*, which takes part in the dorsal articulation of the coxa. Dorsally the pleural ridge terminates in the *pleural wing process* which forms a pivot for certain movements of the wing. Dorsal to the coxal process the pleural ridge gives off a strong apodeme, the *pleural apophysis*, which projects inward above the coxal cavity where it is closely attached to the sternal apophysis.

In the pterothorax the pleuron is well-developed dorsally and it may be in intimate contact or even sclerotically continuous with the tergum by means of the *prealar bridge* which connects the prescutum and episternum in front of the wing-base, and the *postalar bridge* uniting the postscutellum and epimeron behind. Similarly, contact or union is usually established between the episternum and sternum by means of a *precoxal bridge*, and sometimes between the epimeron and sternum by a *postcoxal bridge*.

In the articulatory membrane between the episternum and coxa there is frequently a triangular sclerite, the *trochantin*. In lower insects it may be quite conspicuous and in some insects is articulated to the coxa. In higher insects it tends to atrophy.

Small sclerites, known as *epipleurites,* usually become detached from the dorsal region of the episternum and epimeron in adult winged insects. They lie in the membrane between the pleuron and the wing base and serve for insertion of some of the wing muscles. Epipleurites anterior to the pleural wing process are known as *basalar plates,* those posterior to the process as *subalar plates.*

Acheta assimilis

Remove the head and prothorax and examine the *pteropleura*. Note that the structure of the two pleura is fundamentally the same. The mesopleuron overlaps the metapleuron but the two are connected by membrane and are not consolidated. Examine the mesopleuron and note that it consists largely of two obliquely elongated sclerites separated by a deep sulcus. The anterior sclerite is the *episternum,* the posterior the *epimeron* and the sulcus is the *pleural suture*. Note that dorsally the suture is continued to the base of the wing and ventrally to the proximal edge of the coxa. This is due to the fact that the suture marks the position of a strong internal *pleural ridge* which is produced dorsally to form a pivot for the movement of the wings and ventrally to form a condyle for the articulation of the leg. The processes are known respectively as the *pleural wing process* and the *pleural coxal process*.

Dorsal to the episternum and anterior to the pleural wing process find a small sclerite known as the *basalare* or *basalar plate*. A similar but smaller and less conspicuous sclerite, the *subalare* or *subalar plate* lies dorsal to the epimeron. These sclerites are known collectively as *epipleurites* and are detached fragments of the episternum and epimeron which serve for the insertion of certain wing muscles.

Partly overlapped by the ventral edge of the episternum, and lying between it and the sternum, there is a small triangular plate, the *precoxale*. It is separated by membrane from each of the adjacent sclerites. In the articular membrane in front of the coxa, and partly overlapped by the episternum and precoxale, there is a small elongated sclerite, the *trochantin* which articulates with the coxa by its ventral extremity.

Observe the large *metathoracic spiracle* in the intersegmental membrane ventral and posterior to the epimeron.

DRAWING: Mesopleuron of *Acheta* with the coxa and part of the sternum, showing the features described.

Romalea microptera

Remove the prothorax and the abdomen beyond the first segment. Cut through the mid-dorsal and mid-ventral lines of the pterothorax and first abdominal segment. Use the left half for the external features and boil the other half in potassium hydroxide for studying the internal surface.

Examine the external surface and note that, unlike the condition found in *Acheta,* all of the sclerites of the pteropleuron, except the epipleurites and trochantin, are consolidated, i.e., they are continuous sclerotically, being separated merely by sulci. Furthermore the episternum is consolidated with the sternum.

The pteropleuron consists chiefly of four nearly vertical sclerites separated by three sulci. The middle sulcus is the intersegmental suture, as can be determined by reference to its position in relation to the legs and the intersegmental line between the meso- and metathorax.

Each segmental pleuron is divided by a pleural suture into an anterior *episternum* and posterior *epimeron,* as in the cricket, but the episternum is divided transversely into a dorsal *anepisternite* and a ventral *katepisternite.* A narrow sclerite, the *pre-episternite,* is cut off from the anterior edge of the katepisternite of the mesopleuron. It and its fellow on the opposite side are continuous with a similar sclerite (the presternite) cut off from the sternum. The three form a U-shaped "collar" known as the *prepectus.*

The katepisternite of the metapleuron extends ventrally in front of the coxal cavity forming a *precoxal bridge* which unites with the sternum, the two being separated by the *pleurosternal suture.* In the mesopleuron there is a *precoxale* interposed between the katepisternite and the sternum.

The *epimeron* in the locust is an undivided sclerite which does not meet the sternum ventrally, but in many insects it is divided into anepimerite and katepimerite and may extend behind the coxal cavity, to the sternum forming a postcoxal bridge.

Find in each segment the *pleural wing process, pleural coxal process,* two *basalar plates,* one *subalar plate* and the *trochantin* as described in the previous exercise. Find also the two prominent *spiracles,* one in the intersegmental membrane in front of the mesepisternum, the other in a small triangular plate at the posteroventral angle of the mesepimeron. These belong primitively to the mesothorax and metathorax respectively.

The sclerites surrounding the articulatory membrane of the leg have their edges strengthened by marginal and submarginal inflections. In the mesothorax these ridges completely surround the leg, the coxal cavity being closed behind by the metepisternum. In the metathorax the cavity is open behind. As a result of these inflections a narrow sclerite is cut off in both segments anterior and ventral to the coxal cavity. This sclerite is referred to in the literature as the *pericoxal ring* or *sclerite.*

Examine the internal face of the pleura and note that each sulcus is represented by a well-defined inflection or ridge. The *pleural ridge,* corresponding to the pleural sulcus, is particularly prominent. Find its dorsal prolongation, the *wing process,* and its ventral prolongation, the *coxal process,* which forms a strong condyle for the articulation of the coxa. Dorsal to the coxal process the pleural ridge gives off a strong spur-like process, the *pleural apophysis.* This extends inward above the leg opening and is intimately connected with the *sternal apophysis,* an ingrowth from the sternum. The two apophyses form a strengthening arch above the leg opening, from which certain of the leg muscles originate.

DRAWINGS: (1) External and (2) internal views of the pteropleura showing the features mentioned. In each case include the coxal cavity and a

portion of the sternum to show the relation between these structures and the pleuron.

Romalea microptera

The *propleuron* in the Orthoptera is greatly reduced and largely overgrown
by the pronotum, only the ventral edge of the episternum being visible
externally. The structure, however, is fundamentally the same as in the
other pleura.

Ventral to the anterior half of the edge of the pronotum, in front of and
dorsal to the leg, find a triangular plate, which is continuous mesally with
the basisternite, the spine-bearing sclerite of the sternum. This plate is all
that is visible of the *episternum*, but the position and outline of the pleuron
can be determined usually by indications on the pronotum. In front of the
third sulcus or groove of the pronotum, a triangular area, slightly darker
than the neighboring parts and distinctly punctate, marks the position of
the *episternum*. Behind the sulcus a very narrow horizontal, marginal,
punctate area marks the position of the *epimeron*.

Divide the prothorax by cutting through the mid-dorsal and mid-ventral
lines, boil in caustic potash, remove the soft tissues, examine the internal
surface and find the following structures. The *episternum* is the anterior
triangular piece, the outline of which you saw from the exterior. The
epimeron is a very narrow sclerite posterior to the episternum and adhering
closely to the lower margin of the pronotum. At the junction of the two
there is a well developed *pleural ridge* starting near the apex of the triangular episternum and continuing to the leg socket where it is produced
into the *pleural coxal process* which articulates with the coxa of the foreleg. There is no pleural apophysis distinct from the ridge, but the latter is
very deep and the sternal apophysis is bound to its edge.

> **DRAWING:** A diagrammatic view of the propleuron from the internal
> surface. Show the outline of the pronotum but the inflections of the
> latter need not be shown.

THE STERNUM (Figures 3 and 4)

The sternum is the ventral sclerotized region of the segment. Its morphology is still somewhat obscure and the homologies in the higher insects
difficult to interpret. It seems, basically, to have been formed from four
distinct sclerotizations as follows. (1) A large segmental ventrosternite
sclerotized in the venter of the segment. This may be termed the *medio-*

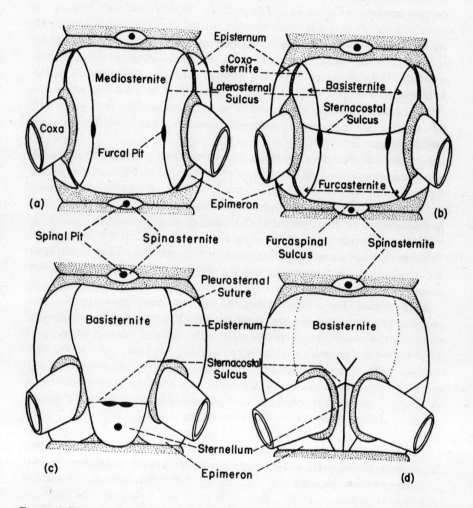

FIGURE 4. Some stages in the evolution of the mesosternum. (a) Union of mediosternite and coxosternite. (b) Development of sternacosta. (c) Loss of laterosternal and furcaspinal sutures. (d) Posterior and ventral migration of coxae resulting in reduction and infolding of the sternellum.

sternite (Figure 4a). (2) A small intersegmental ventrosternite posterior to the mediosternite of the prothorax and mesothorax. This bears an internal process known as the *spina* (Figure 3) and is therefore named the *spinasternite* (Figure 4a). The anterior spinasternite may or may not unite with the prothoracic mediosternite but the posterior one always unites with the mesothoracic mediosternite (Figure 4b). (3) Two *coxosternites* derived from the infracoxal arcs of the subcoxae. These lie lateral to the mediosternite with which they later unite to form the *eusternum*. A pair of *laterosternal sulci* are formed at the lines of union and within each sulcus is a slit-like *furcal pit* which marks the invagination of the *sternal apophyses* (Figure 3), two internal processes which lend support to the region of leg attachment.

An internal strengthening ridge, the *sternacosta,* develops between the anterior edges of the bases of the apophyses and continues laterally across the coxosternites. Thus externally the eusternum is divided transversely by the *sternacostal sulcus* into an anterior *basisternite* and a posterior *furcasternite*. The laterosternal sulci disappear in most insects.

The legs in most insects lie toward the posterior end of the segment, therefore the apophyses also are posterior in position. This results in a reduction of the furcasternite, leaving the basisternite as the most conspicuous sternal sclerite (Figure 4c).

In the higher insects (Figure 4d) the leg bases are closely approximated and the portion of the sternum lying between them probably consists only of the coxosternites, the mediosternite being reduced and inflected along the middle line. In such insects there is usually an extensive sternal plate anterior to the legs. Whether this also consists only of the coxosternites or whether the mediosternite contributes to its structure is not definitely known. In these insects the episternum and basisternite are usually completely fused, as are the epimeron and furcasternite; consequently there are no dividing lines between the pleuron and sternum.

Ferris contends that the entire ventral region in higher insects is derived from the subcoxae. He regards all structures derived from these as the pleuron, and would limit the sternum to the plates here called ventrosternites. He claims therefore that, at least in the higher insects, there are no sternal sclerites.

Paragnetina, Acroneuria or other perlid stonefly

Note that distinct sternal plates are developed in each segment and that, unlike all other segmental plates, the anterior edges of the mesosternum and metasternum overlap the plates anterior to them. The metasternum also overlaps the first abdominal sternum.

The component sclerites of the sterna are distinct and their arrangement is such as to present an almost schematic representation of the probable early stages in the development of the sternum.

PROSTERNUM. Note that this is composed largely of three sclerites which together form the *eusternum.* The two somewhat crescentic lateral sclerites, adjacent to the *coxal cavities,* are *coxosternites* derived from the infracoxal arc of the subcoxa. The median sclerite or *mediosternite* is a ventrosternite sclerotized in the venter of the segment. The mediosternite and coxosternites are separated by the two *laterosternal sulci.* Find the elongated *furcal pit,* marking the position of the sternal apophysis or furcal arm, in the posterior half of each sulcus.

Behind the mediosternite there is a small oval or lenticular intersegmental ventrosternite with a single invagination or pit. This is the *spinasternite* and the invagination is the *spinal pit.* Note that the spinasternite is separated by membrane from the eusternum.

METASTERNUM. Note that the mediosternite is divided into *premediosternite* and *postmediosternite* by the transverse *sternacostal suture* which passes across the anterior ends of the furcal pits and continues across the coxosternites. The sulcus thus divides the entire eusternum into an anterior *basisternite* and posterior *furcasternite,* each of which is a composite plate made up respectively of the anterior and posterior regions of the mediosternite and coxosternites. The laterosternal sulci terminate some distance behind the anterior edge of the basisternite, therefore the mediosternite and coxosternites are completely fused anteriorly. This perhaps marks the beginning of the disappearance of the laterosternal sulci which are rarely present. In most insects the mediosternite and coxosternites are indistinguishably united. Note that there is no spinasternite in this segment.

MESOSTERNUM. The structure here is essentially like that of the metasternum, except for the presence of a *spinasternite* which is united with the eusternum. The united furcasternite and spinasternite constitute the *sternellum.* There is a median sulcus in the sternellum but this is characteristic of the species and of no special morphological significance.

DRAWING: The three thoracic sterna with the intersegmental membranes extended to show the spinasternites.

Romalea microptera

The morphology of the sternum in the higher insects is difficult to interpret owing to the disappearance of some of the primary sutures described in *Paragnetina,* the appearance of secondary sutures marking the position of internal strengthening ridges and the reduction or loss of certain of the sclerites. This difficulty appears even in a relatively generalized insect such as *Romalea.*

PROSTERNUM. All the primary sutures and sclerites are apparently recognizable in the prosternum. A very narrow marginal *presternite* is cut off from the anterior end. Immediately behind this is the *basisternite* which, as found earlier (p. 44), is continuous, in front of the leg, with the episternum. The basisternite bears a large median spine which should be removed to expose the structures behind it more fully. A large *furcal pit* will be found on each side of the spine. A curved suture, not always very distinct, passes through each pit and cuts off a narrow crescentic sclerite lateral to the leg. This suture is almost certainly the *laterosternal suture* and the sclerite the *coxosternite,* but there is a possibility that the suture marks a secondary strengthening ridge in the basisternite. The student should be prepared to find these uncertainties in interpretation, which can be solved only by intensive comparative studies, and should not regard interpretations given here, or elsewhere, as necessarily final.

Extending between the pits, and passing behind the spine, you will find the curved *sternacostal suture* which separates the basisternite from the transverse *furcasternite.*

Identify the median *spinal pit* in the posterior sclerite of the sternum and note that a transverse suture separates the rather large *spinasternite,* in which the pit lies, from the furcasternite anterior to it. The acridids are among the few insects in which the spinasternite of the prothorax is fused with the eusternum.

MESOSTERNUM. The mesosternum has a distinct *presternite,* continuous with the preepisternite. Apart from this the sternum apparently consists of a single sclerite produced posteriorly into two lateral lobes. Find the two *furcal pits* and the *spinal pit* at the posterior border of the median region of the sclerite. Note that these pits are connected by a short curved suture which continues a short distance lateral to the pits and partially separates the lateral lobes from the anterior portion of the sclerite. From its relation to the furcal pits this suture may be interpreted as the *sternacostal suture.* The lobes would, therefore, be the lateral portions of the *furcasternite,* and the body of the sclerite would be the *basisternite.* The spinasternite and the median portion of the furcasternite have disappeared and the three apophyses all arise from the internal ridge marked by the sternacostal suture.

DRAWING: The prosternum and mesosternum.

Acheta assimilis

Remove the ventral half of the thorax of two specimens by cutting longitudinally through the pleura dorsal to the coxae. Boil one specimen in potassium hydrate for a study of the internal features.

PROSTERNUM. Note that the prosternal area is not completely sclerotized but contains a considerable amount of membrane. This condition is common in the prothorax of insects and is probably the result of secondary desclerotization. Find the sclerites whose description follows.

The *premediosternite* is the prominent, transverse, anterior sclerite which is continuous laterally with the edge of the episternum. Behind this sclerite and separated from it by the short, curved *sternacostal suture,* are two posteriorly divergent sclerites. These are lateral fragments of the *postmediosternite.* Examine the internal surface and note that the *sternal apophyses* arise from their posterolateral edges. Lateral to the mediosternite are two crescentic lightly-sclerotized *coxosternites,* very similar in position and form to those of *Paragnetina.* They are semimembranous and not always easily distinguishable. In the membrane behind the mediosternite there is a small median shield-shaped *spinasternite.* On its inner face it bears the *spina,* a short process with a flattened palm-shaped ental surface.

MESOSTERNUM. Note that from the external view the sternum apparently consists of a single four-sided sclerite, the *basisternite.* Examination of the internal surface, however, will show that behind this there is a narrow sclerite bent entally and bearing the paired *sternal apophyses* as well as the *spina.* A common external invagination serves the three processes since the bases of the apophyses are juxtaposed and the spina arises from their dorsal wall at the point of junction. This juxtaposition of the apophyses to form a forked structure arising from a common base is a very common condition in higher insects and is the basis for the term *furca* generally used for them. The posterior sclerite bearing the three processes is obviously the sternellum composed of the greatly reduced *furcasternite* and *spinasternite.* Examine the inner surface and note the close relationship between the sternal and pleural apophyses.

DRAWINGS: 1. Internal surface of the prosternum. 2. Internal surface of the mesosternum with the sternellum extended. Show the relationship between the sternal and pleural apophyses.

THE THORAX OF A SPECIALIZED INSECT

Tipulidae (crane flies) (Diptera)

The preceding studies of the thorax have been concerned with comparatively generalized insects and have been designed to illustrate the fundamental structure of the thorax. In the higher insects the structure becomes more complicated and often difficult to interpret. The thoracic sclerites may be greatly distorted in position as well as in proportions. There may be additional subdivisions of the sclerites, and sclerites originally separate may become fused and their limits obliterated. It is impracticable here to study examples from each of the higher groups, but the thorax of a crane fly will be studied in detail and its structure interpreted in the light of the principles already studied. Any of the common large crane flies may be used, as the differences in the structure of the thorax in different species are relatively slight. In some species the thorax is variegated and there may be a sharp dividing line between two differently colored regions of the same sclerite. Do not confuse such lines with sutures. The whole specimens should be supplemented by sagittal and frontal sections boiled in potassium hydroxide.

PRONOTUM AND PROPLEURON. The *pronotum* and *proepisterna* together form a narrow arch or "collar" behind the neck. In some species the arch is a continuous sclerite, in others the episterna are more or less completely marked off from the pronotum by sutures. The small, triangular, often inconspicuous *epimeron* lies in its normal position posterior to the episternum and separated from it by the short *pleural sulcus*. Identify the sulcus by its relation to the articulation of the coxa and by the presence of the pleural apophysis.

Find the large *lateral cervical sclerite* in the neck and note that it has an articulation with the episternum. This relationship between the two sclerites is typical.

METANOTUM. The metanotum is even less conspicuous than the pronotum. It forms the narrow dorsal arc behind the halteres (the club-shaped hindwings) and in front of the first abdominal tergum.

MESONOTUM. The mesonotum occupies all that area between the pronotum and metanotum. Its great size in the Diptera is correlated with the fact that these insects are normally strong fliers and only the forewings are developed as organs of flight.

The pronotum is deflected behind and thus has a vertical posterior plate which forms the anterior face of a deep groove between the pronotum and mesonotum. This plate terminates in a short inflection which bears a small median *phragma*. The inflection is evidently the *antecosta,* but there is no acrotergite distinct from the posterior plate of the pronotum. The phragma is much smaller than would be expected in such a strong-flying insect. It no longer serves for the insertion of the longitudinal wing muscles but only for the origin of a pair of small neck muscles. The thick mass of longitudinal flight muscles arises secondarily along the entire length of the anterior sclerite of the scutum.

The posterior face of the dorsal groove between the pronotum and mesonotum is formed by the anterior edge of the scutum. Forming the floor of the groove between the antecostal sulcus and the scutum there is a very narrow, usually unpigmented or lightly pigmented sclerite which is the median portion of the *prescutum*. Lateral to the groove the prescutum forks. The anterior branch runs ventrally adjacent to the pronotum. The posterior branch lies along the anterior lateral border of the scutum and terminates just in front of the wing base. The area between the two branches is desclerotized, the amount of desclerotization varying in different species. The *mesothoracic spiracle* lies in this area. Note that though greatly modified the prescutum forms an alar bridge, in front of the wing base, between the notum and episternum.

Note that the *scutum* is partially or completely divided into a number of secondary sclerites. A pair of sulci, orginating near the middle of the lateral margins, in front of the wing bases, run posteromesally. They converge and in some species meet each other in the middle line, forming a *transscutal sulcus* which divides the scutum into an anterior and a posterior sclerite. A somewhat similar pair of sulci arise laterally in the anterior sclerite and run posteromesally. These do not meet but, in some species, continue posteriorly until they join the transscutal suture, thus dividing the anterior sclerite into a median and two lateral sclerites. These sulci seem to correspond to the sutures known as *notaulices*. The posterior sclerite of the scutum is frequently divided into right and left halves by a *median sulcus*.

The median shield-shaped *scutellum* is easily recognized behind the scutum. Note that, as in the more primitive insects studied, the posterior border of the scutellum is continued laterally into the axillary cord of the posterior margin of the wing base.

Posterior to the scutellum lies the *postscutellum* which is extraordinarily well-developed and is divided by longitudinal sutures into dorsal and lateral sclerites. The lateral sclerites are often divided by vertical sutures into anterior and posterior portions. They occupy most of the space between the bases of the wings and halteres, and the lateral portions form what is in effect a *postalar bridge* uniting the tergum and the epimeron.

Examine a specimen treated with potassium hydroxide and find the well-developed *phragmata* at the antecosta between postscutellum and metanotum.

Examine a sagittal section of the thorax and find the prominent longitudinal muscles which have their origin on the inner surface of the median region of the anterior sclerite of the scutum and are inserted on the phragma of the postscutellum, except for one band which is inserted on the posterior edge of the postscutellum itself.

MESOPLEURON. The mesopleuron occupies its normal position; the sclerites and the *pleural suture* are well-developed and easily recognized. The *episternum* is partially divided by an oblique suture into a dorsal *anepisternum* and ventral *katepisternum*. The latter is indistinguishably united with the sternum and there is no pleurosternal suture. The epimeron also is divided into a large *anepimeron* and very small *katepimeron*. Ventral to the katepimeron, and lying between the bases of the middle and hind legs, there is a somewhat triangular sclerite, the *meron*. This is really a detached portion of the coxa or basal segment of the leg. In some species the katepimeron and meron may be partially or completely fused.

Find the *pleural coxal* and *pleural wing processes,* the *subalar plate* and the *basalar plates,* the *pleural ridge* and the *pleural apophysis.*

METANOTUM AND METAPLEURON. Examine the metanotum again and note that it consists of a single narrow sclerite forming the posterior border of the thoracic dorsum. In correlation with the degeneration of the hindwings the metanotum is reduced and not subdivided into sclerites, but its acrotergite forms the prominent and well-developed postscutellum of the mesothorax. The remaining portion of the metanotum is rolled into a narrow cylinder as can be seen by observing the cut edge of a sagittal section. Laterally the metanotum is indistinguishably fused with the *epimeron,* a narrow undivided sclerite which forms the posterior border of the lateral side of the thorax. In front of the epimeron, and separated from it by the *pleural sulcus,* is the small *episternum* divided by a distinct sulcus into *anepisternum* and *katepisternum*. The anepisternum is deeply cleft behind, and the *metathoracic spiracle* lies in the cleft. The *halteres* are borne dorsal to the pleural sulcus.

DRAWING: Lateral view of thorax showing the features mentioned.

STERNUM. The sternum is greatly modified in comparison with that of the more generalized insects studied. It is, however, possible to interpret its structure on the basis of the theory of the sternum outlined earlier. Examine both natural and cleaned (potassium hydroxide) specimens so that both external and internal elements can be seen, and verify the following description.

The *prosternum* consists of two median sclerites. The long narrow anterior sclerite is infolded so that only the narrow margins show externally on each side of the median groove. The comparatively wide spaces between this sclerite and the coxae are completely membranous. The posterior sclerite is triangular, its apex directed posteriorly. A sulcus running along its anterior margin separates it from the anterior plate and the *sternal apophyses* are borne at its anterior angles associated with this sulcus. It would appear that in this segment the coxosternites are completely de-sclerotized, the transverse sulcus is the *sternacostal sulcus,* the anterior infolded sclerite is the *premediosternite* and the posterior triangular plate the *postmediosternite.* There is no evidence of a spinasternite.

The mesothoracic coxae are posterior and ventral in their location and almost touch along the mid-ventral line. As a consequence the *mesosternum* consists of a broad anterior plate in front of the coxae and a very narrow posterior plate which lies chiefly between the coxae but has narrow lateral extensions which form the anterior margins of the coxal cavities. A transverse sulcus separates the two plates and examination of the internal surface will show that the sternal apophyses are associated with it. It is, therefore, the *sternacostal sulcus,* the large anterior plate is the *basisternite* and the posterior plate lying between the coxae is the *furcasternite.*

There is no pleurosternal suture, consequently the basisternite is united with the katepisternum to form a continuous sclerite known to dipterologists as the "sternopleura." Presumably the basisternite includes both mediosternite and coxosternite elements but some authors maintain that it is formed from the coxosternites only.

A deep median sulcus extends from the posterior region of the basisternite through the furcasternite and the entire metasternum. It marks the position of a deep infolded ridge. This infolding of the sternum is probably associated with the close approximation of the coxae, and the infolded region therefore represents the reduced mediosternite, at least in part. The external furcasternite probably represents the postcoxosternites only.

Note that the wider posterior region of the furcasternite bears two lateral processes for articulation with the coxa. This second or *ventral condyle* of the leg occurs in certain insects.

The *metasternum* is greatly reduced, as the metathorax is small and the hind legs occupy most of the ventral surface. Surrounding the coxa there is a complete ring of sclerotized tissue which includes the *episternum* and *epimeron,* narrow *precoxal* and *postcoxal bridges* and a small sternal plate. The whole ring very probably represents the subcoxa. The sternal plate is even more deeply infolded than that of the mesothorax. Near the middle the plate expands to form the *ventral articulatory condyles* of the coxae. A sulcus passing through these articulatory processes divides the sternum into anterior and posterior sclerites and continues inward across the infolded portion. The *sternal apophyses* borne on the latter are apparently associated with this sulcus. The sulcus is therefore the *sternacostal sulcus,* the external sclerites are the *precoxosternites* and *postcoxosternites* while the inflected plate is probably the *mediosternite.*

DRAWING: A ventral view of the entire sternum.

6 The Wings

GENERAL CONSIDERATIONS

The wings of insects originate as lateral hollow outgrowths or evaginations
of the dorsal body wall. Each wing therefore has at first a dorsal and a
ventral lamina both of which have the same structure as the integument;
i.e., an outer layer of nonliving *cuticle* and an inner layer of living epithelial cells, the *epidermis*. The latter is bounded internally by a delicate
basement membrane. As the wing develops the two laminae meet and their
basement membranes unite except along certain lines where the laminae
remain separate. Thus a series of channels is formed in the developing
wing. These channels serve for the passage of tracheae and nerves and
for the circulation of the blood. Their cuticular walls later become thickened to form the *wing veins*. Most of the epithelial cells die in the adult
and the wing is largely cuticular. It is still, however, a living organ which
must be nourished by the blood which circulates through its veins.

The arrangement of the wing veins is very widely used as a taxonomic
aid, therefore wing venation forms an important part of the study of sys-
tematic entomology. The morphologist should have some general knowledge of the primitive venation and of the nature of the changes that have
taken place in the venation of recent insects. In spite of the great diversity
in wing venation it has been possible, largely through the researches of
Comstock and Needham, to homologize the veins in most insects and to
construct an archetypal pattern which serves as the point of departure
for the numerous modifications found in the venation of recent insects.
Figure 5 represents this hypothetical primitive type as depicted by Comstock and Needham with some minor changes proposed by later workers.

The principal veins arranged in order from the anterior margin are as follows:

1. *Costa* (C). Typically an unbranched vein in or near the anterior margin.
2. *Subcosta* (Sc). Typically two-branched (Sc_1 and Sc_2).
3. *Radius* (R). Forks near the base; the anterior branch (R_1) is undivided, the posterior branch or *radial sector* (R_S) forks twice to form four branches (R_2 to R_5).
4. *Media* (M). Forks to form a *media anterior* (MA) and *media posterior* (MP). The media anterior divides into two branches; the media posterior forks twice to form four branches. The media anterior is seldom present and it is customary to label the branches of the media posterior M_1 to M_4.
5. *Cubitus* (Cu). Two branches (Cu_1 and Cu_2) but Cu_1 usually divides into Cu_{1a} and Cu_{1b}.
6. *Anal veins* (A). Behind the cubitus there is a varying number of typically unbranched anal veins. These have been called *vannal* veins by Snodgrass, who claims also that the first anal vein (1A) does not belong to the same series as the others and calls it the "postcubitus."

Cross-veins connect some of the longitudinal veins and, as a result, the wing surface is divided into a number of areas bounded by veins. These areas are known as "cells" and are designated by the name of the vein bordering them anteriorly.

From this archetypal venation specialization may take place in the following ways:

1. By addition, usually an increase in the number of branches of the longitudinal veins and in the number of cross-veins. Sometimes new longitudinal veins are added, e.g., in dragonflies, Neuroptera, etc.
2. By reduction, (a) through loss of some veins or their branches, e.g., in cecidomyids, aleurodids, etc.; (b) through coalescence of veins, e.g., in many Hymenoptera, higher Diptera, etc. When veins coalesce they may follow tortuous courses and are difficult to identify.

There may be addition in one area of a wing and reduction in another.

TOPOGRAPHY OF THE WING

Pieris rapae

Examine the forewing of this or some other butterfly. Spread the wing horizontally at right angles to the body. Note that it is triangular in shape and therefore has three margins and three angles. The anterior margin,

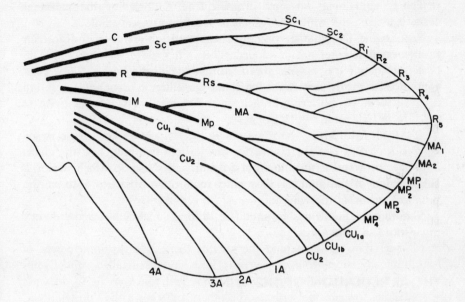

FIGURE 5. Hypothetical primitive wing venation. For explanation see text.

strengthened by the costa, is the *costal margin*, the lateral margin is known as the *outer margin* and the posterior one as the *inner margin*. The angle by which the wing is attached to the thorax is the *humeral angle*, that between the costal and outer margins is the *apex*, while the third is the *anal angle*.

Melanoplus sp.

The hindwing of any long-winged grasshopper may be examined. Find a small notch along the outer margin and note that this marks the end of a furrow which runs the length of the wing. This is the *anal furrow* (Comstock) or *vannal furrow* (Snodgrass) along which the wing folds. It is found in most wings, though not always as distinct as in the one studied. Its normal position is behind the cubitus and it divides the wing into an *anal area* containing the anal veins, and a *preanal area*. These areas are called by Snodgrass the *vannus* and *remigium* respectively. The remigium, containing the most prominent veins, including the marginal costa, is usually stiff while the vannus is usually soft and flexible.

Next to the thorax, the wing base has a membranous area in which several small sclerites are developed. This is the *axillary membrane.* The posterior margin of the membrane forms the corrugated *axillary cord* continuous with the posterior edge of the scutellum.

Musca domestica

Examine the wing of any muscoid fly and find the deep notch near the basal region of the vannus. This notch cuts off a posterior lobe in the proximal region of the wing known as the *jugum.*

Note that the hindwings are modified to form small club-shaped sensory organs known as *halteres.*

THE ARTICULATION OF THE WING

The wings of insects must make complicated movements, not only in flight, but in the less vigorous activities of flexion, extension and folding. To bring about these movements there are associated with the base of the wing a number of sclerites which serve as fulcra and levers, or for the attachment of muscles. Among these are the notal and pleural wing processes, the basalar plates and the subalar plates, which have already been discussed. Other elements are the bases of the wing veins and a series of small sclerites in the axillary membrane known as the *pteralia* or *axillaries.* These function chiefly in the flexion, extension and folding of the wings. In insects such as the Ephemerida and Odonata in which the wings are not folded, the axillaries are not as well developed as in those insects which fold their wings when at rest.

Hexagenia (Mayfly)

Pin the specimen in the dissecting tray in such a way that when the fore-wing is extended horizontally the axillary region is fully exposed. The vein in the anterior margin of the wing is the *costa.* The two immediately behind are the *subcosta* and *radius.* Note that the costa is articulated proximally with a small sclerite, the *humeral plate,* which is hinged to the thorax; manipulate the wing and note that the humeral plate moves only in a vertical (dorsoventral) direction. The bases of the subcosta and radius are closely associated and are, in turn, associated with a large sclerite which appears to be an expansion of the base of the radius. Proximal to this sclerite, and articulated with it, is a narrow curved sclerite which abuts against the anterior notal wing process. Still another sclerite lies posterior to the last one. This is very narrow and thread-like and extends horizontally in the membrane of the wing base, then turns anteriorly to be associated with the bases of some of the veins behind the radius. These three sclerites are known as *axillary plates.*

Manipulate the wing and note that it can be brought to the vertical position with relative ease, but cannot be folded naturally over the body. The Ephemerida and Odonata belong to an archaic group, the Palaeoptera, the wings of which when at rest are held vertically and cannot be folded horizontally over the body. All other Pterygota belong to the group Neoptera and, except in some secondarily modified species, such as the butterflies, fold the wings across the body when at rest. The axillary plates in these are specially modified to this end.

DRAWING: The lateral edge of the thorax and the base of the forewing showing the features mentioned.

Romalea microptera

Examine the forewing and identify the following veins. The *costa* lies a short distance behind the anterior margin. Behind it are three veins very close together proximally but separating beyond the middle of the wing. These are, in order, the *subcosta, radius* and *media.* The costa and radius are convex veins, i.e., strongly developed on the upper surface, while the subcosta and media are concave. Turn to the underside and note that the subcosta is very prominent with an enlarged base from which the costa appears to branch. This thickened base is also very prominent on the dorsal side where it seems to be a continuation of the costa. Note that the radius and media are also united at the base.

Behind the media there are two veins, probably the *cubitus.* Finally there are three *anal veins,* the third lying in the hind margin of the wing.

Remove the pterothorax, cut through the pleura and pin the dorsal half in the dissecting tray with the right forewing extended so as to expose the axillary region fully, and identify the following *pteralia.*

The *first axillary* is triangular in form with a narrow process given off from its anterior angle. This process articulates with the base of the subcosta, while the triangular posterior region articulates with the lateral edge of the scutum. This region of the scutum corresponds to the anterior notal wing process which is not prominently developed in *Romalea.*

The *second axillary* is an irregular sclerite lying lateral to the first with which its mesal edge articulates. Anterolaterally it is joined to the common base of the radius and media by a narrow flexible sclerotic bridge. Normally, when the two veins are separate, the second axillary articulates with the end of the radius. Examine another specimen and note that this axillary has a sclerotization in the ventral side of the membrane which pivots on the pleural wing process.

The *third axillary* lies in the posterior region of the membrane. It extends transversely and then bends anteriorly, the portion beyond the bend being joined to the bases of the three anal veins. The transverse portion is folded on itself and proximally it articulates with the narrow posterior end of the second axillary.

The *fourth axillary.* Normally the third axillary articulates with the posterior notal wing process but sometimes, as in *Romalea,* a small fourth axillary intervenes between the third and the lateral edge of the thorax. It may be the detached notal process.

Median plates. Two sclerites lie lateral to the second axillary and anterior to the third. The *anterior median plate* is attached to the common base of the media and radius and extends obliquely in a posterolateral direction. The *posterior median plate* is a triangular sclerite lying between the second axillary, the third axillary and the anterior median plate. It is closely united to the anterior edge of the third axillary. There is an oblique membranous suture between the two median plates along which the base of the wing folds when it is flexed over the body. Manipulate the wing and note how easily it can be flexed. The flexor muscles are inserted in the third axillary. When they contract they pull the axillary and posterior median plate toward the body and tilt them upward. This pulls the anal area toward the body and causes the wing to fold along the membranous strip between the anterior and the posterior median plate.

DRAWING: The lateral edge of the notum and the proximal half of the outstretched wing showing the veins and pteralia.

MODIFICATIONS IN WING STRUCTURE

The four wings of primitive insects resembled each other in size, shape, texture and venation, but in nearly all modern insects there is some dissimilarity between the fore- and hindwings. Most insects show some differences in the venation of the two pairs. Differences in size and shape are common. There may be a progressive reduction in the size of one pair until in some insects it is reduced to a mere vestige, e.g., in some Ephemerida, Diptera, male Coccidae.

Differences in texture occur in several orders. In Coleoptera and Dermaptera the front wings (elytra) are hard and horny. In the Orthoptera the front wings (tegmina) are stiff and parchment-like. In the Heteroptera the front wings (hemelytra) are partly thickened, partly membranous.

Primitive insects probably moved the two pairs of wings independently but most modern insects have the wing movements so coordinated that they may be said to have attained virtual or actual dipterism. In the Diptera, male Coccidae and Strepsiptera one pair of wings has been reduced to mere vestiges which do not function as organs of flight. In Coleoptera, Dermaptera and some other insects only the hindwings are used in flight. Other insects have devices for hooking the fore- and hindwings together so that they move synchronously. The chief of these devices are as follows:

a. The jugum of the forewing may be produced into a finger-like process which clasps the hindwing against the forewing, e.g., *Sthenopis* (jugate Lepidoptera).

b. The hindwing may bear, near the base of the costal margin, a stout bristle or tuft of bristles (the "frenulum") which fits into a retinaculum on the forewing (e.g., most moths).

c. The hindwing may bear a row of hooks, the "hamuli," on its costal margin which fit into the incurved posterior edge of the forewing (e.g., honeybee).

d. The proximal region of the costal margin of the hindwing may be greatly expanded, extending forward beneath the forewing. This overlapping insures synchronous movements of the two wings (e.g., butterflies).

e. In some insects (e.g., the honeybee) the arrangement of the wing muscles is such as to insure synchronous movements of the wings.

Comparison of wing structure

Study the fore- and hindwings of the following insects in relation to the modifications discussed above. Related species may be substituted for any of those mentioned.

Bittacus (scorpion fly, Mecoptera); *Melanoplus* (grasshopper, Orthoptera); *Euschistus* (stinkbug, Hemiptera); *Phyllophaga* (may beetle,

Coleoptera); *Hexagenia* (mayfly, Ephemerida); *Sthenopis* (jugate Lepidoptera); *Agrotis* (miller, frenulate Lepidoptera); *Danaus* (monarch butterfly, Lepidoptera); *Apis* (honeybee, Hymenoptera); *Musca* (housefly, Diptera).

DRAWING: Make a semidiagrammatic drawing of the fore- and hindwing of each species. Details of venation need not be shown but differences in texture should be indicated. Regarding the wings of the scorpion fly as the most generalized, make a brief statement of the modifications found in the others.

7 Abdominal Appendages and Thoracic Legs

GENERAL CONSIDERATIONS

Each trunk segment of the early embryo bears, typically, a pair of lateral appendages which appear first as unsegmented, finger-like outgrowths of the ectoderm. As development proceeds the appendages of the gnathal and thoracic segments assume the form characteristic of these organs as they appear in the newly-hatched insect.

Persistent remnants of abdominal appendages are found in most Apterygota. In Pterygota the embryonic abdominal appendages are evanescent and, except for the cerci borne on the eleventh segment, and certain elements of the genitalia borne on the eighth and ninth, no obvious trace of them appears in the adult. Abdominal appendages are found, however, in many larval insects. The prolegs of Lepidoptera, sawflies and scorpion flies are generally believed to be segmental appendages serially homologous with the legs and the mouth appendages. This is held to be true also of the appendages found in certain other larval insects, but Hinton has claimed recently that all the so-called prolegs are adaptive larval structures having no relation to the true legs. In no insect are the abdominal appendages similar in structure to the thoracic legs.

The earliest fossil arthropods had a segmented leg comparable to that of recent species, but it is not certainly known whether the segmentation was abrupt, and complete in a single mutation or whether it developed gradually. Almost certainly the segmented leg of arthropods evolved from the parapodia of primitive annelid-like ancestors. These parapodia were probably simple tubular outgrowths like those of the early arthropod embryo. We may assume, provisionally, that the segmentation of the insect

MANUAL OF INSECT MORPHOLOGY

leg may have taken place as follows. With the appearance of the sclerotized cuticle the limb took on a dorsoventral articulation with the body wall which allowed for protraction and retraction of the limb as a whole. Such limbs could be used in swimming, or could pull the body along, but could not raise it above the substratum. Later the limb may have been divided into a proximal *coxopodite* and a distal *telopodite,* having an anteroposterior articulation with each other, and could now raise the body above the substratum. Still later, further segmentation of the telopodite into *trochanter, femur, tibia, tarsus* and *pretarsus* increased the efficiency of the limb in walking or climbing. At some time the coxopodite divided into a *subcoxa* and *coxa,* but the subcoxa was incorporated into the body wall leaving the coxa as the basal segment of the six-segmented leg. It is not certain, however, that the subcoxa was ever a functional segment of an ambulatory leg. It may represent detached basal portions of the coxopodite incorporated in the body wall.

ABDOMINAL APPENDAGES

Nesomachilis (Thysanura)

Examine the ventral view (if a specimen is not available consult Snodgrass, Imms or other text). You will find on each of the first seven segments a pair of large flattened plates, each plate bearing distally a small cylindrical tapering *stylus* and a short blunt *contractile vesicle.* The large plates are the *coxopodites* of the abdominal appendages. They are attached proximally to a narrow triangular sclerite, the *sternum,* which in this insect consists of the *ventrosternite* only. The stylus is a secondary structure articulated to the coxopodite and movable by muscles inserted in its base. The vesicle, which is retractile and therefore not usually visible, is probably a device for absorbing moisture.

DRAWING: Ventral view of a segment showing the structures described.

Heterojapyx

Note that the two styli are attached to a single ventral plate indicating that the coxopodites and ventrosternite have united to form the definitive sternum.

DRAWING: Ventral aspect of one segment.

Thermobia

Here the sternum of the anterior abdominal segments consists of a single plate as in the Pterygota and there is no evidence of its composite origin. The sterna of the posterior segments, however, bear styli as in *Heterojapyx*.

Corydalis larva

Note that the integument of the abdominal segments consists of unsclerotized rings. The first eight bear tapering lateral processes, attached to a bulbous swelling or tubercle of the lateral body wall. This tubercle has been interpreted as the *coxopodite* but this is by no means certain. If it is, the abdominal segment illustrates what must have been the structure of a segment of the unsclerotized ancestral arthropod, namely, a dorsal region, a ventral region, and two pleural regions largely occupied by the bases of the appendages. Note that the spiracles are borne on the dorsal areas above the "leg base."

The tapering lateral process of the tubercle is the *stylus*. Ventral to the stylus the tubercle bears a tuft of filamentous *gills;* remove these gills and note that they are borne on a trilobate outgrowth of the tubercle. The musculature of this outgrowth resembles that of the retractile vesicle, but the two structures are probably not homologous.

Examine the appendages of the tenth abdominal segment. Note that there is a definite basal segment which bears a stylus essentially like that of the anterior appendages. On the distal extremity of the basal segment, there is a short blunt lobe bearing a pair of curved claws. The musculature of this lobe is somewhat similar to that of the gill-bearing lobe and the two may be homologous.

DRAWINGS: 1. An anterior appendage with most of the gills removed.
2. A posterior appendage.

Larva of Protoparce or other lepidopteron

Caterpillars bear several pairs of abdominal appendages, commonly referred to as "prolegs." Examine any common species with well developed prolegs. Note that the appendage is, in most species, attached to a lobe of the body wall. The first region of the proleg is in the form of a short cylinder which is partly sclerotized, but the extent of sclerotization differs in different species. On the assumption that the proleg is a true segmental appendage, this segment is known as the *coxa*. It is followed by a short membranous area, which in turn is followed by a distal plate known as the *planta*. This also is partly membranous, partly sclerotized. It bears a series of heavily sclerotized hook-like structures known as *crotchets*.

DRAWING: A proleg showing its attachment to the body wall.

Larva of Sialis

Note that the first eight abdominal segments bear leg-like segmented appendages. These segments should not be regarded as equivalent to the segments of the thoracic legs. The basal segment has been interpreted as the coxopodite and the remainder as a segmented stylus but this is open to considerable doubt.

It may be stated here that other larval insects bear a variety of leg-like outgrowths which are not homologous with the legs but are adaptive larval structures, and that some structures, such as styli, crotchet-like hooks, etc., borne on abdominal appendages may not be homologous with similar structures of other insects but may be convergent adaptive structures.

DRAWING: An abdominal appendage.

Acheta assimilis

Examine the long tapering *cerci* at the posterior end of the abdomen and note that they are inserted in a membrane between the tenth tergum, the epiproct and the paraproct. The cerci are appendages of the eleventh segment but owing to the partial or complete atrophy of this segment in many insects they appear to be more closely associated with the tenth. They are frequently lost. In *Acheta* a very narrow basal ring is marked off by a suture from the remainder. This ring has been interpreted as the coxopodite but this is very doubtful; the suture more probably marks the position of a ridge for the attachment of muscles.

Check your drawing of the abdomen of *Acheta* and see that the cerci are correctly drawn.

The cerci vary in form and degree of development in different species. Check this on other insects whose abdominal structure you have studied.

THORACIC APPENDAGES

Romalea microptera

Examine the mesothoracic leg of this or some other locust. Extend it at right angles to the body and determine the anterior, posterior, dorsal and ventral surfaces.

Note that the pleuron and sternum surround a *coxal cavity* into which the base of the leg is set. An *articular membrane* connects the base of the leg with the rim of the coxal cavity and provides for free movement of the limb.

The first or proximal segment of the leg is known as the *coxa*. Note its size and form. Find the *basicostal* sulcus which runs parallel to the proximal edge of the coxa and cuts off a narrow marginal sclerite known as the *basicoxite*. Internally the sulcus is represented by a ridge, the *basicosta*. The coxa articulates by a single hinge joint with the pleural coxal process. Note that the basicosta and basicoxite are thickened and modified to form the articular surface at this joint. A *coxal sulcus* extends from the joint to the distal edge of the coxa in *Romalea,* but is not generally present in other insects.

The second segment is a short cylindrical one known as the *trochanter*. It has two lateral articulations with the coxa forming a hinge joint which permits movement in the vertical direction.

The *femur* or third segment is the largest in the leg. The trochanter and femur are quite closely united in this insect and are not freely movable on each other.

The next segment, the *tibia,* is long and slender but heavily sclerotized and rigid because this is the segment which gives the propulsive push in walking or leaping. The tibial muscles lie within the femur, which accounts for the large size of this segment. Note the two rows of strong spurs or spines along the ventrolateral edge of the tibia. The articulation with the femur is by means of lateral condyles. Examine the nature of the joint and the provision to insure the complete flexion of the tibia against the femur.

The fifth segment or *tarsus* is divided into three subsegments. Examine the ventral surface and note that it bears a number of swellings known as *tarsal pads*. These are paired on the first and second subsegments, unpaired on the third. The fact that the first subsegment bears three pairs of pads probably indicates that it is formed by the fusion of three subsegments, since the typical number appears to be five. The last subsegment bears a small dorsal sclerite with a distal median process, known as the *unguifer,* with which the claws articulate.

Beyond the tarsus there are several structures, collectively known as the *pretarsus,* which represent a sixth segment of the leg. Viewed dorsally the pretarsus is seen to consist of two strong curved *claws* or *ungues* and a thick median lobe, the *arolium*. On the ventral side, at the base of the arolium and between the ungues, find a quadrangular sclerite, the *planta*.

Proximal to the planta, and disappearing into the cavity at the distal end of the tarsus is a second sclerite, the *unguitractor*. Cut carefully through each side of the last tarsal segment and remove the tarsal pad so as to expose the unguitractor. Observe that the end of the uguitractor is produced into a slender filiform apodeme which extends through the tarsus into the tibia. This is the *unguitractor apodeme* and is really the "tendon" of the muscle which retracts the pretarsus, that is to say, the muscle which contracts when the insect clings to an object with its claws.

DRAWINGS: 1. The anterior face of the leg showing the visible structures. 2. Dorsal and ventral views of the last tarsal segment and the pretarsus, with the tarsal pad cut away to expose the unguitractor.

Blaberus craniifer or other cockroach

Examine the anterior face of the coxa of the middle or hind leg, i.e., the face which is directed ventrally when the coxae are flexed against the body. Find the *basicostal sulcus* and the *basicoxite*. Note that while the basicostal sulcus runs parallel with the base of the coxa in front of the pleurocoxal articulation, it bends distally at the articulation and runs obliquely to the hind (dorsal) margin of the coxa. The portion of the basicoxite behind the articulation is thus converted into a triangular sclerite which is now known as the *meron*. Note that the meron never takes part in the coxo-trochanteral articulation.

Find the pleuron which consists of a fairly broad episternum and narrower epimeron separated by the pleural sulcus. The episternum is partially divided into *anepisternum* and *katepisternum*. Partly fused with the latter you will find a large triangular sclerite, traversed by a deep longitudinal groove, lying parallel to the anterior edge of the base of the coxa. This is the *trochantin,* which is larger and better developed here than in most other insects. Its ventral end makes an articulation with the coxa so that the latter has two basal articulations, the *pleurocoxal* and the *trochantinocoxal.*

The trochantin, like the pleuron, is derived from the supracoxal arc of the subcoxa, and in the cockroach the two remain partly united.

DRAWING: The pleuron and coxa showing the features mentioned.

Panorpa sp. (scorpion fly) (Mecoptera)

Examine the mesothoracic coxa of *Panorpa* and observe that it is divided longitudinally into two practically equal sclerites, an anterior sclerite which takes part in the coxotrochanteral articulation and a posterior sclerite or *meron* which does not.

DRAWING: Lateral view of coxa.

A tipulid or crane fly

Examine again the drawings of the crane fly previously studied and note that the meron here has separated from the coxa and forms part of the body wall. It may be partially or wholly united with the katepimeron.

Eristalis tenax (drone fly) (Diptera)

Examine the pretarsus and note that the arolium is lost but instead there are two lateral lobes or *pulvilli* attached basally to the *auxilliae,* a pair of small plates near the bases of the ungues. Note further that the unguitractor bears a median spine, the *empodium.*

DRAWING: Pretarsus of *Eristalis*, ventral view.

Bibio sp.

Examine the pretarsus and note that the empodium is in the form of a flattened lobe (pulvilliform).

DRAWING: Pretarsus of *Bibio,* ventral view.

Functional modifications of legs

Many insects have their legs modified to subserve functions other than walking. The following are examples of some of the more common types of adaptation. In addition to the special adaptations described, examine the various segments and note the variety of forms they may assume.

Romalea or Melanoplus sp.

The hindlegs are saltatorial, i.e., modified for leaping. Note the enlargement of the femur as compared with that of the other legs. This provides room for the large extensors of the tibia, the principal muscles used in leaping. The tibia is strongly sclerotized since the force of leaping is exerted against

69

it. Note the strong spurs at the end of the tibia for gaining purchase against the substratum.

DRAWING: A hindleg.

Benacus sp.

This is a predaceous insect with raptorial forelegs, modified for grasping the prey. Here also the femur is enlarged. This is to accommodate the flexors of the tibia, which is strongly flexed against the femur in holding the prey. Note that the whole leg is strongly sclerotized, that the pretarsus consists of a single curved claw, and that the tibia, tarsus and pretarsus are consolidated to give strength and rigidity.

The hindlegs are natatorial, adapted for swimming. Note that the femur, tibia and tarsus are flattened to serve the function of an oar. The width is further increased, without appreciable increase in weight, by fringes of hair along the edges of the tibia and tarsus.

DRAWINGS: A foreleg and a hindleg.

Mantis religiosa

The foreleg here is raptorial but the tarsus and pretarsus take no part in the grasping action. The tibia ends in a sharp curved spine and the opposing edges of the femur and tibia are provided with long sharp spines.

DRAWING: A foreleg.

Pediculus humanus

The legs here are modified for clinging to the hair or to the fibers of the clothing of its host. The tibia is stout and at one side bears a thumb-like process with a spine at its distal end. There is a single *tarsal segment,* to which the "thumb" is opposed, and a curved *pretarsal claw*. Tarsus and pretarsus work against the "thumb" in much the same way as the human forefinger works against the thumb in grasping an object.

DRAWING: A foreleg.

Gyrinus sp.

The hindlegs here are even more highly specialized for swimming. The femur, tibia and the first four subsegments of the tarsus are all broad and flattened and their edges are beset with flattened setae which are folded back against the leg when not in use. Note that the tarsus is articulated in such a way that when not in use it can be drawn back against the side of the tibia so that only the distal half projects beyond the tibia.

DRAWING: A hindleg.

Passalus cornutus

The insect lives in decaying wood and uses its forelegs in helping to excavate its galleries. The foreleg is therefore adapted for digging (fossorial). Note that the segments are strongly sclerotized and rigid and that the tibia is flattened, with several tine-like processes. The tarsus is slender and normal in structure. Many soil-inhabiting insects have similar forelegs. In some of these the tarsus is permanently lost, in others it is worn off by the digging operation.

DRAWING: A foreleg.

Cicada sp., nymph

The immature stages of the cicadas have a subterranean habitat and their forelegs are markedly modified for digging. The femur is enlarged and very stout and is provided with strongly sclerotized tines. The tibia too is heavily sclerotized with a strong terminal tine. Compare this leg with the corresponding one in the adult.

DRAWING: A foreleg.

Gryllotalpa sp.

This also is a subterranean insect and the forelegs are perhaps more highly specialized than the legs of any other insect. The trochanter in some species is produced distally into a flattened spade-like structure. Apart from being very stout the femur is not greatly modified, but the tibia is short and stout, bearing distally two or three strong flattened and pointed tines. The first two segments of the tarsus are also produced into strong tines, and the tine of the first segment can work against one of the tibial tines to function as shears in cutting through fine rootlets.

DRAWING: A foreleg.

71

Dytiscus sp. male

The forelegs are an example of marked sexual variation. The first three tarsal segments are greatly expanded to form a flat disc provided with a number of suckers on its under surface. It enables the male to cling to the female. Compare the corresponding legs in the female.

DRAWING: A foreleg.

Apis mellifera (honeybee)

Examine the legs of the worker and find the specialized structures described below.

(a) The *pollen comb* for removing the pollen from the body hairs is made up of several rows of stiff hairs on the inner surface of the first segment of the hind tarsus. (b) The *corbiculae* or pollen baskets form the concave outer surfaces of the hind tibiae. (c) The tibiotarsal articulation of the hind leg is so arranged that the approximated ends of the two segments form a pair of nippers known as the *wax pincers*. (d) The apex of the middle tibia bears a strong *spur* used in scraping pollen from the baskets and also in cleaning the wings. (e) On the front leg there is the *antennal comb*, a notch in the proximal end of the flexor surface of the basal segment of the tarsus. The notch may be closed by the *velum*, a process from the adjoining end of the tibia. (f) A *brush* of stiff hairs, used in cleaning the antennal comb, is to be found on the distal end of the extensor surface of the front tibia. (g) The extensor surface of the basal segment of the front tarsus bears a row of spines used as an *eye brush*.

DRAWING: As much of each leg as is necessary to show the structures named.

SOME MUSCLES OF THE LEG

Acheta assimilis

The extrinsic leg muscles originate in the notum, the pleuron, the sternum, the sternal apophyses and the spina. They are inserted chiefly in the rim of the coxa but some are inserted in the trochanter. They act as promotors, remotors, rotators and adductors of the leg.

The intrinsic muscles occur as pairs or paired groups within the coxa, femur and tibia and are inserted respectively on the proximal edge of the trochanter, tibia and tarsus. The extent to which muscles arise within the trochanter depends on the degree to which the latter is developed as a distinct segment. These intrinsic muscles act as flexors and extensors of the segment in which they are inserted. When the trochanter is reduced and more or less fused with the femur, the coxotrochanteral muscles are in part responsible for the movements of the femur.

Remove the head and most of the abdomen, cut through the mid-dorsal and mid-ventral lines of the thorax and use the two halves to supplement each other in the study of the muscles. Prepare a second specimen in the same way, remove the soft parts by boiling in caustic potash and use the skeleton to check the attachments of the muscles.

Examine the metathorax and remove any fat or other tissue that obscures the muscles. Find and remove the tergosternal muscle which lies internal to all of the others and which originates on the antecosta of the postscutellum and is inserted on the sternal apophysis. Its removal more fully exposes three prominent dorsoventral muscles which arise in the notum and follow a somewhat oblique course to the coxal cavity. Their origin is partly hidden by the longitudinal dorsals which should be removed. Their insertions are partly hidden by the sternal apophysis and the muscles which arise from it; these may be dissected away carefully but in doing so note that some of the muscles which arise from the apophysis are themselves inserted in the base of the leg. They are therefore part of the extrinsic leg musculature and the student may, if he desires, study their arrangement, and deduce their action before cutting them away.

The anterior of the three muscles mentioned above is a notocoxal muscle which takes its origin in the scutum and is inserted in the anterior edge of the coxa. It functions as a *notocoxal promotor* of the leg, i.e., its contraction pulls the leg forward. Detach the head of the muscle from the scutum and raise the muscle. External to it a long narrow muscle will be found whose origin lies close to that of the first and which is also inserted in the anterior edge of the coxa. The two sets of muscle fibers are inserted in a common apodeme and may be regarded as one double-headed muscle. Identify the apodeme on the skeleton. It is characteristic of most of the muscles of the appendages, which have a very specific action, that they are inserted by means of tendon-like apodemes or ingrowths of the cuticle.

The posterior of the three muscles is also a notocoxal muscle which originates in the scutum immediately posterior to the anterior muscle or promotor. It is inserted by an apodeme into the posterior edge of the coxa and is the *notocoxal remotor* of the leg. It is also double-headed. Remove the promotor and remotor so as to expose the middle muscle more fully. It will be seen to originate from the scutum external to the origin of the two other muscles and to pass through the coxa to be inserted on the ventral edge of the trochanter by a flat apodeme. It also is double but the two heads are of equal size. Since the trochanter is greatly reduced and is no longer an independent segment, this muscle functions as an *extrinsic extensor of the femur*.

The removal of the three extrinsic leg muscles will expose other dorsoventral muscles external to them. These are concerned in part with wing movements, but leg muscles are also included among them.

Make a longitudinal section through the entire leg making the incision through the vertical or dorsoventral plane. If this is difficult the segments may be studied individually. Two sets of muscles originate within the coxa, a ventral group inserted on the ventral edge of the trochanter and a dorsal group inserted on the dorsal edge. These are *intrinsic extensors* and *flexors of the femur* respectively. Two muscles originate in the femur. The large dorsal muscle has groups of relatively short fibers converging on a large flat central apodeme which arises from the dorsal edge of the tibia. This is the *extensor of the tibia* and the force of its contraction is largely responsible for the leaping of the insect. The enlargement of the hind femur in leaping insects is to accommodate this very strong muscle. The ventral femorotibial muscle is inserted on the ventral edge of the tibia. It functions as the *flexor of the tibia* and is not as strongly developed as the extensor. Within the tibia there is a dorsal *levator of the tarsus* and a ventral *depressor*. If difficulty is experienced in dissecting the tibia the dissection may be limited to the distal end where the insertion of these muscles may be seen. There is in addition a small muscle originating near the proximal end of the tibia and inserted in a long ligamentous apodeme which originates in the unguitractor and traverses the tarsus and tibia. This muscle is the *flexor of the claws*.

DRAWINGS: 1. The inner surface of the metathorax showing the extrinsic leg muscles studied.
2. A dorsoventral section of the leg showing the intrinsic muscles.

8 External Female Genitalia

GENERAL CONSIDERATIONS

The external genital organs in the female consist typically of three pairs of elongated processes which, with certain basal sclerites in the body wall, constitute the ovipositor (Figure 1). The ovipositor serves for the outward passage of the eggs and for their deposition in suitable situations; therefore it is frequently adapted for digging or boring in order to deposit the eggs in the soil, wood, leaf tissues or other objects.

A true ovipositor is not found in all insects but the Thysanura, which lie near the ancestral stem of the Pterygota, possess an ovipositor which, though generalized, is built on the same plan as that of the Pterygota; therefore it is assumed that when the ovipositor is absent in the latter it has been lost. This is borne out by the fact that some individual species of an order that normally has an ovipositor either lack the ovipositor or have it in a rudimentary condition and, conversely, in certain orders which characteristically lack an ovipositor there are a few species which possess one.

The morphology of the ovipositor in the Thysanura provides a very definite clue to the interpretation of the pterygote organ. In the Machilidae each abdominal segment from the second to the ninth bears a pair of appendages, such as were described earlier, consisting of a flattened coxopodite and a terminal stylus. The appendages of the eighth and ninth segments do not differ from those of the anterior segments in general appearance, except perhaps in minor details of size and shape, and are obviously serially homologous with them. The coxopodite of each of these two appendages, however, bears from its anteromesal angle an elongated endite process or *apophysis*. The four apophyses are concave on their inner surfaces and are associated to form an elongated, backward-projecting tube which constitutes the *ovipositor*. The two pairs of apophyses because of their association with the genitalia are known as *gonapophyses*. There is a tendency for the ninth coxopodite to be elongated.

The ovipositor in the Pterygota is formed from three pairs of elongated sclerotized processes known as *valvulae* (Figure 1). In Orthoptera the three pairs are associated to form the egg tube but in other orders only two pairs are thus associated, the third having some accessory function.

The *first valvula* is borne on a small sclerite, the *first valvifer,* which originates from the eighth segment but is often displaced posteriorly. The *second valvula* and the *third valvula* are borne on a common basal sclerite known as the *second valvifer* which originates from the ninth segment.

The development of the ovipositor has been followed carefully in several species of Orthoptera. The first valvulae originate as a pair of small papillae on the posterior edge of the eighth sternum. They increase in size at each moult and differentiate into basal valvifers and distal valvulae. The second and third valvulae of each side originate as a bilobate papilla. The outer lobe, which will develop into the second valvifer and third valvula, may bear a stylus at its distal extremity and there can be little doubt that it represents the coxopodite. The stylus is lost before the insect matures.

It appears, therefore, that the first valvifer of the pterygote ovipositor is the reduced coxopodite of the eighth segment and the first valvula is the gonapophysis borne on this coxopodite. The second valvifer and third valvula in the Orthoptera form a continuous structure which is obviously the greatly elongated coxopodite of the ninth segment. In other insects the third valvula is articulated to the end of the second valvifer (Figure 1) and it has been claimed that the valvula is the persistent stylus borne on the end of the coxopodite. In some Coleoptera, however, in which the two are distinct there is some evidence of the presence of a minute vestigial stylus at the end of the third valvula. The second valvula is obviously the gonapophysis of the ninth segment.

This is the most generally accepted interpretation of the ovipositor, but many early writers maintained that it is an outgrowth of the ventral region, i.e., the ventrosternite, of the eighth and ninth segments. Some recent writers have reverted to this view. They claim that the gonapophyses are sternal outgrowths and not endites of the coxopodites. They would interpret the close association of the two structures in Thysanura as secondary.

THE OVIPOSITOR

Thermobia domestica

This is a common lepismatid, distinguished from *Lepisma saccharina* by the dark mottling on the dorsal side. *Lepisma* may be substituted as the structures are essentially alike.

The female may be distinguished by the long median ovipositor on the ventral side. Note that styli are borne on the seventh, eighth and ninth segments. The seventh sternum, which overlaps the base of the ovipositor, resembles the anterior ones in consisting of a single sclerite without differentiated coxopodites. Behind the seventh sternum are two pairs of stylus-bearing plates, the *gonocoxites,* i.e., the coxopodites of the eighth and ninth segments. Remove the seventh sternum so as to expose the base of the ovipositor.

The ovipositor consists of two pairs of concave processes or *gonapophyses* fitted together by tongue and groove joints to form a tube. The two gonapophyses exposed in ventral view are the anterior ones. Note that they are attached to the mesal angles of the bases of the gonocoxites of the eighth segment.

DRAWING: Ventral view of the two pairs of gonocoxites and the ovipositor in position.

Cut away one anterior gonocoxite behind the attachment of the gonapophysis so as to expose that belonging to the ninth segment. Find the posterior gonapophysis which is attached to the dorsal side of the anterior one. If possible separate the two.

Note that the posterior gonocoxite is longer than the anterior one and is divided into two sclerites, a small triangular anterior sclerite and a larger stylus-bearing sclerite. An oblique suture separates the two in such a way that the narrow anterior end of the larger sclerite lies mesal to the smaller one. The base of the posterior gonapophysis is attached to the somewhat thickened anterior edge of the smaller sclerite.

Gustafson identified the smaller sclerite as a fragment of the sternum, but in many Thysanura it is not detached from the stylus-bearing sclerite and the relation of the gonapophysis to it is similar to the relation of the corresponding structure to the second valvifer in pterygote insects. If Gustafson's interpretation is correct the valvifers and gonapophyses here and in Pterygota may conceivably be ventrosternal and not appendicular in origin.

DRAWING: The posterior gonocoxite and gonapophyses.

Conocephalus

Any other available tettigoniid may be substituted. Apart from the size and shape of the ovipositor, differences between the species lie chiefly in the extent and distribution of the sclerotization in the roof of the basal region of the united second valvulae, and in the form of the intervalvulae, which may or may not be completely fused with the sclerites of the second valvulae.

Examine the posterior end of the abdomen from the lateral view. Identify the tergal and sternal sclerites behind the sixth segment. Note that the *subgenital plate* is the apparent eighth sternum, but some authorities claim that the eighth sternum is reduced and the subgenital plate in this family is a secondary sclerite formed by a fold which grows out from the membrane between the seventh and eighth sterna.

Lift the subgenital plate and note that it forms the floor of the genital chamber, a shallow invagination which communicates with the channel of the ovipositor on the one hand and with the oviduct on the other.

Examine the conspicuous elongated ovipositor and identify the *first valvulae* on the ventral side and the *third valvulae* on the dorsal side. These are closely attached to each other by tongue and groove joints and together form the outer wall of the hollow *shaft* of the ovipositor. Note the enlarged base of the first valvula, partially concealed by the subgenital plate. Its anterior border continues into the pleural membrane of the eighth segment to which the appendage belongs. Dorsally the base of the first valvula is attached to a small sclerite which lies behind the ninth tergum and between it and the second valvifer. This sclerite is the *first valvifer,* the rudiment of the gonocoxite of the eighth segment, which is displaced posteriorly. The anterior edge of the valvifer forms a thickened ridge. Ventrally this ridge passes beneath the ninth tergum and forms an articulation with the tergum at its posteroventral border. The dorsal end of the ridge forms an articulation with the second valvifer.

The *second valvifer* and the *third valvula* are not separated by a suture but form a continuous process. The enlarged base, indefinite in extent, is the valvifer. Near the dorsal edge of the base of the valvifer there is a short longitudinal groove marking the position of a strengthening ridge which provides for the articulation with the first valvifer mentioned earlier. Anterior to the articulation, the narrow dorsal region of the valvifer passes into the body cavity as a thin sclerotized apodeme, the *superior apophysis,* for the attachment of muscles.

Separate the first and third valvulae and find the *second valvulae,* two slender processes somewhat shorter than the others. These also work in a tongue and groove joint against the first valvulae.

DRAWING: Lateral view of the abdomen posterior to the sixth segment, showing the visible structures of the ovipositor with the first and third valvulae spread apart slightly to expose part of the second valvulae.

Cut off the posterior end of the abdomen behind the sixth segment and boil it in potassium hydroxide. The valvulae now can be easily spread apart. Examine the specimen first from a dorsal view and note that the bases of the second valvifers are connected dorsally by a T-shaped sclerite, the *posterior* or *superior intervalvula*. The *superior apophysis* can now be seen clearly extending anteriorly from the articulation with the intervalvula. Spread the two valvifers apart to expose the common basal region of the second valvulae. It will be seen that these valvulae are completely fused at their base to form an arched roof over the egg passage. Remove the right valvifer carefully and note in doing so that there is an extensive membranous connection between the valvifer and the base of the valvulae. The dorsal wall of the base of the second valvulae is completely sclerotized except for the two membranous areas by which it is attached to the valvifers. This complete sclerotization of the dorsal wall is not found in all tettigoniids. The degree of sclerotization varies and in some forms there is only a narrow transverse bridge between the two lateral rami, hence the sclerotization of the roof is known as the *pons valvularum*. The median region between the two membranous areas is a narrow sclerotized process closely united with the end of the median process of the intervalvula. Thus the second valvulae articulate with the second valvifers through the mediation of the intervalvula.

The lateral borders of the base of the valvulae are formed by narrow sclerotized rods or *rami*.

DRAWING: Dorsal view of the common base of the second valvulae with the left valvifer attached but displaced slightly to the left.

Examine the ventral side after removing the first valvulae. Note that the ventral wall of the common base is membranous except for the rami which form its lateral borders. Proximally these curve inward and articulate with another small transverse sclerite which unites the ventral edges of the second valvifers. This is the *anterior* or *inferior intervalvula*. Anterior to the intervalvula a very short triangular process of the valvifer projects into the body cavity. This is the *inferior apophysis* of the valvifer.

DRAWING: Ventral view of the basal region of the second valvulae showing its relation to the valvifers and intervalvula.

79

Magicicada septendecim

Examine the ventral side of the posterior region. Note that the last visible sternum is the seventh, which forms the *subgenital plate*. The eighth and ninth terga are well-developed, the large ninth extending ventrally until its lateral edges almost meet and partially cover the ovipositor. The two heavily sclerotized *first valvulae* lie in the middle line, their mesal edges joined by a tongue and groove joint. Partly ensheathing them are the *second valvifers* and the *third valvulae,* which in turn are overlapped in part by the ninth tergum.

Remove the end of the abdomen from two specimens by cutting through the fifth segment. Cut through the eighth tergum and forward along the left lateral line, and through the sterna a short distance to the left of the right spiracles. Remove the excised ventral region and expose the base of the ovipositor. Next cut through the overlapping ventral portion of the ninth tergum to expose fully the second valvifer and third valvula. Boil one specimen in potassium hydroxide and use it to check the observations made on the untreated specimen.

Trace the first valvula anteriorly and note the enlarged base which is attached laterally to a curved sclerite extending backward to the anterior edge of the ninth tergum. This is the *first valvifer.* Lift the remaining portion of the seventh sternum and find the membrane connecting its inner surface to the lateral edge of the eighth tergum. This represents in part the ventral region of the eighth segment invaginated into the genital chamber. Note that the lateral edge of the first valvifer is attached to this membrane.

Attached to the posterior side of the base of the valvula and also to the inner surface of the valvifer, there is a short stout process which extends posteriorly and articulates with the anterior edge of the ninth tergum. The region of the tergum with which it articulates is cut off from the remainder by a transverse suture marking the position of a strong inflection with the end of which the second valvifer articulates.

The *second valvifer* and *third valvulae* lie lateral to the first valvula. They are concave mesally and partly ensheathe the first valvula. Note that opposite the articulatory ridge of the ninth tergum just mentioned there is a corresponding ridge in the valvifer. The articulation between the second valvifer and the ninth tergum is formed by the ends of these ridges. Behind the articulation the valvifer is connected by membrane to the ninth tergum. Note that the third valvula is distinctly marked off from the valvifer, unlike the condition found in the Orthoptera.

The shaft of the ovipositor is formed from the first and second valvulae only. The second valvifer and third valvula form a sheath for this shaft.

The valvula is provided with sensory hairs and is probably used to test the twigs in which the eggs are laid.

> **DRAWING:** 1. The untreated specimen showing the visible portions of the ovipositor and their relations to the neighboring segmental sclerites. Move the second valvifer and third valvula of the left side slightly to the left to expose the first valvula fully.
>
> 2. The first valvifer and first valvula in lateral view.

Remove the first valvulae from the specimens in order to expose the *second valvulae*. Observe their origin from the mesal side of the proximal region of the second valvifers and note the basic resemblance between the second valvifer, third valvula and second valvula in this insect and the coxopodite, stylus and gonapophysis of the ninth segment in *Thermobia*. It is somewhat doubtful, however, whether the third valvula can be homologized with the stylus of *Thermobia*.

The two second valvulae are completely united except at their proximal ends which are connected by membrane. They thus form the roof of the egg passage.

> **DRAWING:** A lateral view of the second valvifer, second valvula and third valvula.

9 External Male Genitalia

GENERAL CONSIDERATIONS

The genital orifice of the male lies in the posterior region of the ninth abdominal sternum, except in Collembola and Protura where it opens in the fifth and the eleventh segment respectively. Primitively each gonoduct opened independently to the exterior, but the double opening is retained only in the Protura, Ephemerida and some Dermaptera. All other insects have a single median orifice which lies typically at the extremity of the *penis* or *phallus,* the intromittent organ used to introduce the sperm into the genital chamber of the female. In some orthopteroids it lies in the ventral body wall but is surrounded by structures which together are the homologue of the penis of other insects. Collembola and Odonata lack the penis, the so-called penis of the latter being a solid structure borne on the second abdominal segment and having no relationship to the true penis.

The penis is paired in the Protura, Epemerida and Dermaptera. In other insects there is a single median organ to which Snodgrass would restrict the term "phallus."

The double penis of Ephemerida and Dermaptera originates as a pair of tubercles or penis valves on the posterior margin of the ninth sternum. The mesodermal gonoducts or *vasa deferentia* terminate blindly in a pair of ampullae lying against the base of the tubercles. The tubercles increase in size with successive moults and invaginate at the tips to form the ectodermal *ejaculatory ducts* which grow inward and make contact with the mesodermal ducts. In the Dermaptera each· penis valve divides distally into a lateral and a median lobe and the ejaculatory duct invaginates in the median lobe which, with the basal portion, forms the tubular penis. The lateral lobe remains attached to, and forms a part of, the penis and is known as the *paramere*. The penes of the Ephemerida may become partially or completely united but the two orifices or *gonopores* and ejaculatory ducts persist. In *Hemimerus* and in the Forficuloidea among the Dermaptera the penes are completely fused. The two gonopores persist in the former but in the Forficuloidea the left duct atrophies and the corresponding gonopore disappears leaving a single median orifice.

The *median penis* or *phallus* in its early development resembles the double penis, originating, like it, as a pair of tubercles or *phallomeres* on the posterior border of the ninth sternum, but the ampullae lie in close contact, one on each side of the median line, and the ejaculatory duct is formed as a single median invagination of the sternum between, and independent of, the phallomeres. This is the only important difference between the two types of penes and it is probable that the one is a modification of the other and that the penes are homologous in all insects.

The phallomeres in Thysanura are undivided and later unite along their dorsal and ventral edges to form the simple tubular penis of this group. In other insects they divide distally so that each consists of a basal portion on which a lateral and a median lobe are borne. In some Orthoptera and in Hymenoptera there are three lobes, lateral, dorsal and ventral. The phallomeres develop independently in the Mantidae and Blattidae. They do not unite to form a tubular penis, and the ejaculatory duct opens between their bases. In other insects the undivided bases of the phallomeres unite dorsally and ventrally to form the *phallobase* or *caulis,* while the median lobes (or dorsal lobes if there are three pairs) unite similarly to form the *aedeagus,* the two forming a continuous tube. The cavity of this tube communicates proximally with the gonopore; distally it opens to the exterior through the *phallotreme,* the orifice of the aedeagus.

The lateral lobes of the phallomeres develop into *parameres* which in the adult may remain attached to the phallobase, but in some insects migrate to the body wall where they form a pair of clasper-like organs. The ventral lobes of Hymenoptera develop into a pair of movable lobes known as the *volsella.*

This uniform method of development has been observed in several groups but in others it is more complicated and what is here regarded as the primitive method is obscured.

The phallus will, of course, have an outer and an inner wall known respectively as the *ectophallus* and *endophallus*. The endophallus which is usually membranous, sometimes extends far into the body cavity and is eversible. In some insects the base of the aedeagus is retracted into a cup-shaped pocket of the phallobase known as the *phallotheca*. The outer wall of the phallotheca is known as the *theca,* the inner wall as the *endotheca.* The latter also is frequently membranous and eversible.

The morphology of the penis is obscure. There can be little doubt that the true penes of all insects are homologous, but there is still some uncertainty as to whether the penis is a new structure, i.e., an organ *sui generis,* or a derivative of some antecedent structure. Various authors have tried to derive it from the appendages of the ninth or tenth segment or from the retractile vesicles of the Thysanura, but the evidence is inconclusive.

A pair of claspers borne on the ninth segment of Ephemerida are universally interpreted as segmental appendages. Somewhat similar claspers are borne by many other male insects and these, for the most part, have been regarded as homologues of those in the Ephemerida. In many of these insects, however, it has been shown that the claspers originate as lateral lobes of the phallomeres and Snodgrass now believes that they are all true parameres.

The male genitalia may include other structures, in addition to the penis, known collectively as *periphallic structures.* These are usually processes of various kinds which may be borne on any of the posterior segments from the eighth to the eleventh.

Only a few examples of male genitalia can be studied here but these will give some indication of the great variety in the structure of these organs. They are of primary importance in taxonomy and the student of any group must make himself thoroughly acquainted with the structure of the genitalia of the group.

THE PENIS AND ASSOCIATED STRUCTURES

Thermobia domestica

The male can be distinguished by the absence of the ovipositor and by the fact that styli are borne only on the eighth and ninth sterna. The eighth sternum otherwise resembles those anterior to it.

The venter of the ninth segment is membranous and bears a pair of coxopodites or *gonocoxites.* Cut away the eighth sternum to expose the gonocoxites completely. Find the relatively stout median *penis* in the form of a simple tube growing out of the mebranous ventral region of the ninth segment and extending posteriorly dorsal to the gonocoxites. Note the wide orifice, and the dorsally bilobate distal margin.

> **DRAWING:** The gonocoxites and penis, with one gonocoxite pushed aside to show the complete outline of the penis on that side.

Hexagenia

The male can be distinguished by a pair of segmented appendages borne on the ventral side attached to the distal end of the ninth sternum.

Examine the insect from the dorsal side and note that the last obvious tergum is the tenth. Turn to the ventral side and note that the lateral edges of this tergum extend to this side. Attached to each of these lateral edges there is an unsclerotized plate, the two meeting in the mid-ventral line. These plates are probably the *paraprocts,* in which case they belong to the eleventh segment. Note the long, slender, multiarticulate *cerci* borne behind the tenth tergum. Dorsally, between the bases of the cerci, find a small papilla bearing a short median process. The papilla represents the reduced *epiproct* and the process is the *caudal filament* or *telofilum.*

Pin the insect, ventral side up, in the dissecting tray. Examine the five-segmented, mesally curved *claspers* or *harpagones* borne on the posterior edge of the ninth sternum. The basal segments of the two claspers are completely united to form a continuous plate which has been often wrongly interpreted as a tenth sternum. These united segments probably represent the coxopodites of the appendages, while the distal segments represent the styli. The coxopodites in many species of mayflies are free from each other.

Find the two *penes,* whose bases lie dorsal to the coxopodites. In some species of *Hexagenia* they are only slightly curved and extend posteriorly as far as the end of the second segment of the claspers. In others they are shorter and curved like a hook. Their enlarged *bases* can be seen extending laterally beyond the edges of the coxopodites.

DRAWING: A ventral view showing part of the ninth segment and the region posterior to this. Include all structures described above which can be seen from this view.

Remove the claspers carefully to expose the bases of the penes. Note that these are greatly enlarged and extend laterally to the posterior portion of the lateral edges of the ninth tergum, with which they are articulated. The bases are joined mesally by a narrow bridge.

DRAWING: Ventral view of the two penes.

Anisolabis

The terminal region is greatly modified. On the dorsal side the last well-developed tergum is the tenth. Behind this are the large assymetrical forcipiform *cerci*. On the ventral side the large ninth sternum forms the *hypandrium*. The penes are concealed in the genital chamber dorsal to this plate. Cut away the hypandrium to expose more fully the terminal ventral sclerites. Between the bases of the cerci you will find two small median sclerites. Their homologies are somewhat obscure. The posterior plate is undoubtedly the *epiproct* or part of it, and the anterior plate is probably also a part of the epiproct since the cerci articulate with it. Lateral to the epiproct and mesal to the tenth tergum are two triangular sclerites which are probably the *paraprocts*. Cut away one paraproct to expose the base of the cercus and note how the latter articulates with the epiproct.

> **DRAWING:** Ventral view of the posterior extremity, with the ninth sternum and one paraproct removed, showing the features mentioned.

The double penis will be seen in the region from which the ninth sternum has been removed. Each consists of an elongated, partially sclerotized basal region and two distal lobes. The outer lobe which is lightly sclerotized and clasps the other is the *paramere*. The inner lobe is membranous and tubular, its cavity continuous with the slender *ejaculatory duct* which extends through the basal tubular region. The inner lobes are asymmetrical, the left being longer than the right and, when at rest, bent back against the basal tube. The basal regions of the two penes may be together homologized with the phallobase of the median penis and the two inner lobes with the aedeagus.

Note that proximally the two penes are united by a weakly sclerotized apodeme which projects into the body cavity.

> **DRAWING:** The double penis showing the features mentioned.

Blaberus craniifer

Examine the tip of the abdomen and identify the bilobate *epiproct* and asymmetric *hypandrium*. The latter is probably formed as the result of the fusion of the ninth sternum and the gonocoxites; it bears a pair of minute *styli*.

Cut through the abdomen behind the fifth segment and pin the posterior portion in the dissecting tray. Lift the epiproct and bend it back to expose the *paraprocts* and protruding portions of the phallus. The *paraprocts* lie transversely beneath the epiproct. They are asymmetrical, the right one bearing a strongly sclerotized hook. Note the relations between the epiproct, paraprocts and cerci.

There is no tubular penis. The gonopore opens in the body wall and is surrounded by three independent lobes, a *median ventral* and a *right* and *left dorsolateral*. Qadri describes the development of the phallus in two other cockroaches, *Blatta orientalis* and *Periplaneta americana*. Development starts in the usual way, two undivided phallomeres being formed, but later each phallomere is divided into dorsal and ventral lobes. The cleft in the right phallomere descends to the base dividing it into two separate lobes. One of these takes up a position ventral to the gonopore while the other shifts dorsally. These are represented by the median ventral and the right dorsolateral lobes in *Blaberus*. The lobes of the left phallomere, the left dorsoventral in *Blaberus,* retain their common base and do not become separated from each other.

The extent of phallic structures exposed on lifting the epiproct will vary in individual specimens. It should be possible to see the end of the median ventral lobe which contains a strongly sclerotized rod and is partly surrounded by two rows of minute spines. The right dorsolateral lobe may also be partially exposed as the mouth of a membranous sac with a strongly sclerotized hook-like structure protruding from it. The left dorsolateral will probably be invisible as it is concealed beneath the left paraproct.

DRAWING: Posterior end with the epiproct turned forward, showing epiproct, paraprocts, cerci, hypandrium and visible portions of phallic lobes.

Cut away the dorsal body wall, boil the specimen in caustic potash and remove the remains of the hind-gut and any persisting noncuticular tissue. Cut the paraprocts away carefully to expose the phallus fully.

Identify the rather wide *ejaculatory duct* which opens through the gonopore dorsal to the median ventral lobe. The *median ventral lobe* is partly membranous, and concave dorsally, with two rows of minute teeth or spines along the lateral and posterior edges of the concavity. On the floor of the concavity there is a strongly sclerotized ridge, irregular in form, which is continued as an apodeme into the body cavity on the ventral side of the ejaculatory duct.

The *right dorsolateral lobe* is in the form of a long, tapering, tubular sac terminating in a sclerotized hook. It projects into the body cavity and the distal half is invaginated into the proximal half, but the end of the hook may protrude slightly through the mouth of the sac. With the points of a pair of fine forceps grasp the hook and pull gently to evert the sac.

87

The *left dorsolateral lobe* is thick and blunt and irregular in shape. It is largely membranous but bears several sclerites. There is a shallow cleft in it but the two lobes are attached to the common base.

> **DRAWING:** The phallic organs from the dorsal side with the lobes spread apart. Show the ejaculatory duct and the position of the gonopore.

Gyrinus

Examine the posterior extremity of the male and find the genital chamber which lies dorsal to the seventh sternum. The tips of three sclerotized processes can be seen just within the orifice of the chamber or protruding slightly from it. Their outline can be seen through the semitransparent sternum. (There are only two processes in the female and they do not extend as far forward.)

Remove the abdomen and pin it, dorsal side up, in the dissecting tray. Starting at the anterior end cut through and remove the dorsal integument as far back as the fifth segment. The digestive tract and the testes will be exposed; remove them carefully and find, ventral to them, a pair of wide tubes which converge and unite to form a more slender median tube. The latter is the *ejaculatory duct* and should be left intact.

Cut away the median portion of the fifth to the seventh terga, making the incision slightly mesal to the lateral line. This will expose the relatively large median *phallus,* into the proximal end of which the ejaculatory duct passes. Examine the three processes mentioned earlier; the median one is the *aedeagus,* the lateral ones the *parameres.* Anteriorly they are enclosed in a sheath, the edges of which do not quite meet on the dorsal side. This is the *phallobase;* note its oblique orifice at the anterior end. The aedeagus and parameres are retracted within the phallobase and their common base, into which the ejaculatory duct disappears, can be seen through the proximal orifice of the phallobase. The phallobase therefore forms a *phallotheca,* and its outer wall, largely sclerotized but partly membranous, is the *theca.*

Before dissecting further examine the muscles of the phallus, the chief of which are as follows: (a) Muscles originating near the lateral ends of the antecostae of the seventh tergum and sternum and inserted in the common base of the aedeagus and parameres. (b) Muscles with a similar origin inserted in the anterior end of the theca. (c) Muscles originating in the posterior region of the seventh tergum and sternum and running forward to be inserted in the anterior end of the theca. (d) Intrinsic muscles originating in the posterior end of the theca and inserted in the base of the aedeagus and parameres. (e) Transverse muscles between the edges of the theca on the dorsal side. Determine the action of these muscles.

Muscles that interfere with a clear view of the phallic structures may now be removed. Turn the phallus over and note that the theca is complete on the ventral side. Examine the aedeagus on this side and observe the shallow median groove into which the *phallotreme* opens.

DRAWINGS: Dorsal and ventral views of the phallus.

Grasp the aedeagus or parameres with the forceps and pull gently until these structures are fully everted. Note the basal connections of the three processes.

DRAWING: Lateral view of extended phallus with the parameres depressed sufficiently to show the aedeagus clearly.

Pteronidea

Each phallomere in the Hymenoptera divides into three lobes. The lateral lobes form the parameres, the dorsal lobes unite to form the aedeagus and the ventral lobes form the volsella.

Examine the posterior end of the abdomen and identify the large *hypandrium,* the ninth sternum, which forms the floor of the genital chamber. The eighth tergum is well-developed, with a posterior median lobe which partly overlaps the reduced ninth and tenth terga. The tenth tergum is the slightly sclerotized terminal plate beneath which the anus opens. It bears a pair of small pygapods at its lateral angles. The ninth forms a narrow arch in front of the tenth, its lateral ends in contact with the ninth sternum.

In the Tenthredinidae and some other Hymenoptera the phallus has rotated through 180 degrees so that the morphologically ventral side comes to lie dorsally. This condition is said to be "strophandrious." The terms "dorsal" and "ventral" as used here will refer to the definitive or secondary, and not the primary, condition.

Pin the insect, dorsal side up, in the dissecting tray and cut away the posterior portion of the dorsal integument and expose the large ovoid phallus. Free the phallus from all adhering tissue except the ejaculatory duct so that it can be turned over easily. Complementary study of the dorsal and ventral sides is necessary to understand the arrangement of the sclerites and other structures. A superficial examination will show that the compact phallus consists of a proximal *phallobase* to which is attached distally a median *aedeagus* and two large lateral *parameres*.

The *phallobase* is not continuously sclerotized but consists of five sclerites and a median dorsal membranous region. The sclerites form a basal ring, two parameral plates and two volsella plates. The *basal ring* surrounds the anteroventral orifice through which the ejaculatory duct enters the phallus. Its lateral edges can be seen on the dorsal side forming the margin of the proximal third of the phallus. Mesal to the basal ring on the dorsal side are the *parameral plates* which extend posteriorly to the outer edges of the bases of the parameres. Follow these plates around to the ventral side where they form two large sclerites behind the basal ring. Each sclerite is divided into two lobes connected by membrane. The lateral lobe and the membrane articulate with the large movable *paramere,* which forms the lateral portion of the posterior end of the phallus. The mesal or *parapenial lobe* curves dorsally and can be seen on the dorsal side as a triangular process lateral to the base of the aedeagus. On the dorsal side, mesal to the edges of the parameral plates and partially overlapped by them, there are two long narrow sclerites, the *volsellar plates*. Each plate terminates posteriorly in two lobes. The ventral lobe or *cuspis* is a continuation of the sclerite, but the dorsal lobe or *digitus* is articulated to the sclerite and therefore movable. These sclerites and lobes together form the *volsella*. The wall of the phallobase is completed dorsally by a membrane between the mesal edges of the volsellar plates. Ventrally it is completed by membrane between the parameral plates, but the degree of approximation between the edges of the plates varies in different species.

The *aedeagus* is a well developed median organ borne distally by the phallobase. It is in the form of a gutter, the concavity being on the dorsal side, but the edges may approach each other fairly closely. The aedeagus is membranous but each edge is strengthened by two narrow sclerites which terminate in free spine-like processes. The outer sclerite is short but the inner is continued anteriorly as a long apodeme, the end of which is visible in the phallobase canal. These sclerites are known as *penis valves* but this term is used for the phallomeres and is unacceptable here.

The interpretation of the penis given here follows that of Snodgrass but Michener and others have offered somewhat different interpretations.

DRAWINGS: Dorsal and ventral aspects of the phallus.

Magicicada septendecim

Examine the tip of the abdomen and note that the segments beyond the eighth are invaginated into the latter which partially conceals them. Cut through the abdomens of two specimens in front of the seventh segment and use the posterior portions for study. Remove the free portions of the eighth tergum and sternum (the hypandrium). Boil one specimen in potassium hydroxide and use it to supplement the observations on the untreated specimen.

Note that the ninth segment consists, in part, of a continuous sclerotized ring, there being no pleural membrane. The tergal region is completely sclerotized and terminates in a large hood-like spine which projects above the tenth and eleventh segments. The posterior portion of the ventral region is invaginated into the segment to form the large genital chamber within which the phallus lies. The tenth tergum is short, largely sclerotized, and its lateral edges are continued into a pair of large sclerotized hook-like processes which project ventrally and curve anteriorly. These processes or claspers grasp the end of the phallus, the tip of which can be seen protruding between them. The eleventh segment is small and only partially sclerotized; the anus opens between two membranous flaps at its extremity.

DRAWING: A lateral view of the last three segments showing the structures described.

Examine the genital chamber and note that while it is open ventrally in the posterior region, it continues into the anterior region of the ninth segment as a blind pouch. Note that the floor of this pouch is formed by two sclerites. The posterior sclerite is narrow and transverse. Attached to its anterior end is a larger sclerite which runs in an anterior direction then curves ventrally. These sclerites constitute the *basal plate* of the phallobase.

Cut away the right lateral wall of the ninth and tenth segments and find the tubular *intromittent organ* which is attached proximally to the anterior end of the basal plate. It runs anteriorly for a short distance, then makes a loop and runs posteriorly within the mid-dorsal groove of the genital chamber. It is held in place by the claspers on the tenth segment. Its diameter gradually increases toward the posterior end. At the distal end it bears a pair of sclerotized *serrate processes* which extend ventrally. A membranous fold formed from its inner wall projects between the serrate processes.

Examine the basal plate in the treated specimen and note that the narrow posterior sclerite gives off an *apodeme* which passes into the base of the intromittent organ. Find also the *ejaculatory duct* which enters the organ ventral to the apodeme.

The homologies of the components of the phallus are difficult to interpret.

91

Snodgrass believes that the intromittent organ is the elongated *phallotheca,* its inner wall being the *endotheca.* He thinks the aedeagus is rudimentary and represented only by the apodeme.

DRAWING: The treated specimen with the right wall removed, showing the features mentioned.

The commoner cicada, *Tibicen linnei,* shows some differences from the periodical cicada. The two ventral processes of the tenth tergum are united to form a single process. The "phallotheca," which is longer and more slender, and lacks the serrate processes, bends ventrally parallel to the ventral process of the tenth segment, and is held in place by a pair of small claspers borne on this segment. The apodeme and the sclerite on which it is borne are absent. Apart from these differences the general structure is similar to that of the periodical cicada and this species may be substituted if the other is unavailable.

10 The Head

GENERAL CONSIDERATIONS

Structure of the cranium

ORIENTATION. The head is said to be "hypognathous" when the mouthparts are borne on its ventral margin and are therefore directed ventrally. This is the primitive orientation and in the following pages, unless otherwise stated, reference to position or direction of head structures relates to a head of this type. In many insects the head is orientated in such a way that the mouthparts are directed anteriorly. Such a head is said to be "prognathous." In a few insects the mouthparts are directed posteriorly on the ventral side and the head is then said to be "opisthognathous."

THE GENERALIZED PTERYGOTE CRANIUM. The cranium is the sclerotized skeleton of the head to which the antennae and mouthparts are attached. Typically an *occipital suture* (Figures 6b and 8), which runs from a point immediately in front of the posterior articulation of the mandible (P.a.m.$_2$) along the sides and top of the cranium to the corresponding point on the other side, divides the head into an anterior *facial* or *frontoparietal region* and a posterior *occipital region*. Ferris believes this suture to be the intersegmental line between the mandibular segment and an oculoantennal segment but there is no confirmation of this from embryological studies. Its close association with the mandibular articulation suggests that the inflection which it marks may be a functional strengthening ridge. Nevertheless it is convenient to study the two regions separately in order to trace consecutively the changes which take place in each.

THE FRONTOPARIETAL REGION. This region includes the large bulging front, sides and top of the head. It bears a pair of compound eyes laterally and a pair of antennae mesoventral to the eyes. Usually there are one median and two lateral ocelli between the compound eyes.

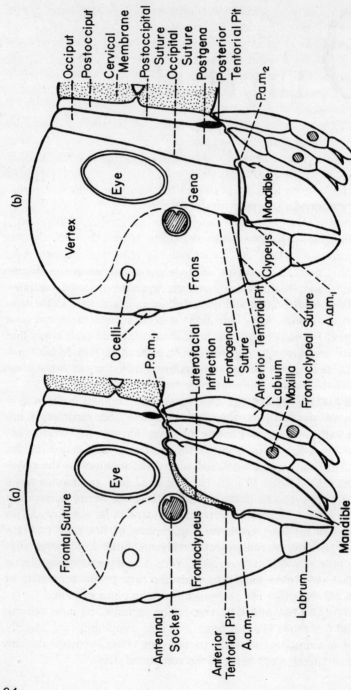

FIGURE 6. Lateral view of (a) hypothetical primitive head and (b) head of a generalized pterygote insect. A.a.m.₁, primary position of the anterior mandibular articulation; P.a.m.₁, primary position of the posterior mandibular articulation; P.a.m.₂, secondary position of the posterior mandibular articulation.

The frontoparietal region consists essentially of a single large sclerite divided ventrally by two vertical *frontogenal sutures* (Figure 6b) into a median *frontoclypeus* (Figure 6a) and two lateral *genae*. The ventral edges of the genae lie at the level of the mouth in the generalized head but the frontoclypeus projects ventrally beyond the level of the mouth and is usually divided transversely by the *frontoclypeal suture* into a dorsal or postoral *frons* and a ventral or preoral *clypeus* (Figure 6b).

The frontogenal sutures mark the position of internal strengthening ridges, the *frontogenal inflections* (Figure 7a) which extend vertically from the lateral edges of the clypeus to the outer edge of the antennal sockets. Their ventral ends form the anterior articulations of the mandibles (A.a.m.$_1$). The anterior tentorial arms join the frontogenal inflections near their ventral extremities at approximately the level of the mouth and are marked externally by the *anterior tentorial pits* (Figure 6b). The ventral edges of the genae may be turned inward to form a strengthening ridge, the *subgenal inflection* (Figure 7a). Sometimes the inflection is submarginal and marked externally by a *subgenal suture* which cuts off a narrow sclerite, the *pleurostoma,* from the ventral region of the gena.

The frontoclypeal inflection and the subgenal inflections are at the same horizontal level (Figure 7a). They meet and fuse with the frontogenal inflection near the point of attachment of the tentorial arms. These ridges and struts are therefore continuous and converge on the anterior mandibular articulation (Figure 7a, A.a.m.$_1$) thus reinforcing the cranial wall against the force exerted by contracting muscles, especially the adductor muscles of the strong crushing mandibles.

The dorsal undivided region of the face is the *vertex* and each lateral half of the vertex together with the gena of that side is known as a *parietal*. In immature insects and some generalized adult insects there is a Y-shaped suture in the head known as the *ecdysial suture*. The stem runs in the middle line of the top or dorsal side of the cranium and at some point between the eyes it forks, the two branches running in a lateroventral direction. The stem is the *coronal suture* (Figure 7a), and the arms the *frontal suture*. The latter, primitively, probably terminated at a point between the eyes and antennae, near the dorsal end of the frontogenal sutures, but in modern insects the course followed varies greatly. The ecdysial suture is the line of weakness along which the cuticle splits at ecdysis. The pigmented exocuticle is not developed along this line, therefore it appears as a pale line against the darker sclerite through which it passes. It is not formed by inflection and is not associated with an internal ridge.

A *mid-cranial inflection,* marked externally by a sulcus, is found in the face of many insects. It extends for various distances down the face, and in

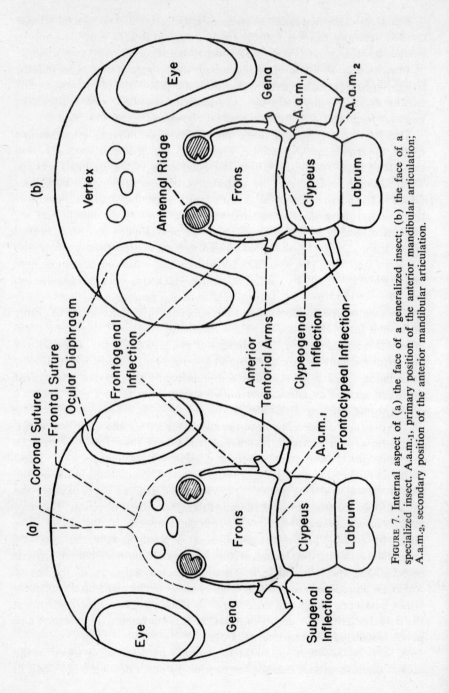

FIGURE 7. Internal aspect of (a) the face of a generalized insect; (b) the face of a specialized insect. A.a.m.$_1$, primary position of the anterior mandibular articulation; A.a.m.$_2$, secondary position of the anterior mandibular articulation.

immature insects, the coronal and sometimes part of the frontal suture are carried inward with the inflection. The mid-cranial suture, which is a sulcus, should not be confused with the coronal which is a line suture.

This interpretation of the cranial structure differs from that commonly found in the literature and is based on the recognition of the nature of the ecdysial and frontogenal sutures. The primitive arthropod head, including that of some apterygote insects, resembles the head shown diagrammatically in Figure 6a. There is at first a single mandibular articulation ($P.a.m._1$) dorsal and posterior to the level of the mouth. The face or front of the head is elongated and extends ventrally far beyond the posterior portion of the head with which the mandible articulates. The mandible is attached by membrane to the lateral edge of the face between the articulation and the mouth level and this edge is inflected for strength (laterofacial inflection). In lepismatids and pterygotes the mandible made a second articulation (Figure 6a, $A.a.m._1$) with the edge of the face at the mouth level and in pterygotes the region ventral to the eye and posterior to it descended ventrally until the two mandibular articulations (Figure 6b, $A.a.m._1$, $P.a.m._2$) were at the same horizontal level. Thus a pair of lateral regions, the *genae,* were added to the face and the lines where these united with the edges of the original face are marked externally by the *frontogenal sutures* (Figure 6b). A transverse *frontoclypeal inflection* between the anterior mandibular articulation divides the frontoclypeus into a dorsal *frons,* lying between the frontogenal sutures, and a ventral *clypeus* which is free laterally.

In the literature the frons and genae are defined, not by the position of the frontogenal sutures, but by the so-called epicranial suture. Usually this is the ecdysial suture but other sutures have been confused with it. Because of this confusion and because of the very different positions taken by the frontal suture the "frons" and "genae" as thus defined are indefinite and inconstant regions. In addition, since the ecdysial suture is absent from the cranium of most adult insects, the limits of these sclerites cannot be determined in such adults. The frontogenal sutures on the other hand are usually present. If they are lost, a line drawn from the anterior mandibular articulation to the lateral edge of the antennal socket determines their position (Figures 6 and 7).

The genae in most of the higher insects have grown ventrally beyond the level of the mouth and partly or entirely embrace the clypeus. The mesal edges of the genae and the lateral edges of the clypeus unite, the lines of union being marked by a pair of *clypeogenal inflections* (Figure 7b) and *sulci.* The inflections are continuous with the frontogenal inflections and form with them the *laterofacial inflections.* The clypeus is now bounded

97

laterally and dorsally by an inverted U-shaped *epistomal suture* and the anterior tentorial pits lie in the laterofacial sutures approximately at the junction of their two components. In the heads of these insects both mandibular articulations have been carried ventrally, the anterior articulation (Figure 7b, A.a.m.$_2$) being with the end of the clypeogenal inflection. In some insects a *transfrontal inflection* between the antennal ridges limits the frons dorsally.

THE OCCIPITAL REGION. The occipital region is typically separated from the frontoparietal by the *occipital suture* (Figures 6b, 8) which may extend around the cranium, may be limited to its lateral portions, or may be absent.

The occipital region is somewhat horseshoe-shaped, partly surrounding the *foramen magnum* or *occipital foramen* (Figure 8), the large orifice connecting the cavities of the head and thorax.

A *postoccipital suture* (Figure 8), roughly parallel to the occipital suture, divides this region into an anterior *occipital arch* and posterior *postocciput*. The suture is associated with a deep *postoccipital inflection* which serves for the attachment of muscles and the strengthening of the posterior edge of the cranium. The inflection is united at each end with one of the posterior tentorial arms, therefore the *posterior tentorial pits* lie in the ventral ends of the suture.

The narrow dorsal region of the occipital arch is known as the *occiput* while the two lateral and wider regions are the *postgenae*. The posterior articulation of the mandibles and the articulation of the maxillae are with the postgenae. A strengthening marginal or submarginal thickening or inflection of the postgena is known as the *hypostomal inflection*. If submarginal it is marked externally by a *hypostomal suture* (Figure 8) running from the mandibular articulation to the posterior tentorial pit, and a narrow *hypostoma* is cut off from the edge of the postgena. The inflection takes part in the articulation of the mandible.

The postocciput is usually a very narrow sclerite, to the free margin of which the neck membrane (Figures 6b, 8) is attached. It bears a pair of small lateral processes, the *occipital condyles* (Figure 8), which articulate with the lateral cervical sclerites in the neck membrane and serve as pivots for the movements of the head.

The cranium is open posteriorly and ventrally, the mouthparts being suspended from the ventral margin. The entire free margin is strengthened by a continuous series of ridges, the postoccipital, hypostomal, subgenal and frontoclypeal inflections.

There are many variations in head structure, including differences in the proportions of the various regions, the suppression of some sutures and the appearance of new sutures. In higher insects the occipital foramen is

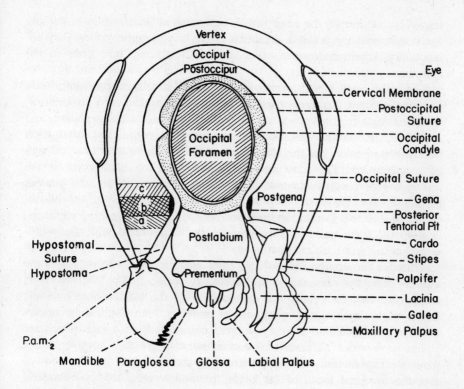

FIGURE 8. Posterior aspect of the hypognathous head. a, b, and c are areas which may undergo rotation and elongation in the prognathous head (see Figure 9).

entirely surrounded by sclerites and in prognathous insects there is a ventral wall to the cranium. Examples of some of the commoner modifications will be found in the insects selected for study.

Metameric constitution of the head

The head is a compound structure and includes several metameres which originally were postoral in the annelid-like ancestors as well, probably, as the prostomium of these ancestors. There is, however, no general agreement as to the number of these metameres nor as to the extent of the contribution, if any, made by the prostomium. Some authors have tried to identify the transverse sutures of the head with intersegmental lines but most authors agree that, with the possible exception of the postoccipital suture, they are secondary, resulting from the formation of functional inflections in the cranium.

The embryo when first formed is a flat band of cells on the ventral side of the egg. Soon this germ band becomes differentiated into an anterior, broad bilobate region known as the *cephalic lobes* or *blastocephalon,* and a narrow, ribbon-like posterior region, the *blastocorm.* The latter soon becomes segmented but the blastocephalon never shows any external sign of segmentation. The most anterior segment of the blastocorm is the *intercalary* or *second antennal segment,* the next three are the *gnathal segments.* The intercalary segment is early incorporated in the blastocephalon, the two forming the *protocephalon.* Later the gnathal segments, bearing the three pairs of appendages, are incorporated with the protocephalon to form the definitive head.

Thus far the composition of the head is quite clear except that some authors deny the presence of an intercalary segment. The controversy is concerned with the origin and composition of the blastocephalon. Some embryologists believe that it contains as many as three postoral metameres because it may contain as many as three pairs of coelomic sacs, which are generally regarded as criteria of metamerism. There are, however, other plausible explanations of the presence of these sacs. Hanström showed that the antennal lobes of the brain, previously regarded as metameric ganglia, resemble structures found in the prostomial ganglion of the Polychaeta and concluded that the antennae are prostomial and not metameric appendages. If this is so, the antennal region of the head, and parts anterior to it, all of which are derived from the blastocephalon, must be the homologue of the prostomium of the Polychaeta. Butt, however, has recently claimed to have found evidence that the labrum is the united appendages of the intercalary segment.

Thus at one extreme it is claimed that the head is composed of seven postoral metameres, with or without contributions from the prostomium; at the other, that it consists of the prostomium and three or four metameres. While it is still desirable to keep an open mind, the evidence for the prostomial origin of the blastocephalon appears to be quite strong.

THE FRONTOPARIETAL OR FACIAL REGION
Acheta assimilis

Examine the relation of the head to the trunk and note its typical hypognathous orientation. Pull the head forward gently and examine the *cervical or neck membrane* which connects the cranium to the prothoracic skeleton. Note the small cervical sclerites in the membrane. The two most prominent, and which are most constantly present in insects, are the *lateral cervical sclerites* which articulate anteriorly with two small occipital condyles on the posterior margin of the cranium, and posteriorly with the episternum of the prothorax. These sclerites form a pivot for the movements of the head.

Remove the head for study and note that it consists of an anterior bulging frontoparietal region, and a smaller, flat occipital region to which the neck membrane is attached. On the frontoparietal region find the long multi-articulate *antennae,* the two large *compound eyes* and the three small *ocelli* or simple eyes. Remove the antennae completely to expose their sockets. Note that there is a suture surrounding the compound eyes which cuts off a very narrow *ocular sclerite.* A similar *antennal sclerite* surrounds the antennal sockets.

Find the *labrum,* the flap-like sclerite movably hinged to the ventral edge of the face. Raise it and expose the heavily sclerotized mandibles beneath. Identify the anterior and posterior articulations of the mandible with the cranium.

Find the *occipital suture* which runs around the cranium, terminating on each side just anterior to the posterior mandibular articulation. The suture runs along a ridge at the back of the head and separates the frontoparietal and occipital regions.

Examine the frontoparietal region and identify the *clypeus,* the median quadrangular sclerite. The labrum is hinged to the ventral margin of this sclerite. The membranous suture between the clypeus and labrum is the *clypeolabral suture* and the sulcus which bounds the clypeus dorsally is the *frontoclypeal suture.* Note that the clypeus is partially divided by two transverse grooves into a dorsal *postclypeus* and a ventral *anteclypeus.* The dorsolateral angles of the clypeus project laterally and take part in the articulation of the mandibles.

The *ecdysial suture* may not be visible in the untreated head of the adult but will be seen later in the head treated with potassium hydroxide. If it is not visible examine the head of a nymph. It consists of a pale line running along the middle of the dorsal region of the head to a point between the eyes, where it forks into two divergent branches which run obliquely to the margins of the lateral ocelli. The median line is the *coronal suture,* the branches constitute the *frontal suture.* Note that the coronal line in the nymph is continued along the mid-dorsal line of the thorax.

That part of the face which lies dorsal to the frontoclypeal suture is

101

divided into three ventral lobes by two short vertical sutures which extend from the extremities of the frontoclypeal suture, just above the mandibular articulations, to the lateral margin of the antennal sockets. These are the *frontogenal sutures.* The median lobe is the *frons* and the lateral lobes the *genae.* The large undivided dorsal region is the *vertex.*

The term *parietal* is sometimes used for one-half of the vertex with the gena of the same side. When a coronal suture is present it separates the two parietals.

The ventral edges of the genae are bounded by *subgenal sutures,* continuous with and in the same horizontal plane as the frontoclypeal suture. Between the subgenal suture and the base of the mandible there is a small triangular sclerite known as the *pleurostoma.*

DRAWING: Anterior view of the face.

Remove the mandibles carefully from the cranium and separate the frontoparietal and occipital regions, making the incision behind the compound eyes. Boil the frontoparietal region in potassium hydroxide and examine the internal surface after removing any persistent soft tissue. The prominent sclerotic framework within the head is the tentorium, which will be studied later. The *anterior arms* of the tentorium arise by a broad base from the ridge which marks internally the position of the frontoclypeal and subgenal sutures. Turn to the outer surface and note that the position of the arm is marked by a deep cleft which extends through part of both sutures. This is the *anterior tentorial invagination* or *pit.* Add it to your drawing of the external features.

Cut through one tentorial arm a short distance from the base and remove the other one completely at its junction with the frontoclypeal and subgenal inflections.

The *ecdysial suture* will probably be more evident in the boiled head as a very thin pale line. Note that it is not associated internally with an inflection.

Examine the eye and find the thin flange which projects obliquely inward from the margin of the socket. This is the *ocular diaphragm* whose position is marked externally by the ocular suture. Note that the antennal sockets are also surrounded by a narrow internal *antennal ridge.*

Identify the *frontoclypeal* and *subgenal inflections* which form a continuous internal ridge marked externally by the corresponding sutures. Find the *frontogenal inflection* which joins this ridge at the junction of the two other inflections and runs dorsally to the lateral portion of the antennal ridge with which it merges. On the ventral side of this system of ridges, directly

102

opposite the frontogenal ridge, find a small rounded protuberance which is the *anterior condyle* of the mandibular articulation. It should perhaps be regarded as the ventral extremity of the frontogenal inflection.

DRAWING: Internal view of face showing the structures described.

Anisolabis maritima

The head is prognathous and the areas which are dorsal and anterior in the cricket are both dorsal in the earwig. The terms "anterior" and "posterior" as used here will therefore have the same morphological significance as the terms "ventral" and "dorsal" as used in describing the head of the cricket. In examining this and the succeeding heads look for the structures described in the cricket as well as the special features to which your attention is drawn.

Find the *clypeus* and note that it is divided into a sclerotized *postclypeus* and a membranous *anteclypeus*.

In the mid-dorsal line of the vertex you will find a sulcus in the position occupied by the coronal suture in the cricket. This is the *mid-cranial suture* which marks the position of an inflection which has carried the coronal suture inward so that it is not evident externally. Its extreme tip can be seen emerging from the sulcus and forking to form the *frontal suture*. The latter curves laterally and terminates near the mesal margins of the eyes in close proximity to the posterior ends of the *frontogenal sutures* which run anteriorly, around the lateral margin of the antennal sockets, and terminate at the lateral ends of the frontoclypeal suture just behind the anterior mandibular articulation. They can be seen more clearly from the lateral view of the head. The *anterior tentorial pit* is a long fissure in the frontogenal suture extending from its anterior end parallel to the antennal socket.

Superficially the frontal and frontogenal sutures appear to be continuous and are commonly thus described in the literature under the name of "frontal suture." The fact that one is a line suture and the other a sulcus distinguishes between them.

Note that the genal region is partly membranous and there is no subgenal sulcus or pleurostoma. The membranous area has been called by Ferris the *subocular sinus*.

DRAWING: Frontoparietal region of the head.

Mantis religiosa

The mantid head presents two new features. There is a pair of sulci on the vertex, mesal to the eyes, which extend a short distance down the face. These are the *temporal sutures* and they occur in some other insects. The *frontogenal sutures* extend, as in the cricket, from the anterior mandibular articulations to the lateral edges of the antennal sockets. A *transfrontal suture* extends between the antennal sockets. Since the frontogenal inflections merge with the antennal ridges and the transfrontal inflection extends beween the antennal ridges, this inflection may be regarded as forming the dorsal boundary of the frons. A similar inflection is found in some other insects.

The *anterior tentorial* pit is, as in the earwig, an elongated slit extending through most of the length of the frontogenal suture.

DRAWING: Anterior view of head.

Leptinotarsa (larva)

Observe the *ecdysial suture* which consists of a short coronal suture and a *frontal suture* whose arms diverge widely and terminate at the dorsal edges of the antennal sockets. Observe also the *mid-cranial sulcus* which extends from the end of the coronal suture to the frontoclypeal suture. It is marked internally by a deep inflection which terminates in the frontoclypeal inflection. Note that in this and other larvae the antennae are borne well forward on the genal region and that the eyes are represented by stemmata which also are usually well forward.

DRAWING: Anterior view of head.

Leptinotarsa (adult)

The ecdysial suture is absent but the *mid-cranial suture* persists though it is not as distinct as in the larva. It meets the *frontoclypeal suture* which arches dorsally in such a way that the relation of the two sutures resembles superficially that of the coronal and frontal suture. This combination in the heads of some beetles has been confused with the ecdysial suture and described as the "epicranial suture."

Examine the internal surface of the face and note the relationship between the two inflections. Find the prominent *mandibular condyles* at the lateral ends of the frontoclypeal inflection. A very slender thread-like process arises from the ridge opposite the condyle. This is the greatly reduced *anterior tentorial arm*. The thickness and rigidity of the cuticle reduces the need for internal scaffolding in most beetles, and in many species the frontoclypeal inflection is the only prominent ridge.

Note that the ventral edge of the gena is inflected, the *subgenal inflection* being continuous with the frontoclypeal.

The ventral position of the eyes and antennae suggests that in this insect the vertex has expanded ventrally at the expense of the frons and genae. This may explain the absence of the frontogenal inflection.

   DRAWING: Internal view of face.

Apis mellifera (worker)

Find the *clypeus,* the large median plate ventral to the antenna. Note that its sides are not free as in the more generalized insects but are joined to the mesal edges of the genae. The lines of demarcation between the clypeus and the genae are the vertical components of an inverted U-shaped sulcus, the *epistomal suture*. Toward the dorsal end of this suture find the *anterior tentorial pits*. Note that they do not lie entirely in the suture, their dorsal ends being somewhat lateral to it. From these dorsal ends a pair of very short sutures run to the lateral margins of the antennal sockets. These are the greatly reduced *frontogenal sutures*.

The explanation of this structure is as follows. In a generalized insect like the cricket the genae have grown ventrally to the level of the mouth, which is also approximately the level of the tentorial pits and the fronto-clypeal suture. In the honey bee this ventral growth has continued and the lateral edges of the clypeus have fused with the mesal edges of the genae. The sutures thus formed between the sclerites, i.e., the vertical components of the epistomal suture, are the *clypeogenal sutures*. The clypeo-genal suture is continuous with the frontogenal suture, the two constituting the *laterofacial suture*. The tentorial pit lies at the junction of the two sutures. The horizontal component of the epistomal suture is the *fronto-clypeal suture* in its normal position near the level of the mouth.

The anterior articulation of the mandible has shifted to the ventral end of the clypeogenal suture.

   DRAWING: Anterior view of the head.

Remove the frontoparietal region, boil in potassium hydroxide, examine the inner surface of the face and identify the inflections corresponding to the sutures described above.

Note that the very short *frontogenal inflection* unites with the lateral side of the antennal ridge as in the cricket, and that the *tentorial arm* is attached at the junction of the frontogenal and *clypeogenal inflections*. On the mesal side of each laterofacial ridge, ventral to the base of the tentorial arm, there is a small tubercle which is probably the ventral extremity of the frontogenal inflection, i.e., the original *mandibular condyle* corresponding to that in the cricket.

DRAWING: Internal view of the face showing the inflections.

Protoparce quinquemaculata (larva)

The most conspicuous feature of the face is the *mid-cranial sulcus* which forks at its ventral end to form an inverted V, the two arms enclosing a median triangular sclerite. The midcranial inflection has carried the coronal suture and part of the frontal suture inward but the *frontal suture* emerges from it dorsal to the fork and can be seen as a pale line lateral and more or less parallel to the V-shaped sulcus. The *tentorial pits* lie near the middle of each arm of the V but may not be very evident. Their positions may be checked later on the inner surface.

The triangular sclerite and the V-shaped sulcus have been variously interpreted. For a long time the sulcus was believed to be the frontal suture and the sclerite the frons. Snodgrass interpreted the sulcus as the epistomal suture and the sclerite as the clypeus. Hinton believes the sutures to be secondary, cutting through the frontoclypeus, and the sclerite to be a median portion of the frontoclypeus.

Judging by the position of the frontal ganglion and the anterior tentorial pits in relation to that of the morphological mouth, and by the origins of the cibarial and anterior pharyngeal dilators, it appears that the region of the sclerite dorsal to the tentorial pits is the frons and that ventral to the pits the clypeus. The entire sclerite is therefore the *frontoclypeus,* and the arms of the V are *laterofacial sutures,* the dorsal ends of which have been drawn together as a result of the very deep mid-cranial inflection.

Note that the frontoclypeal suture is not developed but that the clypeal region is traversed by a *transclypeal suture.* The clypeal region dorsal to the suture is the *postclypeus,* that ventral to the suture the *anteclypeus.* The latter consists of a narrow sclerite followed by a membranous area to which the labrum is attached.

DRAWING: Anterior view of the face.

Cut through the cranial wall, remove the frontoparietal region and examine its inner surface. Identify the inflections corresponding to the sutures described above. Note particularly how large an area of the vertex is carried inward by the mid-cranial inflection.

DRAWING: Internal view of the face.

THE OCCIPITAL REGION

Acheta assimilis

Remove the head with the neck membrane attached to it. Identify the labium and maxillae on the posterior side of the head, and the large *foramen magnum* or *occipital foramen* which is enclosed dorsally and laterally by the cranial wall and ventrally by the base of the labium. Note that the neck membrane is attached to the dorsal and lateral edges of the cranium and to the proximal margin of the labium. The sclerotic cranial wall is not completed ventrally, the sclerite bounding the foramen being more or less horseshoe-shaped. This is the primitive condition. The remnants of the neck membrane may now be removed.

Make a longitudinal incision through the middle of the labium and remove the right half of the labium and the right maxilla. This will partially expose a strong transverse bar near the ventral edge of the foramen. It is known as the *tentorial bridge* and is formed by the union of the two posterior tentorial arms. It is, of course, an internal structure and does not close the foramen externally. Find the posterior articulation of the right mandible and trace the course of the *occipital suture* again.

Find the deep inflection of the cranial wall, close to and parallel with the margin of the foramen. This is the *postoccipital inflection,* marked externally by the postoccipital suture, which divides the occipital region into an anterior *occipital arch* and a posterior *postocciput.* The neck membrane is attached to the margin of the postocciput.

In *Acheta* the postocciput is reduced, forming little more than the posterior wall of the inflection. Divide it by cutting through the middle, and bend the right half back, i.e., away from the occipital arch. Its relation to the remainder of the cranium will be more evident and the postoccipital suture will be fully exposed on this side. Near its ventral ends the postocciput bears a pair of small triangular processes, the *occipital condyles,* which articulate with the lateral cervical sclerites.

The junctions of the tentorial bridge with the postoccipital inflection are marked externally by the *posterior tentorial pits* which lie at the ventral ends of the postoccipital suture. This relation to the suture appears to be constant in spite of the changes which take place in this region. Find the pits and note that the proximal angles of the labium meet the cranial wall at the level of the pits.

The *occipital arch* lies between the occipital and postoccipital sutures and forms the major portion of the occipital region. It is a single sclerite consisting of a narrow dorsal area, the *occiput,* and two wider triangular areas, the *postgenae.* The *articulation of the maxilla* is with the postgena just ventral to the tentorial pit. The *posterior articulation of the mandible* is with the ventral edge of the postgena.

Find the *hypostomal sulcus* which extends from the mandibular articulation to the posterior tentorial pit and cuts off a narrow marginal sclerite, the *hypostoma,* from the postgena. In *Acheta* the hypostoma is little more than a marginal thickening but in many insects it is a more distinct sclerite. The hypostomal sulcus marks the position of an internal hypostomal ridge, the lower end of which provides the socket for the mandibular condyle. It will be observed that the postoccipital, hypostomal, subgenal and fronto-clypeal inflections form what is, in effect, a continuous strengthening ridge to the free margin of the cranium.

DRAWING: Posterior view of the head with the right maxilla and the right half of the labium removed, and with the right half of the postocciput turned posteriorly.

Protoparce quinquemaculata

In many insects, although the hypognathous condition is retained, the occipital foramen is closed ventrally and the labium is separated from the neck membrane by sclerotic tissue. The closure is effected by the mesal growth of the hypostomae.

In lepidopterous larvae the ventral portion of the head is complete but the posterodorsal region is reduced. This reduction is slight in *Protoparce,* but in some larvae it is carried so far that the entire vertex proximal to the fork of the ecdysial suture is lost. The occiput is probably always lost.

Remove the head of *Protoparce* with the neck membrane attached. Remove the labium and maxillae which are closely associated with each other. Boil the head thoroughly in potassium hydroxide, clear away any remaining soft tissues and examine the posterior aspect.

Find the *postgenae,* to the ventral edges of which the mandibles are articulated, and note that they are not separated from the genae by an occipital suture. Note that the foramen is closed ventrally by two triangular sclerites whose bases are attached to the mesal edges of the postgenae and whose apices meet in the middle line. Find the *tentorial bridge,* the slender bar which stretches across the cranial cavity dorsal to the triangular sclerites. From the position of the bridge find the *tentorial pits.* Note that the sulci which bound the triangular sclerites laterally run from the posterior mandibular articulation to the tentorial pits. They are therefore the *hypostomal sulci* and the sclerites are the *hypostomae* which have extended mesally to form a *hypostomal bridge* beneath the foramen.

Note that the tentorial bridge lies between the ventral ends of two deep inflections. These are the lateral portions of the *postoccipital inflection.* The dorsal portions are lost as the result of the reduction of the cranium in this region, and the postocciput has disappeared as an external sclerite.

Dorsal to the postoccipital inflections there is a marginal inflection of the cranium continuous with the mid-cranial inflection. It appears superficially to be continuous with the postoccipital inflections but careful inspection will show that it is not. It is more probably a secondary strengthening ridge but may be the dorsal portion of the occipital inflection.

DRAWING: Posterior view of the head with the labium and maxillae removed.

Apis mellifera (worker)

Examine the posterior aspect of the head after removing any muscle or other soft tissue about the foramen. Note the small size of the foramen and the enlarged area of the occipital arch; note also that the foramen is completely surrounded by sclerotic tissue.

Find the *postoccipital suture* which cuts off a narrow *postocciput* dorsal and lateral to the foramen. The slit-like *tentorial pits* in the suture mark its ventral limits and those of the postocciput. The base of the proboscis fits into a U-shaped depression, the *fossa of the proboscis.* Pull the proboscis ventrally to expose the fossa and note that the lateral walls of the latter with which the maxillae articulate are sclerotized. These sclerites are the inflected *hypostomae.* The *hypostomal sutures* between them and the postgenae run from the mandibular articulation to the tentorial pits.

The two hypostomae meet and fuse beneath the foramen, forming the *hypostomal bridge.*

Note that the postgenae send short triangular processes mesally into the subforaminal bridge. Only the middle portion of the bridge, therefore, is formed from the hypostoma; in some other Hymenoptera the postgenal processes apparently meet to complete the bridge externally, and the hypostomal portion is invaginated into the head cavity.

DRAWING: Posterior view of the head with the base of the proboscis extended.

VENTRAL REGION OF THE PROGNATHOUS HEAD

The cranium of the hypognathous head has no ventral wall. It terminates ventrally in the *peristome,* which is formed by the clypeal and lateral cranial borders surrounding the mouth, to which the mouthparts are attached. In typical prognathous insects, such as the Coleoptera, the occipital foramen retains its vertical orientation but the head is rotated dorsally so that the primitively cephalic aspect is now dorsal and the peristome opens anteriorly instead of ventrally. This change is accompanied by the elongation and dorsal rotation of the postgenal and, to some extent, of the postoccipital region, and by the development of a ventral wall to the cranium, between the postgenae, which closes the foramen ventrally.

Judging by the structure of the ventral wall of the prognathous head it appears that the rotation and elongation may have been restricted to different regions of the postgena in different insects. In some, the region ventral to the posterior tentorial pits (Figure 8 a) seems to have been involved, in others the region of the pits (Figure 8 b), and in still others the region dorsal to the pits (Figure 8 c).

In some orthopteroid insects the area involved is ventral to the pits which retain their primitive position. The base of the labium retains its relationship to the pits and to the cervical membrane. No gula is formed but the postlabium is greatly elongated (Figure 9 a).

When the region of the pits is involved the pits become greatly elongated in the gular sutures. The labium is carried forward, its basal angles being adjacent to the ventral ends of the pits. The area between the labium and the neck is sclerotized to form the gula (Figure 9 b).

When the change occurs dorsal to the pits, the pits and the labium are carried forward and again a gula is formed (Figure 9 c).

110

Anisolabis maritima

Prepare the head as for *Acheta* (p. 107) and examine the ventral aspect. Find the *postoccipital suture* and the *tentorial pits* which have essentially the same relations to the cranium as they have in *Acheta*. Note that the opening into the head is vertical. Actually the foramen is oblique because the head has been tilted upwards, but this is compensated for by two sclerites in the neck membrane. The anterior sclerite, the gula, is attached to the submentum but not to the cranium.

Those portions of the postgenae which, in *Acheta*, lie ventral to the tentorial pits are, in *Anisolabis*, greatly elongated and lie in the horizontal instead of the vertical plane, so that the mouthparts are directed anteriorly. The two postgenae now form a partial ventral wall to the head but are still widely separated and the foramen is incomplete ventrally. As in *Acheta*, the labium is suspended from the neck membrane at the level of the tentorial pits and the maxillae also retain their primitive position, articulated with the hypostoma just anterior to the pits. As a result of the elongation of the postgenae, both the mentum and the stipes are also elongated. The posterior articulation of the mandible is still with the ventral (now anterior) margin of the postgena and is therefore far removed from that of the labium and maxilla.

Find the *hypostomal suture* which extends from the posterior articulation of the mandible to the tentorial pit and cuts off a narrow hypostoma from the mesal edge of the postgena.

The elongation of the postgenae had already begun in the cricket, but there is no rotation of the head. Apart from the greater length of postgenae, labium and maxillae, and the rotation of the head, the structure of the head in the earwig is essentially the same as in the cricket.

DRAWING: Ventral view of the head with the right maxilla and the right half of the labium removed.

Phyllophaga anxia

Remove the heads from two insects. Make a lateral incision through one head, separate the ventral region, boil it in potassium hydroxide and clear it of all soft tissue. Use the two specimens in studying the structure of the ventral region of the head.

Note that the occipital foramen is vertical and is completely closed ventrally. The ventral wall of the cranium consists of three sclerites, a median *gula* and two lateral *postgenae,* the three separated by a pair of *gular sutures.* Find the *postoccipital suture* and the *postocciput,* visible as a very narrow plate bordering the foramen laterally and dorsally. Note that the postoccipital and the gular sutures are continuous. Internally the gular sutures are marked by high ridges. The tentorial bridge formed by the posterior tentorial arms arises from the anterior ends of these ridges and retains its primitive attachments at the lateroventral margins of the foramen. Because of this structure, it is assumed that the elongation and rotation of the postgenae involved the region of the tentorial pit and that the ventral ends of the postocciput therefore accompanied the elongating postgenae. The gular sutures therefore would be elongations of the postoccipital suture and the gular ridges elongations of the postoccipital inflections. Since the labium is attached at the ventral ends of the postocciput it has been carried forward and is now attached to the ventral edge of the gula.

This theory accounts adequately for the origin of the gula. With the upward tilting of the head, usually accompanied by the elongation of the postocciput, the space bounded laterally by the postocciput and anteriorly by the base of the labium would be filled in by an anterior extension of the neck membrane. Sclerotization of this membrane to form the gula would restore the vertical orientation of the foramen. This happened in *Anisolabis* but the small gula in this insect is free from the cranial wall whereas in most prognathous heads it is united laterally with the postocciput. The submentum also is frequently united in part or in whole with the hypostomal region of the cranial wall and in many species the suture separating the gula and submentum is lost.

Less convincing theories of the origin of the gula have been proposed. Some authors suggest that it is a basal sclerite of the labium as if, for example, the submentum in *Anisolabis* should be divided transversely and fused with the hypostomata. Others claim that it is formed by the mesal growth of the hypostomata as in the honey bee. These theories both presume that the tentorial arms have migrated along the hypostomal ridges while the first does not.

DRAWING: A ventral view of the cranium with the labium attached.

Dytiscus

The ventral region of the cranium has a structure essentially similar to that of *Phyllophaga*. Note the following differences.

There are two deep *postoccipital inflections* at the lateral margins of the foramen, and these are definitely continuous with the gular ridges. The *tentorial bridge* lies farther forward. There may be a shallow groove or depression between the gula and the submentum but the two are not separated by a distinct suture. When the two sclerites are thus united they are often referred to as the *gulamentum*. In all cases a transverse line through the ventral ends of the posterior tentorial pits may be regarded as the boundary between the gula and the submentum.

   DRAWING: Ventral aspect of the head.

Suppression of the gula

It will be remembered that in the bees and wasps there is a tendency for the postgenae to grow mesally and obliterate the hypostomal bridge. A similar tendency is found in the prognathous head. The gula in the two specimens studied is a broad sclerite but there is a tendency for it to contract in width and finally disappear as the postgenae grow mesally and meet in the middle line. Successive stages may be seen in the following heads.

   Harpalus. The gula here is still quite distinct but much narrower. There is a *mid-gular suture* which may mark an invagination resulting from its lateral compression.

   Necrophorus. The postgenae have met in the proximal region of the head and have forced out the gula which is reduced to a narrow triangular sclerite between the distal ends of the postgenae.

   Cantharis or *Chauliognathus.* The mesal edges of the postgenae have united completely and the gula is almost or quite suppressed.

THE TENTORIUM

The tentorium consists of a set of strengthening struts within the cranium. It is not a true endoskeleton as it is formed by two pairs of integumental invaginations known as the *tentorial arms*. It serves not only for strengthening the cranial wall against the pull of the mandibular adductors and other muscles but also for the origin of certain muscles and for the support of the pharyngeal region. The *anterior arms,* as we have seen, originate just dorsal to the anterior articulation of the mandibles while the *posterior arms* arise at the ventral ends of the postoccipital inflections, their points of origin being marked by the *tentorial pits.* In many insects the anterior arms give rise to a third pair of processes, the *dorsal arms,* which are attached to the inner wall of the face near the antennal sockets. Since these are not independent invaginations their attachment to the cranium is not indicated externally by pits.

The tentorium undergoes many modifications and in some insects it is greatly reduced. It has been examined in part in several of the heads already studied. At this time two relatively primitive examples will be studied in detail.

Protoparce quinquemaculata (larva)

Remove the soft tissues by boiling in potassium hydroxide. Find the *tentorial bridge,* a slender transverse bar across the cranial cavity near

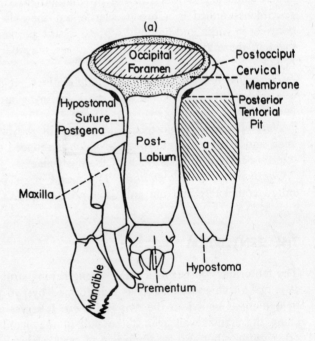

FIGURE 9. Prognathous Heads.   (a) Rotation and elongation have taken place distal to the tentorial pits. No true gula is formed, but the postlabium is greatly elongated and the other mouthparts carried forward.

the ventral edge of the foramen. Cut away the postgenal areas, the maxillae and the labium, leaving the bridge intact.

The tentorial bridge is formed by the fusion of the *posterior tentorial arms,* the origins of which are marked by the *posterior tentorial pits.* The *anterior tentorial arms,* originating near the middle of the *laterofacial inflections,* have been previously identified. Note that they unite with the tentorial bridge a short distance from the ends of the latter, so that the combined structure is shaped like the Greek letter π.

DRAWING: The tentorium showing its relation to the cranium.

Acheta assimilis

Remove the mouthparts carefully and completely, either before or after boiling the head in potassium hydroxide.

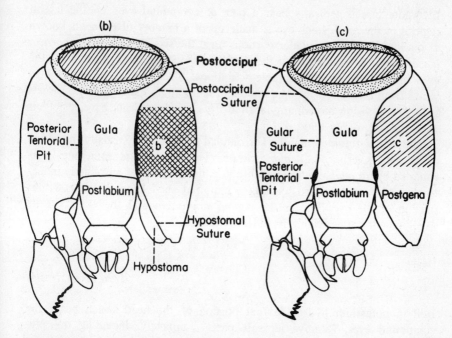

(b) Rotation and elongation have taken place in the region of the pits. These are greatly elongated in the gular sutures, the labium is carried forward and a true gula is formed.

(c) Rotation and elongation have taken place proximal to the pits. The pits and the labium are carried forward and a true gula is formed proximal to them.

Find again the posterior and anterior arms and the tentorial invaginations which were seen in earlier exercises. Note that the *posterior arms* unite to form the stout, vertically flattened *tentorial bridge.* The *anterior arms* converge posteriorly and fuse to form a horizontally flattened triangular plate, known as the *body of the tentorium.* This in turn unites with the dorsal edge of the tentorial bridge.

From the dorsal side of the anterior arms another pair of processes, the *dorsal arms,* are given off. They extend anterodorsally to meet the cranial wall in the lateral regions of the antennal ridges with which they unite.

DRAWING: Posteroventral view of the tentorium of *Acheta* showing its relations with the cranium.

COMPOUND EYES

Pterygote insects typically bear a pair of compound eyes on the lateral regions of the head. Each eye is made up of a number of elements known as *ommatidia* whose cuticular portions form the six-sided *facets,* or *corneal lenses,* seen on the surface of the eye. The shape, size and position of the eyes are subject to considerable variations. The number of facets also varies from a very few in some insects to many thousands in others. Insects with strong vision have many-facetted eyes. A few insects have lost their eyes and are totally blind.

The ocular foramen may be surrounded by a narrow, usually thickened or heavily sclerotized, *ocular sclerite.* This in turn is sometimes surrounded by an *ocular suture* which marks the position of an oblique inflection which slopes inward forming a marginal shelf beneath the cuticular portion of the eye. This is the *ocular diaphragm* and the extent of its development varies widely in different insects.

Acheta assimilis

Boil in potassium hydroxide that portion of the head which bears the compound eyes. Remove all soft parts completely, including the pigmented material on the inside of the eye. Examine the outer surface of the eye and note the ocular sclerite which is little more than a slight thickening of the margin of the ocular foramen.

On the inner surface find the *ocular diaphragm* which surrounds the *ocular foramen,* the opening through which the sensory structures of the eye pass to the facets.

Examine a portion of the cuticle of the eye under the high power and note the *facets,* each of which forms part of the lens system of an ommatidium or single element of the compound eye.

DRAWINGS: 1. Diagrammatic cross section of the eye and adjoining cranial wall.

2. A portion of the eye cuticle showing several facets.

Variations in eyes

A few of the more marked variations in the external features of the eyes will be seen in the following examples.

Aeschna sp. (dragonfly). Eyes are greatly enlarged with many facets. The range of vision is increased by the great convexity of the eye which enables light to strike it from many directions.

Camponotus sp. (ant) worker caste. The eyes are greatly reduced in size with relatively few facets.

Apis mellifera (honeybee) drone and worker. Note the sexual differences in the eye.

Gyrinus sp. (whirligig beetle). Each eye is completely divided so that there are apparently two pairs, one dorsal the other ventral.

ANTENNAE

All insects except the Protura, which are doubtfully included among the insects, have a single pair of antennae which are sensory in function. These were probably borne primitively in the dorsal region of the frons, ventro-mesad of the compound eyes, but their definitive positions vary widely in modern insects.

The antenna is set in a *foramen* or *socket* of the cranium and an *articulatory membrane* connects the base of the antenna with the edge of the socket, thus permitting free movements of the antenna. The rim of the socket may be thickened or more heavily sclerotized. This thickening sometimes has the appearance of a distinct sclerite and is often referred to as the *antennal sclerite.* It is associated with the internal reinforcing *antennal ridge* surrounding the foramen seen earlier in the examination of the

117

internal aspect of the face. The rim of the socket may bear an articulatory process, the *antennifer,* which makes contact with the base of the antenna, forming a pivot against which the latter works.

The basal segment of the antenna is known as the *scape,* the second segment as the *pedicel,* and the remaining portion as the *flagellum* or *clavola.* Muscles are inserted on the scape, pedicel and the base of the flagellum. The individual segments of the flagellum are not provided with muscles except in the Diplura and Collembola in which Imms has shown that all segments are provided with muscles. It would seem therefore that in the higher insects the antennae are really three-segmented, the flagellum being a single subdivided segment.

The antennae may have a great variety of forms which have greater taxonomic than morphological significance. The following are some of the terms descriptive of the form of the antennae.

Filiform. Slender, thread-like, the segments nearly uniform in width.

Setaceous. Resembling a tapering bristle. The scape is fairly stout and the remaining segments progressively smaller in diameter.

Moniliform. Segments globose or ovoid so that the antenna has the appearance of a string of beads.

Serrate. The segments are triangular and produced slightly on one side giving the appearance of the teeth of a saw. When the segments are thus produced on both sides the antenna is said to be *biserrate.*

Pectinate. Segments with longer processes like the teeth of a comb. If such processes occur on both sides the antenna is *bipectinate.*

Plumose. The antenna bears numerous long slender processes and thus resembles a feather.

Clavate. Distal segments become gradually broader so that the antenna resembles a club.

Capitate. Distal segments broaden suddenly so that the antenna has a pronounced knob or head at the end.

Lamellate. Distal segments as in the capitate type but produced on one side into flat plates arranged like the leaves of a book.

Aristate. Three short segments, the distal one bearing a lateral bristle-like structure known as the "arista."

Geniculate. Bent abruptly at an angle resembling a bent knee.

Acheta assimilis

Examine the facial region and find the *antennal sockets* into which the bases of the antennae fit. Note the slightly raised rim of the socket and the *articulatory membrane* by which the base of the antenna is attached to the rim of the socket.

The basal segment or scape is distinctly larger than the other segments. It is dorsoventrally compressed and its lateral edges abut against the rim of the socket so that the horizontal movement of the scape is limited. Vertical movement, however, is quite free. Check the movements by manipulating the antenna with a needle. A small *pivotal sclerite* in the articulatory membrane is broadly united with the lateral edge of the base of the scape. It tapers to a point which pivots against the rim of the socket.

The second segment or *pedicel* has a vertical dicondylic articulation with the scape and moves in the horizontal plane.

The *flagellum* consists of an indefinite number of short, cylindrical rings, each slightly recessed into the one behind and united with it by a narrow membrane, so that the flagellum is perfectly flexible.

DRAWING: The antenna showing its relation to the head.

Apis mellifera

Examine the antennal socket and note that the scape here can move in any direction. On the lateral side find a somewhat depressed triangular process of the rim of the socket which articulates with the base of the scape. This is known as the *antennifer* and is the functional equivalent of the pivotal sclerite found in *Acheta*.

Note the relations of scape, pedicel and flagellum.

DRAWING: The antenna showing its relation to the head.

Types of antennae

Examine the antennae of the following insects. Add a drawing of each to those of *Acheta* and *Apis*. Name each type: *Cicada, Silpha, Passalus, Phyllophaga, Archytas, Musca, Tabanus, Meloe* (male and female), *Dicerca, Tenebrio, Necrophorus, Estigmene, Gyrinus, Aedes* (male and female).

119

11 Mandibulate Mouthparts

GENERAL CONSIDERATIONS

The insect mouthparts consist typically of (1) the *labrum* or upper lip with its epipharyngeal lining, (2) the *hypopharynx,* (3) a pair of *mandibles* or principal jaws, (4) a pair of *maxillae* or accessory jaws, and (5) the *labium* or lower lip.

Primitive insects were probably omnivorous, feeding largely on hard substances, and needed strong mandibles adapted for cutting and grinding. Such mouthparts are said to be *mandibulate* or biting. Most modern groups still feed on solid material and retain the mandibulate type of mouthparts, but others feeding on fluid substances have *suctorial mouthparts* greatly modified for sucking and often for piercing also. Both types of mouthparts are subject to considerable variation. The description that follows refers to the generalized mandibulate type.

LABRUM AND EPIPHARYNX. The labrum (Figures 6 and 7) forms an anterior or upper lip to the intergnathal cavity. Typically it is a transverse, often bilobate, flap-like organ suspended from the clypeus by a narrow articular membrane which permits free production and reduction (i.e., anterior and posterior movements) and limited retraction and lateral movements.

The labral integument is reflected along the ventral edge to form an inner lining which extends dorsally through the labral and clypeal regions and terminates at the mouth where it becomes continuous with the dorsal wall of the pharynx. This inner wall is the *epipharyngeal wall* or *palate.* It forms the roof of the preoral cavity and frequently bears a lobe which protrudes into the cavity and is known as the *epipharynx.*

The labrum has been variously interpreted as (1) a part of, or the entire, prostomial or acronal region of the head, (2) the anterior metamere of the head, and (3) the first postoral metamere, or its appendages, which has migrated to an anterior position.

The hypopharynx is a blunt organ situated, like a tongue, within the preoral cavity. It is formed from the displaced ventral regions of the gnathal segments. In some generalized insects it consists of three lobes, a median *lingua* and two lateral *superlinguae*. The latter are lost as free lobes in most insects.

MAXILLAE (Figure 8). The maxilla is always complex in structure. There is a large basal plate which articulates at one point with the hypostoma and is otherwise attached to the cranium by membrane. It is always divided into at least two sclerites. The proximal sclerite, which carries the articulation with the cranium is the *cardo,* while the distal and larger sclerite is the *stipes.* A small lateral sclerite, the *palpifer* is frequently cut off from the stipes and supports the five-segmented *maxillary palpus.* The stipes bears two free lobes on its distal margin, a lateral *galea* and a mesal *lacinia.* Each is movably articulated with the stipes.

The maxillae are segmental appendages derived from leg-like antecedents. The cardo, stipes and palpifer have a common opening into the head cavity and must therefore represent a single basal segment, the *coxopodite.* The galea and lacinia are specialized *gnathobases* or endite lobes of the coxopodite and the palpus is the *telopodite.*

The maxillae act as auxiliary jaws helping to retain food particles in the intergnathal cavity and to pass them inward for mastication by the mandibles.

MANDIBLES (Figure 8). The mandibles are strongly sclerotized unsegmented jaws, their mesal edges usually provided with a distal incisor region with cutting teeth and a proximal molar region with grinding teeth. They have two articulations with the head, an anterior articulation (Figures 6b, 7a, A.a.m.$_1$) with the ventral end of the laterofacial inflection, and a posterior articulation (Figures 6b, 8, P.a.m.$_2$) with the postgena. The two articulations constitute a hinge joint which allows for movements of abduction and adduction only.

The mandibles are segmental appendages whose evolution has continued beyond that of the maxillae. The telopodite was reduced until it finally disappeared, therefore the mandible consists of the coxopodite only. The incisor and molar regions are gnathobases which have remained consolidated with the coxopodite.

LABIUM (Figure 8). The labium forms the posterior wall of the gnathal region of the head. It has a broad basal plate, adnate to the cranium, known as the *postlabium,* which is frequently divided transversely into a proximal *submentum* and a distal *mentum.* The proximal edge of the

postlabium is joined to the neck membrane, ventral to the occipital foramen, and its basal angles are associated with the postocciput adjacent to
the posterior tentorial pits.

Hinged to the distal edge of the postlabium there is a movable structure,
the *prelabium,* which forms the functional lower lip of the intergnathal
cavity. It consists of a basal plate, the *prementum,* on which are borne
(a) a pair of *labial palpi* attached laterally, (b) a pair of *paraglossae*
on the outer portions of the distal edge, and (c) a pair of *glossae* between
these, one on each side of the middle line. The palpi are usually borne
on *palpigers,* lateral sclerites partly or wholly cut off from the prementum.

The labium is formed during embryonic development by the fusion of
a pair of appendages, the second maxillae. The correspondence of its
parts with those of the maxillae is evident, except for some doubt as to
whether the postlabium is a part of the appendage or a ventral sclerite of
the labial segment.

LABRUM AND EPIPHARYNX
Acheta assimilis

Examine the labrum, manipulate it with the forceps and note the narrow
membrane connecting it with the clypeus which permits free production
and reduction of the labrum. Apart from differences in size and shape, the
labrum in mandibulate insects is relatively conservative, showing few
important specializations. In *Acheta* a very shallow median notch divides
its ventral edge into two lobes. In many other insects the notch is much
deeper. Two vertical lines divide the labrum incompletely into median and
lateral areas. At rest the labrum is somewhat retracted beneath the clypeus
and is therefore capable of limited extension.

> **DRAWING:** The labrum and the base of the clypeus in their natural
> positions.

Make two deep vertical incisions in the head passing from the lateral
edges of the clypeus upward between the antennae and compound eyes
to the level of the lateral ocelli, and a transverse incision between the ends
of the others. Carefully remove the portion of the head thus excised. To do
this, it is necessary to cut through the tentorium. The pharynx, or anterior
end of the digestive tract, should be detached with the excised portion.

Examine the inner surface and note that the inner wall of the labrum and clypeus consists of a continuous membranous plate. This is the *epipharyngeal wall* or *palate*. Note that it is continuous through the mouth with the dorsal wall of the pharynx. Note also that the mouth is at the level of the frontoclypeal suture.

Two curved rod-like sclerites divide the palate into a median and two lateral areas. Two groups of short stiff hairs lie in the median area and similar hairs are in the distal region. These are sensory hairs, probably tactile or gustatory, functioning in the testing of food.

A shallow median groove bisects the palate and, in the clypeal region, widens gradually as it approaches the mouth.

At the angles which mark the junction of the clypeus and labrum you will find two heavily sclerotized transverse bars, the *tormae*. They lie between the palate and the outer wall and each sends an anterior process to the lateral edge of the labrum.

DRAWING: The epipharyngeal wall showing its relation to the mouth.

Using the same or a similar specimen remove the clypeal region of the palate proximal to the tormae, which should be left undisturbed. Remove any loose tissue to expose the muscles which lie against the inner side of the frons and clypeus. Trace the origin and insertion of these muscles. One pair originates in the frons on either side of the median line and is inserted in the proximal edge of the outer wall of the labrum. These are the *productors of the labrum* whose contraction pulls the labrum forward. On either side of these there is another pair, one member of the pair originating mesal to the antennal foramen, the other external to the productors. The two converge to a common insertion on the tormae. These are the *reductors of the labrum*. Their contraction closes the intergnathal cavity by pulling the labrum against the mandibles.

DRAWING: Inner surface of the specimen showing the origin and insertion of the muscles.

Cut the labrum longitudinally along the median line and identify the *compressor of the labrum* which originates by a broad head on the outer wall of the labrum and is inserted in the inner wall, i.e., the palate.

DRAWING: Longitudinal section of the labrum showing the compressor muscle.

123

Apis mellifera

Examine the labrum and note that, except for its linear proportions, it is very similar to that of *Acheta*.

Remove the facial region as directed for *Acheta* and examine its inner surface. Note that the labral region of the palate is sclerotized while the clypeal region is membranous.

The morphological mouth of the bee lies at the level of the frontoclypeal suture, but the alimentary tube is continued beyond this point and opens by a secondary mouth dorsal to the level of the clypeolabral suture. This portion of the tube is the *cibarium,* formed by the union laterally of part of the palate and a basal portion of the hypopharynx. This union does not occur in *Acheta* where the cibarium is open at the sides, a generalized condition.

Cut through the lateral walls of the cibarium and remove the posterior wall, exposing the anterior wall formed by the palate. Note that, ventral to the functional mouth, the epipharyngeal wall evaginates to form a protuberant triangular lobe. This is the *epipharynx* which occurs in various forms in many of the higher insects. In the bee it is capable of closing the entrance to the cibarium. It is somewhat triangular in form with a median salient "keel" which extends along the entire dorsal surface, but only part way on the ventral surface. On either side of the keel on the dorsal surface there is a somewhat bulging area beset with short sensory hairs.

DRAWINGS: 1. A surface view of the epipharyngeal wall and epipharynx.
2. A diagrammatic view of a sagittal section through the clypeus and labrum showing the relation of the epipharynx to the epipharyngeal wall.

THE HYPOPHARYNX

Ephemerid larva

Place the insect on its dorsal side with the head extended. Pin the head through the foramen and cut away the labium carefully. The trilobate hypopharynx will be exposed. Note that it consists of a median lobe, the *lingua* and two broad flat lateral lobes, the *superlinguae.*

DRAWING: The hypopharynx.

Romalea

Remove the left mandible and maxilla carefully, taking care not to mutilate other structures. Pin the head with the left side upward and locate the hypopharynx exposed within the preoral cavity. Cut through the median line of the labrum, labium and cranium, leaving the hypopharynx intact. Dissect out any muscles or other soft tissues that interfere with a clear view of the hypopharynx and pharynx.

Note that the hypopharynx is attached posteriorly to the head, the line of attachment running obliquely from the mouth to the base of the prementum. Find a transverse groove, approximately at the level of the clypeolabral suture, which divides the hypopharynx into a narrow proximal portion extending to the mouth where it becomes continuous with the ventral wall of the pharynx, and a bulbous distal portion which lies free like a tongue within the intergnathal cavity. The proximal region may be called the *basilingua,* the distal region the *distilingua.* Both are thickly beset with sensory hairs and for the most part are lightly sclerotized, but each bears a pair of more heavily sclerotized plates which serve for muscle attachment. The sclerites in the sides of the basilingua are known as the *suspensorium* of the hypopharynx. Each forks, forming an *oral arm* which runs dorsally to terminate in the lateral wall of the pharynx, and a *loral arm* which extends posteriorly. The anterior wall of the basilingua, known as the *sitophore,* forms the floor of the cibarium, whose roof is formed by the clypeal region of the palate.

The distilingua divides the intergnathal cavity into an anterior food passage leading through the cibarium to the mouth and a posterior salivary passage into which the salivary duct opens. The base of the distilingua is strengthened by a pair of *lingual sclerites.* Posteriorly the distilingua projects into a small cavity at the base of the prementum. The cavity has a lightly sclerotized wall which is continuous with the salivary duct. It is in effect a widening of the duct which opens into the salivary passage between the distilingua and the prementum. The duct can be distinguished as a pale tube attached near the posterior end of the base of the distilingua.

DRAWING: A sagittal section through the labrum, clypeus and labium, leaving the hypopharynx and the anterior end of the pharynx intact. Show the features mentioned.

THE MANDIBLES
Acheta assimilis

Lift or remove the labrum, examine the closed mandibles and observe how their teeth interdigitate. Find the two articulations with the cranium. The anterior articulation lies opposite the end of the frontogenal suture. The frontogenal inflection forms the condyle or knob which fits into the socket in the mandible. The socket for the posterior articulation is formed by the hypostomal inflection while the condyle is on the mandible.

Remove one mandible and note that it is an unjointed, heavily sclerotized organ with a triangular base. The teeth on the mesal edge are somewhat sharper near the distal extremity but the *incisor* and *molar surfaces* are not sharply differentiated.

DRAWING: The mandible from the inner side showing the base and the articulatory structures.

Remove the labium and maxillae from another head. Make a sagittal section through the head and examine the cut surface after removing the pharynx and the brain, which is evident as a soft white body on the dorsal side of the pharynx. Note that most of the head cavity is filled with a large pyramidal group of muscles which originate in the vertex and postgenae and converge on a flat tendon-like apodeme. The apodeme passes through the lateral foramen (the space between the body of the tentorium and the lateral cranial wall) and is inserted in the inner side of the mesal angle of the base of the mandible. The tentorium should be cut away carefully to expose the course of the apodeme. The muscle is the *adductor of the mandible*.

Remove the adductor and find a much smaller muscle originating in the cranium in front of the occipital suture and inserted by a slender apodeme on the lateral edge of the base of the mandible. This is the *abductor of the mandible*. Examine the relation of these muscles to the hinge joint. It will be seen that the adductor is not only the stronger muscle by far but it has the more advantageous leverage.

DRAWING: Add the stumps of the apodemes to your drawing of the mandible.

Meloe angusticollis or Phyllophaga sp.

Note that the incisor and molar regions are sharply differentiated. The incisor region is a knife-edge cutting tool, while the molar region is flattened mesally, with ridges traversing the flattened face, making it an efficient grinding organ. It is especially well developed in *Phyllophaga*.

Between the molar and incisor regions there is a membranous hairy appendage, the *prostheca*. This was once incorrectly interpreted as a lacinia. A somewhat similar appendage will be found proximal to the molar region.

DRAWING: Mandible of *Meloe* or *Phyllophaga.*

Cicindela sp.

Note that the incisor and molar regions can be distinguished but that each is provided with sharp teeth fitted for cutting and tearing animal tissues rather than for grinding vegetable tissues. This is characteristic of carnivorous insects.

DRAWING: A mandible of *Cicindela.*

THE MAXILLAE

Acheta assimilis

Cut away the labium; remove one maxilla for study and leave the other in place for comparison. Identify the following parts. The proximal region is the *cardo* which lies transversely and makes the single articulation with the cranium in the hypostomal region. Typically a single sclerite, it is divided in *Acheta* by a suture which marks the position of an internal ridge for muscle attachment. The *stipes* is attached almost at right angles to the cardo. Turn the maxilla over and note that the stipes and cardo are attached by membrane to the head in such a way that the two have a single cavity communicating with the cranial cavity. From the lateral side of the stipes a small sclerite, the *palpifer,* is incompletely cut off. It bears the five-segmented *maxillary palpus.* Two free lobes are articulated to the distal end of the stipes. The outer one, the *galea,* is hood-like and relatively membranous. The inner one, the *lacinia,* terminates in two sharp sclerotized teeth. A faint suture runs parallel to the mesal margin of the stipes and marks an inflection in which the adductor muscles are inserted.

DRAWING: A maxilla from the posterior aspect.

Pin a head in the dissecting tray, placing the pins as near the top as possible. Cut away the labrum and all of the front of the head as far as the posterior margins of the eyes. Remove the mandibles and cut away the genae to expose the maxillae, then remove the mandibular adductors carefully.

A long slender muscle should now be exposed originating in the cranium near the origin of the abductor of the mandible and inserted by a slender tendon in the base of the lacinia. This is the *retractor of the maxilla* which pulls the whole appendage dorsally. Remove this muscle and expose the *rotator of the maxilla,* somewhat rhomboidal in shape, originating in the angle of the gena and subgena and inserted by a slender tendon on the anterior side of the cardo at the junction between its two sclerites. It causes the cardo to rotate in such a way as to cause retraction and production of the maxilla; i.e., it draws the organ toward the cranium and at the same time pulls it anteriorly against the mandibles.

The *adductors of the maxilla* are two groups of muscle bands which originate on the body of the tentorium. One group, the *adductor of the cardo,* is inserted in the cardo. As it draws the cardo towards the middle line the angle between the cardo and the stipes flattens out and the maxilla is extended ventrally. It is therefore an extensor of the maxilla also. The other group is inserted in the stipes on the shallow ridge near the mesal edge. This is the *adductor of the stipes.*

Note that the cavity of the stipes is almost filled with the *flexor of the lacinia* which originates in the proximal end of the stipes and is inserted in the lacinia. External to this there are three smaller muscles originating in the stipes. Two of these, the *levator* and the *depressor of the palpus* are inserted in the base of this appendage. The third, the *flexor of the galea,* is inserted in the base of the galea.

DRAWING: Anterior view of the maxilla, showing the muscles.

Cicindela sp.

The *cardo* here is an irregularly shaped sclerite with an articulatory process at its proximal end. The stipes is divided by an oblique suture into two somewhat triangular sclerites. The lateral sclerite, the *basistipes,* has its base next to the cardo. Lateral to it and developed chiefly on the anterior side is the *palpifer* bearing the four-segmented *palpus.* The mesal sclerite of the stipes, the *dististipes,* has its apex at the junction with the cardo. Distally it is continuous with the *lacinia* which bears a large curved spine at its distal end and many small spines mesally. This structure is obviously correlated with the carnivorous habits of the beetle.

Between the palpifer and galea the basistipes narrows to form the first segment of the two-segmented palpiform *galea.*

DRAWING: Posterior view of the maxilla.

Phyllophaga sp.

Identify the *cardo, basistipes, dististipes, palpifer* and *palpus.* Note that the *lacinia* is immovably joined to the dististipes and is reduced to a small blunt tooth-like process. The *galea* is peculiar in that it is provided with a curved row of strong sharp teeth. Evidently it supplements the mandible as a cutting jaw and to this end the cardo and stipes are heavily sclerotized and consolidated to form a rigid base for the action of the galea.

DRAWING: Posterior view of the maxilla.

Meloe angusticollis

Here also the various maxillary components are easily identified. Note that the *galea* consists of two segments. The *lacinia* and the distal segment of the galea are membranous and clothed with a thick brush of hair. This is often true of those insects whose food, in part or in whole, consists of soft material such as pollen. In some species even the mandibles are largely membranous or very lightly sclerotized.

DRAWING: Posterior view of the maxilla.

THE LABIUM
Acheta assimilis

Examine the labium while still attached to the head and note the three median sclerites which form the bulk of the organ. The large proximal sclerite is the *submentum.* Note that it is immovably attached to the cranium, that the neck membrane is attached to its proximal edge and that its proximal angles are associated with the postgenae adjacent to the posterior tentorial pits. The middle sclerite, or *mentum,* is also immovable on the cranium. It and the submentum are subdivisions of a previously single sclerite, the *postlabium.*

129

The third median sclerite is the *prementum* which is movable on the cranium at the suture between it and the mentum. Note the median groove in the prementum which suggests its double origin, i.e., by the union of a pair of stipites. The prementum and the appendages borne by it constitute the *prelabium*.

Find two small sclerites, the *palpigers,* cut off from the lateral sides of the prementum and bearing the three-segmented *labial palpi.*

Distally the prementum bears two pairs of appendicular lobes. The inner lobes are the *glossae,* the outer two-segmented ones are the *paraglossae.*

DRAWING: The labium from the posterior aspect.

Dissect a head as directed for the study of the maxillary muscles. Remove the maxillae and their muscles. Find on each side two muscles which originate in the tentorial bridge and are inserted in the prementum, one on its proximal edge, the other on the base of the paraglossae. These act as *retractors* and *productors* of the prelabium. They are the only extrinsic muscles and are probably the homologues of the retractor and adductors of the maxillae.

A pair of intrinsic muscles originate near the middle of the submentum and are inserted in the proximal edge of the prementum. They are *reductors of the prelabium.* The muscles lying within the prementum are similar to those of the maxillae, viz., the *flexors of the paraglossae,* the *flexors of the glossae,* the *levators* and *depressors of the palpi.*

DRAWING: Inner surface of labium showing the muscles mentioned.

Romalea microptera

Find the *submentum, mentum, prementum, palpigers* and *palpi* as in *Acheta.* Note that the prementum bears distally a pair of broad lobes which almost meet in the middle line. These are the greatly expanded *paraglossae.* Between them the prementum bears a pair of very small papilla-like lobes, the obsolescent *glossae.* Glossae and paraglossae together constitute the *ligula,* but this term is more frequently used when one pair is missing or inconspicuous as in *Romalea,* or when one or possibly both pairs are united to form a single lobe.

DRAWING: Labium of *Romalea.*

Anisolabis maritima

Note the large submentum and much smaller mentum. In this species the stipites of the second maxillae have not united, therefore the prementum consists of two separate lateral halves. Each bears a single large distal lobe. The nature of this lobe is somewhat doubtful but the Dermaptera are usually classified in the orthopteroid group and, since in this group there is a tendency for the glossae to be reduced (as in *Romalea)*, the lobes in question are almost certainly the *paraglossae.*

DRAWING: Labium of *Anisolabis.*

Harpalus sp.

The *submentum* is in the form of a narrow transverse plate. The mentum is much larger and bilobate. The prementum is folded under beneath the mentum but the two prominent *palpigers* are partly exposed, as is the median portion of the prementum between them. The latter is continued distally as a free process which is formed by the union of the *glossae.* The *paraglossae* are large and membranous.

In the evolution of some species of Coleoptera there has been a tendency for the glossae to unite and expand while the paraglossae become reduced and finally disappear. The next two examples illustrate stages in this process.

DRAWING: Labium of *Harpalus.*

Dytiscus sp.

The *submentum* here is not separated by a suture from the gula. The combined sclerite is known as the *gulamentum.* The *mentum,* as in *Harpalus* bears two large lateral lobes and, in some species, a median lobe. The prementum is folded back beneath the mentum and if the latter has a median lobe it may be necessary to cut away part of one side of the mentum to expose the prementum. The *palpigers* are well defined. Here also the prementum and the united glossae form a continuous plate but the *glossae* are greatly expanded, while the *paraglossae* are reduced, membranous and piliferous.

DRAWING: Gula and labium of *Dytiscus.*

Phyllophaga sp.

Note that the *submentum* is well defined. The suture between the *mentum* and *prementum* is well-developed laterally proximal to the palpigers, but very faint in its median region. The prelabium consists of a single plate from which the palpigers are incompletely cut off. Because of the tendency for the paraglossae to be reduced in the Coleoptera it may be assumed that they are completely lost in *Phyllophaga* and that the prelabial plate consists of the completely united prementum and glossae.

DRAWING: Labium of *Phyllophaga*.

12 Suctorial Mouthparts

STRUCTURE OF SOME COMMON EXAMPLES

Apis mellifera

The mouthparts of the Hymenoptera vary from the wholly mandibulate type, as in ants that feed on solid particles, to the wholly suctorial type which reaches its highest development in the long-tongued bees. In all species the labrum is of the general type found in mandibulate insects, as are the mandibles. The suctorial modifications are limited to the maxillo-labial complex.

Examine the head of a worker bee. If a preserved specimen is used it may be necessary to heat it in potassium hydroxide to render the parts of the proboscis more flexible. The labrum and epipharynx were studied in an earlier section.

THE MANDIBLES. Examine the mandibles in position, then detach one for study. Note the stout basal region, the narrow middle region and the expanded distal region. The latter is not toothed but has instead a curved knife edge. Find on the posterior face a narrow longitudinal groove which starts near the inner basal angle and, in the distal region, widens to form an oblique shallow groove. The mandibular gland opens near the proximal end of the groove, along which the glandular secretion flows. The mandible is used for modeling wax and other manipulative functions and only in a minor degree for feeding.

DRAWING: A mandible from the posterior aspect.

THE PROBOSCIS. The occipital region was examined earlier. Note again that the hypostomae are bent at right angles to the elongated postgenae so

133

as to form the sides of the *proboscis fossa,* the floor of which is membranous. The proboscis, when at rest, is folded on itself and retracted within the fossa. If it is thus retracted, grasp the distal part with the forceps and extend it. Note that it consists of three elongated organs, a median *labium* and two lateral *maxillae.* Note also that the labium is not independently articulated with the cranium, but that the whole maxillolabial complex is suspended from the cranium by the cardines and by membrane.

THE MAXILLA. Find the *cardo,* a rod-shaped sclerite which articulates with a small condylar process of the hypostoma. Distally it articulates with the base of the *stipes,* a fairly large elongated sclerite which is somewhat concave on its mesal face. The prominent, elongated, tapering *galea* is attached to the distal end of the stipes and it also is concave mesally. The other elements of the maxilla are reduced or obsolescent. The *lacinia* is represented by a small membranous lobe on the mesal edge of the stipes, and the *palpus* consists of two minute segments on the lateral edge near the origin of the galea.

THE LABIUM. The *postlabium* is represented by a small, triangular, median sclerite set in the membranous floor of the fossa, usually called the "mentum." Dorsal and lateral to this sclerite is a V-shaped sclerite known as the *lorum.* The apex of the "mentum" fits into the angle of the lorum and the ends of the latter articulate with the distal regions of the cardines. The lorum also is probably part of the postlabium, but it is not certain whether the two sclerites correspond to the submentum and mentum of other insects. It will be observed that the lorum links the labium and maxillae. The linking of the two to form a single complex, articulating with the cranium only by the cardines, is characteristic of both larval and adult Hymenoptera, as well as of some other insects.

The *prementum* is the elongated sclerite distal to the "mentum." Distally it bears five appendicular structures. The most lateral of these are the palpi which are borne on a pair of largely membranous *palpigers.* The palpi are four-segmented. The first segment is very long and concave mesally; the second segment is shorter and the remaining two, minute. The median structure borne distally on the prementum is known as the *glossa* or "tongue." It is formed from the united and greatly elongated glossae and is rolled to form a split tube, the edges of which meet on the posterior surface forming a median groove. The glossa terminates in a small circular, spoonshaped lobe known as the *flabellum.* Between the bases of the palpi and glossa there is a pair of *paraglossae.* These are largely membranous and they clasp the base of the glossa.

DRAWING: A posterior view of the proboscis with the parts spread sufficiently to show the details of their structure. Include enough of the occipital region of he cranium to show the relation of the mouthparts to it.

Remove the proboscis and examine its anterior aspect. Note that the prementum appears to be tubular, having the posterior and lateral sides sclerotized while the anterior side is membranous. Find the paraglossae again and note their relationship to the glossa. At the base of the glossa there is a small median sclerite and a short distance proximal to this sclerite there is an inconspicuous median pore in the membranous wall of the prementum. This is the outlet of the salivary duct and its position suggests that the membranous region belongs to the hypopharynx which is in part united with the prementum. The canal of the glossa forms the salivary passage.

DRAWING: Anterior view of the prelabium showing the salivary orifice, palpigers, paraglossae and the base of the glossa.

Danaus plexippus

The structure and arrangement of the mouthparts in most Lepidoptera is uniform, the differences in details being unimportant. An exception is to be found in the primitive suborder Zeugloptera in which the mouthparts show gradations from an almost typical mandibulate structure to the purely suctorial structure of the higher forms. A study of the mouthparts of this primitive group has been therefore very valuable in interpreting homologies in the more specialized groups.

Remove the head, heat in potassium hydroxide if necessary and scrape off any hairs or scales that interfere with a clear view of the structures.

Observe the large median facial sclerite on the anterior side of the head. This is the *frontoclypeus,* bounded laterally by the *laterofacial sutures.* Attached to its distal margin you will find the *labrum,* a very narrow transverse sclerite with a median triangular lobe and a pair of hairy lateral lobes known as *pilifers.* Beyond the labrum is the long coiled *proboscis,* the definitive feeding organ formed from the interlocked *galeae.* Lateral to the base of the proboscis two *labial palpi,* plentifully clothed with scales, project forward.

The *mandibles* are completely lost in *Danaus,* but in some moths vestiges persist as small tubercles immovably joined to the genae between the eyes and the base of the proboscis.

THE MAXILLA. Examine the posterior side of the head and note that the *galea* arises from a sclerite imbedded in the membranous wall of the head. This is the *stipes* which curves laterally and is attached at the proximal end to a small triangular *cardo*. The lacinia and palpus are lost in *Danaus* but in some moths there is a minute vestige of the palpus.

The mesal faces of the galeae are grooved and when the two are interlocked the grooves form the narrow *food canal*. The galeae themselves are hollow, and within the cavities there are numerous short oblique muscles which operate in coiling the proboscis. The stipes forms the outer wall of a blood sinus which communicates with the cavity of the galea. Muscles inserted in the stipes can compress the sinus and force blood into the galea, the pressure thus produced causing the proboscis to uncoil. Cut through the proboscis, examine the cut end under the high power and find the food canal and the cavities of the galeae.

THE LABIUM. Find a small, somewhat heart-shaped sclerite between the stipites in the median region of the posterior wall of the head. Note that the three-segmented *labial palpi* arise from this sclerite, therefore it may be interpreted as the *prementum*. There are no other labial structures.

THE EPIPHARYNX. Remove the posterior region of the head, including the proboscis and find within the head, attached to the labrum, a transparent sclerite having a shape somewhat like that of the bowl of a shallow spoon. This is the *epipharynx*.

> **DRAWINGS:** Anterior and posterior views of the head, showing the visible mouthparts.

Tabanus atratus (horsefly)

All Diptera have suctorial mouthparts but there is wide variation in the structure. In general two principal types may be recognized, (1) the piercing mouthparts of blood-sucking Nematocera and Brachycera, and (2) the sponging mouthparts of the Cyclorrhapha. The latter are non-piercing but some species such as stable flies and horn flies have the same type of mouthparts modified for piercing.

Remove the head of *Tabanus,* examine the face and note the two divergent sutures running from the antennal sockets to the ventral edge of the cranium. These are *laterofacial sutures* and the median plate enclosed by the sulci is the *frontoclypeus*.

The mouthparts project ventrally in the form of a stout median "beak" which is a complex of all of the mouthparts typically present in insects. The most prominent component is the fleshy *labium* and, when at rest, the other mouthparts are enclosed in an anterior groove of this organ. Manipulate the mouthparts and note their positions within the labial groove. It may be necessary to boil the specimen in potassium hydroxide to increase the flexibility of the organs. The most anterior is the *labrum* which forms a lid closing the groove. The *mandibles* are a pair of flat blades beneath the labrum which overlap like the blades of closed shears. Laterally beneath the mandibles are the slender *galeae* and beneath these again is a median stylet, the *hypopharynx*.

THE LABRUM. The labrum is a relatively broad organ tapering to a point at its distal end. Lift it and find the deep median groove on the posterior surface. This is the food canal through which the blood meal flows to the cibarial orifice which lies at the junction of the clypeus and labrum.

THE MANDIBLES. These are flat heavily sclerotized structures, broad at the base and tapering to a sharp point. When closed they form the floor of the food canal. Find their articulation with the cranium and note that it is such that protraction and retraction are not possible as in some other blood-sucking Diptera. Their movement is a lateral one as in mandibulate insects. They scarify the skin and the piercing thrust is made by movement of the head as a whole.

THE MAXILLA. Examine the posterior region of the head and find the very narrow hypostomal bridge which forms the ventral border of the occipital foramen. Find, in the membrane between the elongated postgenae, a pair of slender sclerites which articulate proximally with the postgenae and extend ventrally to the border of the head. These are the basal sclerites of the maxillae and each is divided into a small triangular *cardo* and a larger *stipes*. The stipes is continued distally into the slender *galea* which forms part of the feeding apparatus. The prominent two-segmented *palpus* arises from the lateral side of the stipes. No trace of the lacinia remains.

THE HYPOPHARYNX. This is a slender median stylet, pierced throughout its length by the salivary canal which can be seen through its walls.

THE LABIUM. Examine the posterior region again and note the membranous area between the bases of the maxillae. This corresponds in position to the postlabial region in the generalized insect and may be interpreted as such. The functional labium is therefore the *prelabium*. It consists of a proximal *haustellum* or *mediproboscis* and a distal *labella* or *distiproboscis*. The haustellum is the prementum. It is somewhat cylindrical with a deep median groove, the *labial gutter,* in its anterior face. The posterior and lateral sides are formed by a sclerite known as the *theca*. The distiproboscis consists of a pair of oral lobes which can be spread apart for feeding. Its structure is essentially similar to that of the housefly which will be studied next. Comparative studies suggest that the oral lobes are modified palpi.

137

DRAWINGS: 1. Anterior view of the ventral region of the head showing the mouthparts spread apart.
2. Posterior view of the ventral region of the head showing the maxillae and labium.

Musca domestica (housefly)

Examine a freshly killed specimen, if one is available, or else use a preserved specimen. In either case use a head boiled in potassium hydroxide to supplement your observations on the untreated specimen.

Note that the antennae lie, when at rest, in a median depression of the face which is bounded laterally by two sutures running from the antennal sockets to the ventral edge of the cranium. The depressed sclerite is the frons and the sutures are the frontogenal sulci. Find the occipital foramen and the deep hypostomal bridge and note that the ventral margin of the cranium forms a well-defined sclerotic ring to which the proboscis is attached and within which it can be partially retracted. The proboscis consists of three regions: (1) the proximal *rostrum* or *basiproboscis,* (2) the *haustellum* or *mediproboscis,* and (3) the *labella* or *distiproboscis.*

THE ROSTRUM. The rostrum is largely membranous, widest at its base and tapering distally, its shape approximating that of a truncated cone. There is a horseshoe-shaped sclerite on its anterior face which is interpreted as a *clypeal sclerite.* The anterior region of the rostrum must therefore be composed in part, at least, of the clypeal region of the generalized insect. The relation of the posterior face of the rostrum to the ventral edge of the hypostomal bar suggests that it includes the postlabial region. The rostrum is formed, therefore, from the ventral region of the head and probably includes the clypeus, the postlabium and parts of the genae and postgenae. Its exact homologies, however, are somewhat obscure.

Beyond the tips of the prongs of the clypeal sclerite find a pair of small unsegmented appendages, the *maxillary palpi.* They are associated at their bases with a pair of small sclerites which are regarded as vestiges of the *stipes,* the remainder of which is either lost or desclerotized and incorporated in the wall of the rostrum. There are no other maxillary structures, and no trace of the mandibles remains.

Within the rostrum there is a sclerotic framework known as the *fulcrum* which can best be seen in the treated specimen. The anterior wall is formed by the clypeal sclerite; the two lateral walls may be regarded as inflections of the lateral edges of the same sclerite. The cibarial pump is embraced between the posterior edges of the lateral walls, and the dilator muscles of the pump originate in the inner face of the clypeal sclerite.

THE HAUSTELLUM. The haustellum is the premental region and corresponds to that of *Tabanus*. Note that here also the posterior wall is formed by the sclerotized *theca,* while the anterior wall is excavated to form the *labial gutter.*

THE LABRUM. The labrum is attached at the distal edge of the rostrum and forms a cover to the labial gutter. Lift the labrum and note that it is quite thick with a median food canal forming a deep groove on the inner side. Find a pair of narrow rodlike sclerites which project dorsally within the rostrum from the basal angles of the labrum. These are *labral apodemes* for the insertion of muscles.

THE HYPOPHARYNX. Find the hypopharynx, a slender stylet beneath the labial groove. It is pierced by the salivary canal. The hypopharynx forms a floor to the food canal which communicates with the cibarial orifice or functional mouth.

THE LABELLA. Spread the two lobes apart and note that they are united posteriorly but separated anteriorly as far as the floor of the labial gutter. The two edges can be closely apposed except at the bottom of the cleft where an oval aperture, the *prestomium,* remains permanently open. Note that the labrum and hypopharynx, and therefore the food canal, terminate at the prestomium. The edges of the cleft, including the prestomium, have a heavily sclerotized border, the *discal* or *prestomial sclerite.* The surface of the oral lobes appear to be cross-striated. If they are examined under the high power the striae will be seen to be split tubes held open by sclerotic rings. They are known as *pseudotracheae* and serve for the passage of liquid or finely divided food to the prestomium. Note that the anterior and posterior pseudotracheae empty into collecting tubes which converge on the prestomium, but the middle ones run directly to the prestomium. The prestomial sclerite bears several slender *prestomial teeth* between the ends of the middle pseudotracheae, which themselves terminate in fine teeth.

DRAWINGS: 1. A lateral view of the proboscis with the labrum and hypopharynx lifted out of the gutter. Show the position of the internal sclerites of the rostrum by broken lines.
2. A diagrammatic view of the spread labella.

Siphona irritans (horn fly)

Examine the proboscis of this blood-sucking muscoid and note that its structure is essentially similar to that of the housefly but is modified in such a way as to make it an efficient piercing organ. The *rostrum* is small. The *haustellum* is slender and heavily sclerotized. Its base is enlarged to accommodate some of the muscles used in piercing. The *labella* also are heavily sclerotized and greatly reduced. The *prestomial sclerite* is relatively large and provided with strong cutting teeth.

DRAWING: A lateral view of the proboscis.

Tibicen sp. (cicada)

The head of the Hemiptera (*sens. lat.*) is very greatly modified and its morphology not yet fully understood. That of the cicada is opisthognathous but the directional terms in the text that follows are used as if it were hypognathous, e.g., the term "anterior" refers to the aspect which is definitively ventral.

Remove the head and identify the following sclerites. The anterior face bears a large bulging median sclerite usually called the "postclypeus." It is more probably a *frontoclypeal sclerite* composed of the frons and postclypeus. Ventral to this is a smaller median sclerite, the *anteclypeus*. Lateral to these two sclerites there is a pair of elongated sclerites known as the *lora* or *mandibular plates*. Snodgrass interprets them as lateral plates of the hypopharynx. Two large sclerites, lateral and posterior to the lora, extend ventrally from the region of the compound eyes. They are known as the *maxillary plates* and complete the lateral border and form the posterior lateral walls of the cranium. The evidence indicates that these are formed in part from the maxillary stipites which are completely fused with the postgenae.

The mouthparts consist of a narrow elongated labrum, a complex epipharynx and hypopharynx, a long, segmented, anteriorly grooved labium and two pairs of slender stylets, the mandibles and laciniae. The stylets when at rest lie in the labial groove but their enlarged bases lie in two lateral stylet pouches sunk deep within the head.

THE LABIUM. The labium projects like a beak from the posterior side of the head, to which it is attached by membrane. It consists of two short basal segments and a longer and more slender distal segment. The lips of the groove on the anterior face are closely apposed in the distal segment, but diverge to form a narrow triangular opening in the two basal segments. The homologies of the parts of the labium in relation to those of the generalized insect are unknown.

THE LABRUM. Find this elongated narrow triangular organ which arises from the anteclypeus and closes the opening at the base of the labium.

THE STYLETS. Remove the stylets from the labium with the point of a fine needle inserted into the basal orifice of the labial groove. They may at first sight appear to be a single structure. The two laciniae are interlocked. Each is provided with two longitudinal grooves on its mesal face which form tubular canals in the interlocked stylets. The anterior canal is the *food canal,* the posterior the *salivary canal.* The mandibles slide on the lateral faces of the laciniae by a tongue and groove device. Separate the stylets and note that the tips of the mandibles are provided with barbs which help to anchor them in the host plant. The stylets form the definitive piercing organ.

THE GALEA. Remove the labium and examine the posterior aspect of the head. Note that the distal end of each maxillary plate gives off a slender, ventrally directed process which lies close against the stylets. Snodgrass interprets this process as the galea.

For further studies boil the head in potassium hydroxide.

THE EPIPHARYNX. Remove the anteclypeus and frontoclypeus carefully, making the incision just mesal to their lateral edges. This will expose the anterior surface of the epipharyngeal wall. Note that it is attached to the labrum and anteclypeus only, but projects some distance dorsal to the anteclypeus where it unites with the hypopharynx to form a tube which tapers to the mouth. Note the deeply depressed median region, which is the *epipharynx.* If fits closely into the *sitophore,* a corresponding concavity of the hypopharynx, and forms the roof of the cibarial pump. A number of muscles, originating over the whole inner surface of the frontoclypeus, are inserted in the median line of the epipharynx and function as dilators of the cibarium. When the muscles relax the epipharynx springs back by its own elasticity and closes the cibarium.

Cut carefully along the lateral edges of the anterior portion of the cibarium, remove the epipharyngeal wall and examine its posterior surface noting again the shape of the epipharynx.

THE HYPOPHARYNX. Removal of the epipharyngeal plate exposes the hypopharynx which consists of a broad *basilingua,* attached laterally to the lora, and a narrow free lobe, the *distilingua,* which terminates in a pointed process. Observe the *sitophore,* the concavity in the basilingua which forms the floor of the cibarial pump. On the posterior side of the hypopharynx there is a salivary pump which forces the saliva through the distilingua, the tip of which communicates with the salivary canal in the stylets.

THE MANDIBLE. Using the specimen from which the frontoclypeus has been removed, cut away the hypopharynx and the lora with the large flattened plates attached to them. (These plates form part of the inner wall of the stylet pouches and serve for the origin of muscles which operate the

141

salivary pump). This will expose the bases of the stylets within the pouch. Examine the line of union between the dorsal portion of the frontoclypeus and the regions of the cranium lateral to it and find a deep inflection from which the anterior arms of the tentorium are given off. This is the *laterofacial inflection* and it terminates near the dorsal end of the lorum. Identify the enlarged base of the mandible and note that it is prolonged dorsally into two processes. The mesal or *retractor process* is short but the lateral or *protractor process* is large extending to the level of the ventral end of the laterofacial inflection to which it is attached by a short hinge-like sclerite. This sclerite is bent at right angles to the inflection when the mandible is retracted but straightens out when it is protracted. Test this by manipulating the mandible.

The muscles which move the mandible are inserted on the enlarged base and its processes. A strong protractor muscle originates in the ventral end of the lorum and is inserted along the entire lateral surface of the protractor process. A fan-shaped retractor muscle originating in the vertex is inserted by a long tendinous apodeme in the retractor process. Another retractor muscle, also originating in the vertex, is inserted in the base of the mandible between the two processes.

THE LACINIA. The base of the lacinia lies in the pouch dorsal and posterior to that of the mandible. It also has two processes, both short, in which retractor muscles are inserted. Attached to the posterior side of the base is the *lever arm,* a narrow sclerite which runs transversely and articulates with a vertical process from the inner face of the maxillary plate. It acts as a lever to control the movements of the lacinia. Protractor muscles originate in the ventral end of the maxillary plate and are inserted on the lever arm and on the lateral side of the basal enlargement.

If time permits, the student should dissect another head and identify the mandibular and maxillary muscles.

DRAWINGS: 1. Lateral view of the head with the stylets free.
2. The bases of the stylets.
3. Diagrammatic sketches of the epipharyngeal plate and hypopharynx.

13 The Integument

GENERAL CONSIDERATIONS

The integument protects the insect against desiccation, the entry of toxic substances and the invasion of parasitic organisms. It provides the exoskeleton which supports the body and maintains its form; and the skeletal muscles, which bring about locomotion and other movements, are attached to it. The cellular elements give rise to glands having a wide variety of functions.

During embryogeny the ectoderm forms the outer cellular layer of the germ band. As development proceeds parts of it differentiate into the nervous system and certain other organs. The remainder persists as a continuous outer layer, one cell thick, covering the entire embryo except for the natural orifices, into which it is inflected. This superficial layer of cells constitutes the *epidermis*. Externally the epidermis secretes a noncellular *cuticle,* and internally it rests on a *basement membrane*. These three elements constitute the integument.

EPIDERMIS. The epidermis consists of a single layer of epithelial cells. In adult insects, and between moults in immature insects, when the epidermis is relatively inactive, the cells are usually flattened, the boundaries tend to disappear and the epidermis over most parts of the insect is inconspicuous. At moulting, however, the cells undergo a period of extreme secretory activity synthesizing material for the new cuticle. They become taller (cuboidal, columnar, or pyramidal in form) with well-defined cell boundaries.

BASEMENT MEMBRANE. The thin basement membrane which underlies the epithelium is fibrous and noncellular, but it has been claimed perhaps mistakenly, that in some insects it consists of flat stellate cells united by their processes. Its origin has been ascribed to embryonic mesodermal cells and to blood cells which unite by their amoeboid processes, but there is good evidence that it may be a product of the epidermal cells themselves.

CUTICLE. A new cuticle is secreted at the beginning of each instar in two primary layers, a thin *epicuticle* on the outside and a much thicker layer on the inside, usually called the *endocuticle* but for which Richards has recently suggested the term *procuticle*.

The epicuticle is extremely thin, in most insects of the order of 1 μ in thickness, but it usually consists of three relatively distinct layers. The innermost layer is a tanned lipoprotein which Wigglesworth calls *cuticulin*. This is covered by a *wax layer,* which in turn is covered by the *cement layer* or *tectocuticle.* The cement layer is frequently lacking. The relative impermeability of the integument to the passage of water, salts and other materials is due largely to the epicuticle, and especially to the wax layer. Koidsumi has claimed recently that this layer confers a resistance to infection by muscardine fungi.

The *endocuticle* or procuticle is secreted in layers and therefore has a stratified appearance. It is, in nearly all insects, traversed by vertical striations known as *pore canals* which are formed as the result of the secretion of the cuticle around protoplasmic processes extruded by the epidermal cells. The withdrawal of these processes as the secretion solidifies leaves a large number of patent canals, but in some insects they are not withdrawn and are themselves transformed into solid cuticular material.

The endocuticle consists almost entirely of *chitin* and a water soluble protein. The protein, for which Fraenkel and Rudall suggest the name *arthropodin,* probably varies somewhat in different species and its exact composition is not definitely known. Chitin is a nitrogenous polysaccharide composed of a series of linked residues of monacetyl glucosamine and has the empirical formula $(C_8H_{13}O_5N)_x$. It is highly resistant to most of the common organic and inorganic solvents, but is broken down by concentrated mineral acids and by a solution of sodium hypochlorite containing 5 per cent available chlorine. It is hydrolyzed by hot concentrated potassium or sodium hydroxide to yield chitosan and acetic acid without change of form.

Endocuticle is pliable and relatively soft but in all adult insects, and most immature insects, portions of its outer region are changed chemically and physically to form hard rigid plates or *sclerites*. These hardened portions constitute the *exocuticle* and the term *endocuticle* is now reserved for the unchanged inner layer. Such cuticle now consists of three distinct layers, epicuticle, exocuticle and endocuticle.

The formation of the hard exocuticle results from a rearrangement and closer linkage of the protein and chitin molecules and the tanning of the protein to form an insoluble scleroprotein called *sclerotin* by Pryor. The process is a complex one and not yet thoroughly known in all its details, but the basic events may be summarized briefly as follows. At the time of moulting tyrosine is secreted into the blood, oxidized by tyrosinase and deaminated to form an orthodiphenol. This diffuses through the cuticle until it reaches the inner layer of the epicuticle where it is oxidized by polyphenol oxidase to form a quinone which unites with the arthropodin in the outer region of the endocuticle to form sclerotin. Recent work suggests that in some insects the process varies from this in some of its details.

Cuticle thus tanned is brown in color, and the dull colors of most insects, varying from light brown to black, may be the natural colors of the sclerotin. Other pigments, however, may be present in the exocuticle.

HISTOLOGY OF THE INTEGUMENT

The species suggested here for study show the features mentioned but many other species are equally suitable. This, in fact, is true for most of the histological material studied in this course. In studying histological preparations, it is not always possible to find an ideal section of the structure being studied but the student should be able to reconstruct the organ after examining several sections.

Owing to the difficulty of sectioning cuticle, some of the sections may be torn or distorted. The slides should be searched for a section which shows the structures described in their normal relationships.

In sections of cuticle stained with hematoxylin-eosin the endocuticle is unstained or pale pink in color, the epicuticle is amber or brown and so is the exocuticle, if present. In those stained with Mallory's connective tissue stain, the endocuticle is blue, the exocuticle red and the epicuticle amber or brown.

Caterpillar, muscoid larva, etc. (unsclerotized integument)

Find an area on the slide in which the structure of the cuticle is clearly defined and identify the following.

EPIDERMIS. The size and shape of the cells will vary in different insects, in different regions of the same insect and in different developmental stages. In the third instar muscoid larva the cells are relatively large and

145

flat with bulges in the region of the nucleus. The large size is due to the fact that in these larvae the cells do not multiply but increase in size with growth of the insect. In the caterpillar between moults the epidermis forms a thin layer. The cell boundaries may not be distinct but their positions can be determined in relation to the nuclei and it will be observed that the cells are small and cuboidal or flattened in shape.

Examine a section of a caterpillar cut during the moulting period and note that the cells here are tall (columnar or pyramidal) with well-defined boundaries.

BASEMENT MEMBRANE. Find the extremely thin, noncellular basement membrance underlying the epidermis. It may be seen most clearly on the slide with columnar epithelium.

CUTICLE. Note the relatively thick endocuticle with horizontal stratification and vertical pore canals. The epicuticle is very thin, and amber or brown in color. There will probably be small denticles or tubercles on the surface covered by the epicuticle.

DRAWINGS: Sections showing the structures described.

Acheta assimilis (cuticle)

Examine a Mallory-stained section, find a sclerotized area of the cuticle and identify the three layers. In a newly moulted insect the exocuticle may be thicker than the endocuticle, but in an older insect the reverse is true because secretion of endocuticle continues for some time after ecdysis. In most insects the endocuticle is much thicker than the exocuticle.

Examine a section of the pleural membrane and note the absence of the exocuticle. Small red areas may, however, be observed in the endocuticle, some of these may be the small sclerites observed earlier (p. 24), others are setal sockets.

DRAWING: A section of the cuticle through both the pleural membrane and the adjacent sclerotized region. The three layers may be distinguished by using colored crayons, or by different shading.

MOULTING

When an insect moults, the old cuticle separates from the epidermis which now secretes the cuticle of the next instar, starting with the cuticulin layer of the epicuticle. It secretes also the moulting fluid which digests the old endocuticle. For some time therefore the new instar is enclosed within the cuticle of the old. This stage of the new instar is called the *pharate* stage by Hinton. Eventually the epicuticle and exocuticle, if any, of the old instar are shed at ecdysis.

Pharate caterpillar

Note that the old cuticle has separated from the epidermis and that its endocuticle is in process of being digested. The epidermal cells are distinct with large vesicular nuclei. The cuticulin layer of the new instar has been secreted and the endocuticle is in the process of being secreted.

DRAWING: A section of the integument showing the epidermis and the old and new cuticle.

TANNING OF THE CUTICLE

Acheta assimilis

Examine a section of the integument of a newly moulted insect cut before the cuticle has hardened and darkened. Note that in the Mallory-stained sections the entire endocuticle or procuticle shows the red color characteristic of the exocuticle, except for the pleural membrane which stains blue. This is due to the fact that it is already impregnated with the tanning agents, although the actual hardening has not yet occurred. This happens on exposure to air. The outer endocuticle, which is secreted first, is tanned and it appears that, in *Acheta,* only this has been secreted at the time of ecdysis; the inner or definitive endocuticle is secreted after ecdysis.

Note that the pleural membrane stains blue, showing no evidence of the presence of tanning agents.

DRAWING: The two kinds of cuticle, in color.

INTEGUMENTAL ARMATURE

The cuticular surface may bear a varied assortment of outgrowths and processes which involve the cuticle only. There are no visible modifications of the underlying epidermal cells which secrete them. Some of these are hair-like and are known as *fixed hairs;* others are in the form of minute *denticles* and *tubercles,* examples of which were observed in slides previously examined. None of these outgrowths are movable on the cuticle.

Another kind of fixed armature is the *spine* which, as the name indicates, is a stout outgrowth tapering to a point. The spine is formed by an evagination of the entire integument and is therefore lined with epidermis. Examples of movable or articulated armature are the *spurs* and *setae.*

Romalea (spines and spurs)

Examine the posterior face of the hind tibia and find the two rows of stout fixed *spines.*

Spurs differ from spines only in being movable. They fit into a socket of the cuticle to which their bases are attached by a flexible articular membrane. Identify the spurs at the distal end of the hind tibia.

DRAWINGS: Diagrams of longitudinal sections of a spine and a spur showing their relation to the integument.

Pharate caterpillar (setae)

Setae are the most characteristic armature of the insect and are almost universally present. They are usually hair-like or bristle-like but may assume other forms.

Examine the slide and find a place where a section passes through the long axis of a seta and cuts the integument at right angles to its surface. The seta will be recognized as a hollow hair-like or spine-like outgrowth set in a socket of the cuticle. The edges of the socket or *alveolus* are usually raised above the general surface level of the cuticle. Note that the base of the seta is attached to the bottom of the socket by a flexible *setal* or *articular membrane.* This membrane, with the seta, closes externally a relatively wide canal, the *trichopore,* which traverses the inner portion of the cuticle. Note that an epidermal cell, immediately beneath the trichopore, is enlarged and flask-shaped with a large nucleus, its narrow "neck" extending through the trichopore to the seta. This is the *trichogen* which secretes the seta. At one side of the trichogen is another conspicuous epidermal cell which also extends through the trichopore to the articular membrane; within the trichopore its cytoplasm completely surrounds the neck of the trichogen. This cell is known as the *tormogen* and is responsible for the secretion of the articular membrane.

After the secretion of the seta is completed these cells usually shrink to normal size and are not easily distinguishable from the other epidermal cells. In some insects they apparently degenerate.

DRAWING: A section of the integument showing the setal structures described.

Larva of Hyphantria, Hemerocampa, etc. (glandular setae)

Many insects, especially lepidopterous larvae, possess unicellular glands associated with some of the setae. These also are modified epidermal cells which secrete toxic or irritant substances which are poured out through the setae when the tips of the latter are broken. Glandular setae may occur singly or in groups. They are sometimes borne singly on the tip of a spine or in groups on a raised tubercle or spine.

The glandular setae can be recognized in the section by the large *gland cells* underlying them and usually extending some distance below the general level of the epidermis. Find a section which passes through the long axis of a gland cell and shows the relationship of the cell to the seta. Note that there is a single gland cell associated with each seta and that its cytoplasm extends through the trichopore to the base of the seta. It may be possible to distinguish the trichogen but this may have degeneraed completely.

Most setae are sense organs and, in addition to the cells described earlier, have one or more nerve cells associated with them. The glandular cells can be distinguished from nerve cells by the fact that the cytoplasm of the former takes a basic stain and the nucleus is usually branched or double, an evidence of secretory activity.

DRAWING: A glandular seta with gland cell and adjacent epidermis.

14 The Alimentary System and Malpighian Tubules

GENERAL CONSIDERATIONS

Origin

The *epithelium* of the alimentary canal originates typically from four embryonic rudiments. Two of these are ectodermal; the other two are generally interpreted as entodermal though some embryologists dissent from this view.

1. An anterior invagination of the ectoderm grows posteriorly as a blind tube. This is the *stomodaeum* which forms the epithelial layer of the fore-gut. The orifice of the invagination is the morphological mouth.

2. A similar posterior invagination, the *proctodaeum,* forms the epithelium of the hind-gut, and its orifice is the anus.

3. A group of entoderm cells, the *anterior mesenteron rudiment,* lying against the blind end of the stomodaeum, proliferates cells in a posterior direction.

4. A similar group, the *posterior mesenteron rudiment,* against the proctodaeum, proliferates in an anterior direction. The two mesenteron rudiments meet and unite and eventually produce a closed tube, the cells of which form the epithelium of the mid-gut. Three contiguous but noncommunicating tubes are thus formed. Later the dissepiments between them break down and a continuous tube, patent from mouth to anus, is formed.

The *muscular coats* of the gut are derived from embryonic mesoderm.

The *Malpighian tubules* are the principal excretory organs and not part of the alimentary system. They are discussed here because, in the embryo, they originate as evaginations of the blind end of the proctodaeum and throughout the life of the insect their excretions are voided into the hind-gut.

150

Stomodaeum or fore-gut

Primitively the fore-gut is a simple tube differentiated into a pharynx within the head and an esophagus which passes from the head, through the thorax, to the abdomen where it enters the mid-gut. In most insects, however, there is some further regional differentiation, both structural and functional.

THE INTERGNATHAL CAVITY. The nature of the intergnathal cavity was discussed in an earlier section. The cibarium, it will be remembered, is that part of the cavity which lies between the clypeus and the basilingua. In generalized insects the lateral edges of the clypeus are free, therefore the cibarium is open laterally; but in those higher insects, in which the edges of the clypeus and the genae are united, the cibarium forms a tube continuous with the pharynx and is, functionally, an anterior region of the fore-gut. The functional mouth is now the cibarial orifice.

THE PHARYNX. The pharynx (Figure 10) is that region which lies within the head and for the most part beneath and in front of the brain. It terminates anteriorly in the morphological mouth. The *frontal ganglion* (Figure 10) of the stomodaeal nervous system lies on the pharynx just above the mouth; therefore when a tubular cibarium is formed, the position of this ganglion is one criterion for distinguishing between it and the pharynx. In addition, the *dilators of the cibarium* normally originate in the clypeus while the *precerebral dorsal dilators of the pharynx* (Figure 10) originate in the frons and are inserted in the pharynx posterior to the frontal ganglion or the nerve cords which connect it with the brain.

THE ESOPHAGUS (Figure 10). The remainder of the fore-gut in the simplest digestive tracts is the esophagus, a straight tube leading to the mid-gut, but in most insects it is regionally differentiated, in which case only the tubular portion lying behind the pharynx is known as the esophagus. The first differentiated region is usually an enlargement which serves for the storage of food and is known as the *crop* or *ingluvies*. The size and shape of the crop vary. In adult Diptera and Lepidoptera it is in the form of a sac some distance from the esophagus and connected to it by a slender duct. In many of these it is no longer a food storage organ but subserves other functions.

The crop is often followed by another chamber known as the *proventriculus* which varies greatly in the degree of its development. In some insects it is highly developed with strong sclerotized teeth and thick bands of circular constrictor muscles. In these it acts as a gizzard, triturating food particles on the way to the mid-gut. In other insects it is poorly developed but still provided with strong constrictor muscles which serve as a sphincter

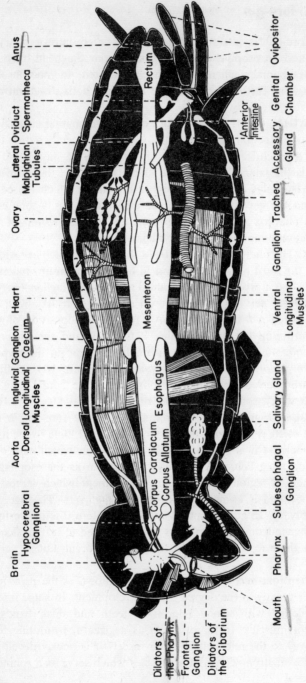

FIGURE 10. The positions and relationships of the principal internal organs.

to regulate the passage of food to the mid-gut. In still others it may serve some specialized function.

The posterior end of the fore-gut, regardless of the degree of specialization, is always invaginated into the anterior end of the mid-gut to form the *esophageal* or *cardiac valve*. It seldom has a true valvular function and, according to Wigglesworth, functions chiefly in directing the food into the lumen of the peritrophic membrane.

Mesenteron or mid-gut

The mid-gut or ventriculus (Figure 10) is that region of the gut in which the digestive juices are secreted. Digestion usually takes place here, though in a few insects digestive enzymes may pass forward into the crop and most of the digestion may take place there. The mid-gut in some Apterygota and some larvae is a straight tube of uniform diameter and structure, but in most insects it is coiled to a greater or lesser extent and is frequently differentiated into two or more regions. The differentiated regions, however, are not the same in all insects. The mid-gut is the seat of absorption also. The secreting epithelial surface may be also absorptive but sometimes one of the differentiated regions is specialized for absorption.

Diverticula of the mid-gut, known as *gastric caeca,* are common. They vary in size, number and position. Primitively they seem to have been devices for increasing the area of the digestive epithelium.

Extending through the mid-gut and into the hind-gut there is, in most insects, a thin chitinous tube free from the epithelial wall. It is known as the *peritrophic membrane* because it encloses the food within the mid-gut and thus protects the delicate epithelial cells from contact with hard or rough particles. In many insects the membrane is secreted by a ring of specialized cells at the anterior end of the mid-gut. In others, it is formed, in part at least, by desquamation of sections of the striated border of the epithelial cells, the sections adhering to each other to form a continuous tube.

Proctodaeum or hind-gut

A posteriorly directed invagination, the *pyloric valve* or *proctodaeal invagination* marks the junction of mid-gut and hind-gut. The latter is always divided into at least two regions, the *anterior intestine* (Figure 10) and the *posterior intestine* or *rectum*. The rectum is typically a relatively wide pear-shaped terminal chamber opening externally through the *anus*. The anterior intestine varies greatly. It may be very short and straight or long and coiled. It is frequently divided into two regions, an anterior *ileum* and a posterior *colon*.

The hind-gut is primarily a passage for conducting to the exterior undigested food as well as excretions from the Malpighian tubules and mid-gut epithelium. It has also the important function of reabsorbing needed water and, presumably, salts from the waste material within it.

Salivary glands

Most insects have glands which empty into the intergnathal cavity and which are known as *salivary glands*. (Figure 10). For the most part these are labial glands which originate as invaginations at the bases of the second maxillae. When the latter unite to form the labium the ducts of the two glands also unite to form a common median duct through which the salivary secretion empties into the salivary passage of the intergnathal cavity. These glands often secrete digestive enzymes or other substances which are in some way accessory to alimentation.

Malpighian tubules

These tubules (Figure 10) frequently retain their original position at the anterior end of the hind-gut, their position marking the junction of mid- and hind-gut, but may shift forward to the mid-gut or to a more posterior position on the hind-gut. The number of tubules may vary from two to upwards of a hundred, but when the numbers are high they are frequently arranged in groups opening into the gut through one or more common ducts. The distal ends are always closed and usually lie free in the body cavity. Sometimes, however, they penetrate beneath the muscular coats of the rectum and lie close against the rectal epithelium forming what is known as a *cryptonephridium*.

CIBARIUM AND PHARYNX

Melanoplus or other large grasshopper

Cut off the head and prothorax. Remove the left half of the prothoracic wall and expose the portion of the gut lying within it. Remove the left mandible and maxilla. Remove the left side of the cranium, including the clypeus and labrum, making the incision mesal to the eye. (With a large head these dissections can be done easily while holding the specimen in the hand beneath a simple magnifier.) Pin the head in the dissecting tray with the cut side up, pushing one pin through the posterior part of the vertex and another through the right cheek by way of the occipital foramen.

Portions of the large mandibular adductor muscle will be exposed; remove them carefully. Flood the specimen with some suitable stain, wash and cover with water.

Follow the stomodaeum from the prothorax into the head and note that within the head it narrows to form the *pharynx*. The posterior portion of the latter is supported by the body of the tentorium, but the anterior portion bends ventrally, passing through the anterior tentorial foramen (i.e., between the two anterior arms and the frons). Expose the pharynx fully by removing such portions of the tentorium as is necessary. Be careful not to disturb the muscles attached to the pharynx.

Identify the *cibarium,* the cavity between the clypeus and basilingua, and the *mouth,* the orifice of the tubular pharynx. Find the brain, a white, lobed body dorsal to the pharynx at approximately the level of the antennae. It gives off a nerve cord, the circumesophageal connective, which runs across the pharynx to enter another ganglion ventral to the pharynx. Near the root of the connective the brain gives off a nerve which soon forks, one branch running forward in a loop to terminate in the minute *frontal ganglion.* Note that this ganglion lies on the pharynx at the level of the mouth, i.e., at the boundary between the pharynx and the cibarium.

It should now be possible to identify the following muscles of the cibarium and pharynx.

The *dilators of the cibarium* originate in the inner surface of the clypeus and are inserted in the clypeal region of the epipharyngeal wall, i.e., the roof of the cibarium.

The *retractors of the mouth angles* originate on the frons and are inserted at the lateral sides of the mouth in the oral arm of the suspensorium of the hypopharynx.

The *precerebral dorsal dilators of the pharynx* originate in the frons and are inserted in the dorsal wall of the pharynx in front of the brain and behind the frontal ganglion.

The *postcerebral dorsal dilators of the pharynx* originate in the vertex and are inserted in the dorsal wall of the pharynx behind the brain.

The *ventral dilators of the pharynx* originate in the tentorium and are inserted in the ventral wall of the pharynx.

The *constrictors of the pharynx* are circular muscles which form the outer coat of the pharynx.

DRAWING: Sagittal section through the cranium showing the features described.

Protoparce (larva) or other caterpillar

Pin the specimen in the dissecting tray with the left side upward, carefully cut away the left mandible and left half of the cranium and expose the stomodaeum and its muscles. Find the brain and the *frontal ganglion* and identify the arched *connectives* which unite the two. Note that the digestive tube does not terminate at the level of the frontal ganglion as it does in the cricket. *The cibarium,* which lies in front of the ganglion, has been converted into a tube continuous with the pharynx, and the functional mouth is now the orifice of the cibarium.

Find the *skeletal dilators* which pass from the cranial wall to the tube and note that the *dilators* of *the cibarium* originate from the distal (i.e., the clypeal) region of the triangular frontoclypeus, while the *dilators of the pharynx,* inserted within the loop of the frontal ganglion connectives, originate from the proximal or frontal region of the sclerite and from the area lateral to it.

DRAWING: Sagittal section of the head showing the structures described.

DIGESTIVE TRACT, MALPIGHIAN TUBULES AND LABIAL GLANDS

Protoparce larva

The specimen used in the last exercise may be used here. Slit the body wall along the mid-dorsal line from neck to anus and pin the specimen flat in the dissecting tray. The prominent digestive tract will be exposed. Observe the slender noduliferous tubules on the surface of the tract. These are the *Malpighian tubules.* Leave them intact but remove any fat that obscures the view of the digestive tube which, it will be noted, is a straight tube extending from the mouth to the anus without coils.

STOMODAEUM. Within the head just studied was a very short *esophagus* behind the pharynx, which widens as it enters the thorax to form the *crop,* a stout tube with a thin transparent wall. The muscular coats, evident on the outer surface, consist of an outer layer of delicate bands of circular muscles, and an inner layer of irregularly branching longitudinal muscles. Posteriorly the end of the fore-gut projects into the anterior end of the mid-gut to form the *esophageal valve* or *stomodaeal invagination*. Make a short incision through the junction of fore- and mid-gut, wash the contained food out with a fine stream of water, and examine the invagination. Note that it is not deep enough nor sufficiently strongly muscled to occlude the gut.

MESENTERON. The mid-gut is a wide, straight tube extending throughout most of the abdomen. The epithelium is thrown up into folds giving the outer surface a corrugated appearance. Find, at the anterior end, a circle of small papillae; cut through one of these and note that it is not a solid body but a small diverticulum of the mid-gut. These bodies are the *gastric caeca* which are minute in caterpillars.

Numerous very fine strands of *longitudinal* and *circular muscles* will be found on the surface of the mid-gut, the latter internal to the former. In addition there are six evenly spaced double bands of stouter longitudinal muscles which run from the anterior to the posterior end and continue on to the fore-gut and hind-gut where they break up into several divergent fibres. The circular muscles are very fine and difficult to distinguish. They are most easily seen by raising one of the stouter bands of longitudinal muscles, when very fine fibers will be seen running at right angles to the longitudinal muscles and for the most part disappearing between the folds of the epithelium. The muscles show more distinctly in a caterpillar having a smoother mid-gut surface than that of *Protoparce*.

PROCTODAEUM. The junction between the mid-gut and the hind-gut can be recognized by the abrupt change in the character of the tract from the opaque, corrugated wall of the mid-gut to the relatively smooth, semitransparent wall of the hind-gut. A slight constriction between the two marks the position of the poorly developed *proctodaeal invagination* or *pyloric valve*.

The short, conical anterior region of the hind-gut has been called the "pylorus" but, as it is part of the hind-gut, *ileum* is a preferable designation. The muscular coats of the ileum are well developed. The longitudinal muscles are external to the circular, but at the anterior end there is an additional group of circular muscles on the outside.

The constriction at the posterior end of the ileum marks the position of the *ileocolic valve* which is provided with powerful muscles. There is an outer layer of longitudinal muscles and beneath this a thick band of circular muscles which forms an efficient sphincter. A second layer of longitudinal muscles lies beneath the sphincter. Two bundles of these can be seen on the dorsal wall of the ileum disappearing beneath the sphincter. Cut longitudinally through the valve, wash away the contained food, and examine the infolded epithelium. Because of the narrow passage and the strong sphincter, the valve is capable of shutting off the passage between the ileum and the colon.

Lateroventrally in this region find a pair of thin-walled sacs, the *urinary bladders,* into which the Malpighian tubules empty. Trace the duct leading from one bladder into the gut and note that it empties into the colon through the epithelial fold of the valve. Apparently, therefore, the ileocolic valve can occlude the orifice of the Malpighian duct also.

The *colon* or second region of the hind-gut is somewhat globular when filled with waste food but tubular when empty. It terminates in the *rectal valve,* a narrow region of the tube surrounded by strong circular and oblique muscles. It is capable of occluding the passage between the colon and the rectum.

The *rectum* is the terminal pear-shaped chamber of the hind-gut opening externally through the *anus.* It is surrounded by a continuous tunic of circular muscles and external to these there are six bands of longitudinal muscles. These are skeletal dilators which take their origin in the body wall of the last segment, run along the wall of the rectum and terminate in the rectal valve region. The musculature is well adapted to the expulsion of fecal pellets.

THE MALPIGHIAN TUBULES. Find the urinary bladders again and note that a pair of Malpighian tubules enters each one. These are slender coiled tubes, their walls studded with numerous small diverticula. Follow their course and note that they run some distance forward on the mid-gut then turn posteriorly to form a series of convolutions surrounding the hind-gut. Their free extremities terminate in convolutions on the outer surface of the rectal epithelium beneath the muscular coat. The ends are blind and the tubules do not communicate with the lumen of the rectum. This perirectal arrangement of the tubules is found chiefly in Lepidoptera and Coleoptera and is known as a *cryptonephridium.* It is presumed to reabsorb from the rectum water and salts needed by the insect which would otherwise be lost with the feces and urine.

DRAWING: The digestive tract and the Malpighian tubules of one side.

LABIAL GLANDS. The labial glands in most insects have a salivary function. In lepidopterous larvae this function is taken over by a pair of small mandibular glands and the labial glands function as silk glands. In the adult they function as salivary glands.

158

Remove the digestive tract from the specimen just dissected or use a fresh specimen, if necessary, and find in the lateroventral region a pair of long, irregularly coiled or convoluted tubes, their distal blind ends extending almost to the posterior end of the abdomen. Follow the course of these *labial glands* forward and note that in the thorax each one narrows to form a slender duct which passes into the head. Cut away the dorsal portions of the head and remove any tissue that obscures the path of the ducts. The ducts unite in the head to form the short common *salivary duct* which enters the labium-hypopharynx complex and opens through the spinneret.

A pair of small glands known as *Lyonet's* or *Fillipi's glands* discharge at the base of the common duct. These are not well developed in sphingid larvae but may be found in most other caterpillars. The silk for the cocoon is secreted by the labial glands; a silk press in the common duct flattens the fibers and it is thought that Lyonet's glands secrete an adhesive substance which cements the two fibers together.

DRAWING: The labial glands.

Acheta assimilis

Select for dissection a large female nymph, if one is available, because the reproductive organs are small and inconspicuous and do not obscure the view of the intestine. They can be easily removed.

Remove the legs and cut through the dorsal body wall from the neck to the eighth abdominal segment, making the incision just dorsal to the pleural membrane. Remove the dorsal region thus excised. Pin the insect in the dissecting tray and, under the microscope, remove carefully the remainder of the dorsum. If an adult has been used, the large ovaries or the testes should be removed and the digestive tract exposed throughout its length.

The structure of the pharynx is similar to that of the locust and its study may be omitted. The *esophagus* will be seen passing from the head into the thorax. It is a narrow tube whose lateral and dorsal walls soon expand to form a capacious *crop* which extends into the abdominal cavity. Note the white lobulate masses of tissue adhering to the sides of the esophagus and crop. These are portions of the salivary glands which will be studied later. The walls of the esophagus and crop are thin and both the outer layer of *longitudinal muscles* and the inner layer of *circular muscles* are in the form of delicate bands which can be distinguished in the specimen.

Behind the crop lies the *proventriculus* consisting of a short anterior

159

tubular portion, the *peduncle,* and a posterior ovoid region, the *gizzard.* Note the strong bands of circular muscles on the proventriculus.

The proventriculus is clasped laterally and posteriorly by the *gastric caeca,* a pair of large diverticula from the anterior end of the mid-gut, which terminate blindly near the hind end of the crop.

Behind the proventriculus there are two spirally coiled regions of the tract which may be called respectively the *secreting* and *absorbing intestine.* The former consists of a short tubular region with the gastric caeca which evaginate from its anterior end. Its surface is densely mottled with minute spots which mark the position of epithelial cell groups.

The absorbing intestine is somewhat wider, the surface is not mottled but along one side there are rows of circular pits which mark the position of tubular invaginations or "villi." A shallow constriction separates it from the secreting region. Posteriorly it narrows to form a valve surrounded by a strong sphincter. The common duct of the Malphighian tubules enters at this point.

The secreting intestine is the mid-gut or mesenteron or an anterior region thereof. The absorbing region has been interpreted as the ileum and as a differentiated region of the mesenteron. Internally the constriction between the two regions resembles the pyloric valve of the caterpillar. In its relation to this invagination, to the posterior (ileocolic?) valve and to the origin of the Malpighian tubules, it resembles the ileum of the caterpillar. On the other hand, the apparent absence of a cuticular intima and its function in absorbing digested food suggest that it is part of the mid-gut. If so, the sphincter marks the position of the true pyloric valve.

Manipulate the region of the sphincter and find a short tube which enters the gut at this point. This is the common duct of the Malpighian tubules. At its distal end it bears a tuft of slender *Malpighian tubules* which are distributed among the coils of the tract.

The short *colon* bends ventrally and continues posteriorly. It discharges into the rectum through a *rectal valve* as in the caterpillar. The wall of the *rectum* is divided into six broad bands, separated by narrow semitransparent strips. The bands mark the position of the *rectal pads.* The musculature is essentially similar to that of the caterpillar.

DRAWING: Dorsal view of the digestive tract, partly extended so as to show all regions, with the Malpighian tubules extended at right angles.

PROVENTRICULUS AND STOMODAEAL INVAGINATION. Cut away the dorsal portion of the mid-gut at the base of the caeca and expose the posterior end of the fore-gut which is invaginated into the mid-gut. Make a sagittal section of the gizzard and the invagination with a sharp scalpel. (Remove the organ, if necessary.) Wash out the contents and examine the inner surface. Note that the wall consists of six longitudinal ridges or folds separated by grooves and by narrow septa. Each ridge contains about ten transverse rows of backward-directed sclerotized teeth. Note further that the ridges (without the teeth) continue posteriorly to form the folds of the invagination which are sufficiently close together to occlude the canal when the circular muscles contract.

DRAWING: Inner surface of one ridge.

SALIVARY GLANDS. Separate the lobes of the salivary glands from the esophagus and crop, being careful not to break their connections with the ventral portions of the glands. Remove the esophagus and crop carefully, and note that the salivary lobes already observed are connected with similar lobes in the ventral region of the thorax. Minute ducts lead from each lobe and these eventually unite to form two main ducts which lie side by side in the ventral neck region and pass into the head ventral to the tentorial bridge. In the neck each duct gives off dorsally a thin-walled blind sac, the *salivary reservoir,* which extends into the thorax. Cut away the dorsal region of the head and follow the course of the ducts. Within the head they unite to form the common salivary duct which empties into the salivary chamber of the intergnathal cavity.

DRAWING: Semidiagrammatic drawing of the glands and their ducts.

Dytiscus sp.

Remove the dorsal wall of the abdomen and pin the specimen in the dissecting tray. Most of the alimentary tract will be exposed and any fatty or other obscuring tissue should be removed carefully. The large crop will be evident in the anterior portion of the abdomen. Cut through the lateral walls of the thorax and expose the thoracic portion of the tract. Examine the structures in place and note the following.

The relatively narrow *esophagus* extends from the head, through the thorax, to the abdomen where it enlarges to form the crop. Behind the crop there is a short conical *proventriculus* and this is followed by the anterior chamber of the *mid-gut* which can be recognized by the large number of finger-shaped *gastric caeca* which cover its walls. At the posterior end of the visible portion of the mid-gut there are four or five transverse folds of the *anterior intestine* with the *Malpighian tubules* among them. Behind these folds is the stout *rectum*. At the left of the mid-gut, and disappearing posteriorly beneath the folds of the intestine, the anterior end of the *rectal caecum* can be seen. Unless distended it appears as a corrugated, tapering blind tube and in the female, it may be partially imbedded in the left ovary.

Remove carefully any persisting vestige of the apparent last abdominal tergum. Find on each side of the rectum a thin-walled tube which empties into the lateral side of the anus. This is the *duct* of the *anal gland*. It extends anteriorly and expands to form a large *reservoir*. The gland itself is a closely convoluted white tubule lying in large part on the reservoir. It enters the duct a short distance posterior to the reservoir.

> **DRAWING:** The alimentary canal and anal glands in their normal positions.

Cut through the esophagus, lift up the gut and extend it carefully. Note that the *anterior chamber* of the mid-gut is relatively wide and bears small finger-shaped caeca over the entire surface. It is folded on itself and followed by the *posterior chamber,* which is narrower with its surface closely beset with small papillae. Find the junction of the mid-gut and hind-gut and note the origin of the *Malpighian tubules* at this point.

The *anterior intestine* is a long coiled tube of uniform diameter. The rectum is relatively very large and is produced anteriorly to form a large tapering *rectal caecum*.

> **DRAWING:** The alimentary canal partly extended to show the various regions.

HISTOLOGY OF THE STOMODAEUM

Acheta assimilis

PHARYNX. Examine a slide of the head which shows the pharynx in cross section. Note that the epithelium is thrown up into six irregular folds or ridges, which if relaxed and flattened out will considerably increase the capacity of the pharynx. The epithelial cells are tall and well-defined in the folds but shorter between the folds. Note the relatively thick cuticular intima, secreted by the epithelium, which lines the pharynx.

The muscular coats are well developed. The circular or constrictor muscles are attached to the wall between the folds. The longitudinal dilator muscles lie internal to the circular muscles on the outside of some of the folds. There is a particularly strong one on the dorsal side of the anterior region of the pharynx. In some sections the skeletal dilators will be seen originating in the cranium or the tentorium and inserted in the pharynx between the folds. This complex and well-developed musculature is correlated with the function of the pharynx in the intake and swallowing of food. Note that the muscles are all striated. There are no smooth muscles in insects.

DRAWING: Cross section of the pharynx.

CROP. Note that the arrangement of the tissues is similar to that in the pharynx but the epithelial cells are small and ill-defined, the intima is thick and beset with minute denticles and some larger spine-like processes, and the muscle coats are more regularly arranged and thinner.

DRAWING: Cross section of crop.

PROVENTRICULUS. Examine the cross section of the gizzard, i.e., the posterior region of the proventriculus. Note the six ridges or folds to which attention was drawn earlier (p. 161) and the narrow septa between them. The intima varies in thickness in different parts of the section, but the great thickness and heavy sclerotization of the *teeth* will be evident in some regions. The *epithelium* also varies somewhat in character in different regions. The *longitudinal muscles* will be found in the concavity on the outside of the folds, while several layers of *circular muscles* surround the whole organ. When the strength of these constrictor muscles is considered in conjunction with the strongly sclerotized teeth it is evident that the proventriculus is equipped to function as a triturating organ.

DRAWING: Cross section of the proventriculus.

HISTOLOGY OF THE MESENTERON

Orthosoma sp. (larval mid-gut)

A section of the anterior region of the mid-gut shows the epithelium in its simplest form. Several other larval insects, e.g., mosquitoes, show a similar structure.

Examine a region of the slide which shows a true cross section and note that the *epithelium* consists almost entirely of large, well-defined, regular columnar cells with large spherical or ovoid granular nuclei. Many of them may contain clear or granular secretion globules in the cytoplasm. Find along the inner surface of each cell a fringe-like border with numerous vertical striations. This is the *striated border* which consists of a series of short rod-like outgrowths from the cytoplasm held together in a clear gelatinous medium. Such a border is known as a "honeycomb border," but in some instances the rods are free and the border is then called a "brush border." The rods are nonmotile and must not be confused with cilia. These columnar cells with striated borders are the typical secreting cells of the mid-gut and are found in all insects.

Between the bases of the secretory cells you will find small cells at irregular intervals which do not reach the lumen of the gut. These are *replacement* or *regenerative* cells which by proliferation and growth produce new secretory cells. These replacement cells are found in practically all insects. The secretory cells, because of their intense activtiy, have a limited life span. In some insects individual cells die at irregular intervals and are replaced by the regenerative cells; in others the entire secretory epithelium is replaced at each moult; and in some Coleoptera there is a periodical complete replacement throughout adult life.

The epithelium rests on a delicate *basement membrane,* and surrounding this there is a thin coat of *circular muscles.* External to the circular muscles there is a layer of *longitudinal muscles* spaced at intervals around the tube.

DRAWING: Cross section of the mid-gut.

Caterpillar (mid-gut)

Study a cross section and find the secretory and replacement cells which are essentially similar to those of the insect just examined. Note, however, that the epithelium is not as uniform as in *Orthosoma* because there are many small clear areas, either unstained or weakly acidophilic, which seem to break the continuity of the cells. These mark the position of *goblet cells,* of which there are several among the secretory cells. The goblet cells vary in size and form, but the typical form may be likened to a narrow cylindrical goblet with a deep solid base and an ovate or lanceolate cavity, the inner end of which communicates with the lumen of the gut. They resemble, in fact, a columnar secretory cell having the striated border invaginated deep within the cytoplasm. The nucleus, usually smaller than that of the columnar cells, lies in the cytoplasm at the base of the cell and thus at a lower level than that of the columnar cells.

The function of the goblet cells is not definitely known. Some authors believe them to be a distinct type of cell with some specialized secretory function. Others claim that they are worn out and degenerating columnar cells.

Ental to the epithelial layer you will find the *peritrophic membrane,* a thin, irregular, noncellular membrane surrounding the food and free from the epithelium.

Circular and *longitudinal muscles,* as in *Orthosoma,* can be distinguished.

DRAWING: A complete cross section of the mid-gut. Details of cell structure may be shown in a segment of the drawing only.

Acheta assimilis (secreting intestine)

Examine slides showing cross sections of the caeca and the secretory region and, if available, longitudinal sections through the mid-gut and caeca. Note that the structure of the epithelium is the same in the caeca as in the tubular region, but in the caeca the epithelium is thrown up into a number of folds which fill the lumen, thus greatly increasing the secretory surface.

The *regenerative cells* are arranged in large groups which, for the most part, are evenly spaced. Each group forms a nest or *nidus* in the center of a cylindrical group of *secretory cells* with striated borders. Thus the epithelium is divided into a number of cell units. In some regions, especially in the outer wall of the caecum, the cells all arise at the same level. The outermost cells of each unit extend vertically to the lumen, but as they are wider at their inner ends, the inner cells become progressively more oblique until those from opposite sides meet and enclose a central core of cells which do not reach the lumen. The outermost cells of this core, or *nidus,* are also inclined toward the center, but they become progressively smaller until at the bottom of the nest there is a group of very small cells with scanty cytoplasm. When there is need for the replacement of secretory cells, the small cells multiply while the outer cells of the nidus increase in size, reach the lumen and become striated.

The epithelial cells rest on a thick layer of connective tissue. Throughout most of the region this tissue is folded inward in such a way as to form cup-like capsules around each cell unit. The secretory cells arise from the wall of these capsules, therefore their bases are not all at the same level. This has the advantage of increasing the number of secretory cells and is responsible for the wavy outline of the inner surface of the epithelium.

The appearance of the epithelium will vary according to the stage of secretion. After the secretion has been discharged and any dead cells replaced, the cells are distinct and the "waves" shallow. When secretion is taking place actively the cells are more elongated and crowded and the "waves" are higher. When the secretion is being discharged the edges of the cells become somewhat ragged in appearance and globules of secretion may be seen exuding from the cells.

DRAWINGS: Two or more sections showing different appearances of the epithelium.

Labidomera clivicollis (milkweed chrysomelid)

Examine a cross section of the mid-gut of this or some other suitable beetle and note that the regenerative cells are evaginated outward through the muscular coats and form minute papillae on the outer surface of the gut. These evaginations are usually referred to as *regenerative crypts.* As the secretory cells die the small regenerative cells at the bottom of the crypt multiply and increase in size. Those nearest the lumen are pushed inward to replace the dead cells.

DRAWING: Cross section of the mid-gut.

Acheta assimilis (absorbing intestine)

Note that the epithelial cells are relatively large and either cuboidal or columnar, depending on the state of activity. The cytoplasm is clear, the cell boundaries distinct, the nucleus round or oval and of moderate size; the striated border is lacking. The sections will pass through the villi mentioned earlier. Most of these will be cut obliquely or transversely and will appear as a circular or oval group of cells surrounded by an amorphous mass. Find a place in which the section passes through the long axis of the villus and note that the villus is a tubular invagination of the epithelium. A large number of branched, hair-like processes radiate from the cells of the villus. A basophilic mass of amorphous substance usually surrounds and obscures these processes, but if a section through the gut of a starved specimen is available the processes are easily seen.

Some sections should show clearly a mass of coarse unstained particles surrounded by the peritrophic membrane and, between the latter and the epithelium, a heavy mass of finely divided deeply staining material, particularly heavy around the villi. The material within the peritrophic membrane is composed of indigestible food particles; the matter outside the membrane is digested food which has passed through the membrane to be absorbed by the epithelium.

As stated earlier, there is still some question as to whether this region is part of the mid-gut or the hind-gut.

DRAWING: A cross section showing the structures described.

HISTOLOGY OF THE PROCTODAEUM

Estigmene or other caterpillar

Examine a longitudinal section passing through the hind-gut and the posterior region of the mid-gut. Note the abrupt passage from the columnar secretory cells of the mid-gut to the very flat epithelial cells of the pylorus or ileum. Behind the junction the epithelium of the ileum is infolded to form the *proctodaeal invagination* which is neither deep enough nor muscular enough to function as a valve.

The intima of the ileum is very thin, and it is possible that some absorption takes place here. The muscular coats are well-developed.

Note that the posterior end of the ileum is narrowed, the epithelium is thrown up into folds and the circular muscles are well developed. This is the *ileocolic valve* which regulates the passage of food along the hind-gut. In some sections the opening of the Malpighian tubules into the ileum, just anterior to the heavy sphincter muscle, may be seen.

The *colon* lies behind the valve. The epithelial cells are larger and more definite than those of the ileum, and the intima thicker. The epithelium is thrown up into folds, the depth and number of which depend on the amount of food in the colon.

DRAWING: A longitudinal section showing the posterior end of the mid-gut, the ileum, ileocolic valve and the anterior end of the colon.

Acheta assimilis (rectum)

Note that the epithelial cells are of two kinds. For the most part they are tall columnar cells arranged in six *rectal pads*. The pads are separated by a narrow strip of small cuboidal epithelial cells which form the bottom of the groove between adjacent pads.

The *cuticular intima* is well developed and so is the *connective tissue* which forms a relatively thick layer around the outside of the epithelium. A band of *circular muscles* lies external to the connective tissue and there are six strands of longitudinal muscles external to the circular ones, opposite the cuboidal epithelium.

DRAWING: A cross section of the rectum.

HISTOLOGY OF THE MALPIGHIAN TUBULES

Acheta assimilis

Study a true cross section, circular in outline. Surrounding the tubule note the *peritoneal coat* of very thin squamous cells with widely separated nuclei. Internal to this there is a delicate but usually distinct *basement membrane* which supports a ring of glandular *epithelial cells*.

The epithelial cells are large and pyramidal in shape. The cytoplasm is usually finely and abundantly vacuolated but varies in appearance depending on the stage of secretion. The outer edge of the cells, next to the basement membrane, is finely striated and the inner edge more distinctly striated.

The *nucleus* is coarsely granular and situated near the inner end of the cell.

DRAWING: A cross section of a tubule.

15 The Respiratory System

GENERAL CONSIDERATIONS

There has evolved in insects and some other terrestrial arthropods a method of respiration by which oxygen is delivered directly to the tissues through a system of branching and intercommunicating tubes which do not contain blood. For these animals the method is obviously highly efficient because muscle metabolism in strong-flying insects is relatively more intense than in any other animal.

The respiratory system consists of branching tubules known as *tracheae* which open to the exterior by paired segmental orifices, the *spiracles* or *stigmata,* and which terminate internally in very delicate branches or *tracheoles* distributed among the tissues. Gas exchange takes place through the walls of the tracheoles and the finer tracheae.

SPIRACLES. There are typically ten pairs of spiracles borne on the mesothorax, metathorax and the first to the eighth abdominal segments. This number may be greater in the early embryo, but is never exceeded in postembryonic life except in some Diplura and, especially in larval insects, it may be considerably reduced.

The tracheae originate in the embryo as invaginations of the ectoderm and the spiracles are the mouths of the invaginations. This primitive spiracular aperture, however, usually sinks inward and comes to lie at the bottom of a shallow pit, the *atrium or spiracular chamber,* which opens to the exterior through the *atrial aperture.* In such insects the term "spiracle" is used to include the atrial aperture, the atrium and the spiracular aperture. The atrium is usually provided with an air filtering device formed from branched and interlocking hairs, and in most sclerotized insects there is a device for closing the spiracular aperture.

TRACHEAE (Figure 10). The tracheae originate independently in each segment. From each embryonic invagination primary branches extend (a) dorsally to supply the dorsal body wall, dorsal muscles, dorsal vessel, etc.; (b) ventrally to supply the ventral body wall, ventral muscles, nerve cord, etc.; (c) mesally to supply the digestive tract and other viscera. Except in a few primitive Apterygota the individuality of the segmental tracheae is not retained in postembryonic life. Anterior and posterior branches from tracheae in adjacent segments unite to form a pair of continuous *lateral tracheal trunks,* into which the spiracles now open. Other longitudinal trunks may be formed and transverse commissures are frequently formed by fusion of branches from opposite sides of the same segment. Thus the whole system is connected in such a way that air taken in through any spiracle can be directed to any part of the body.

The histological structure of the trachea is essentially similar to that of the integument. There is an epithelial layer of flat polygonal cells on the outside continuous with the epidermis and these cells secrete a chitinous intima, continuous with the cuticle, which lines the trachea. The intima is reinforced by a number of ridges, the *taenidia,* which run spirally around the inside of the tubes. The taenidia hold the tracheae open and strengthen the walls so that they cannot be compressed by any force likely to be developed within the insect.

Many flying insects have dilatations, known as *air sacs* in the course of some of the tracheae. These vary greatly in size, number and distribution. Their walls lack taenidia, therefore they collapse when air is expelled and thus function in bringing about the ventilation of the system during respiration.

TRACHEOLES. The tracheae branch repeatedly and finally each branch terminates in a tuft of minute tubules known as *tracheoles* having a diameter of the order of 0.2 μ. The tracheoles originate as excavations in the cytoplasm of a branching *tracheal end cell* which is probably a greatly enlarged cell of the tracheal epithelium. Their cavity is at first shut off from that of the tracheal branch by the intima of the latter, but when the intima is shed at the first moult, communication is made between the cavities.

CLOSED RESPIRATION. Open respiration (breathing through open spiracles) is primitive in insects, but spiracles are lacking in the larval and pupal stages of many insects. Most Collembola and the protopod larvae of certain Hymenoptera have no tracheal system. Respiration in these is entirely cutaneous and the oxygen is distributed by the blood. The larvae and pupae of many aquatic insects (Ephemerida, Plecoptera, Odonata, Trichoptera, some Diptera) have a well-developed tracheal system but no functional spiracles. Respiration in these is cutaneous (through the general integument) or branchial (through gills). The respiratory surfaces are richly supplied with tracheae and tracheoles; the oxygen diffuses into the tracheae and is distributed by them. Gills are of various kinds. They are adaptive structures and those of the various groups are not homologous.

Tracheal gills are thin-walled lamellate or filamentous evaginations of the integument containing a rich supply of tracheae and tracheoles. They may be borne on any segment of the trunk and also on the head. In dragonfly larvae they develop in the wall of the rectum and are known as "rectal gills." Tracheal gill respiration in many aquatic larvae supplements general cutaneous respiration and becomes important when the oxygen concentration of the water is low.

Blood gills, so-called, are evaginations of the integument containing blood but no tracheae. Formerly thought to be respiratory organs, they are now known to have no special respiratory function.

Spiracular gills, sometimes called "tube gills" or "cuticular gills" are found in the pupae of many species, chiefly aquatic Diptera, which live in swift-running streams or in other habitats liable to periodical drying out. They are capable of functioning both in and out of the water. They vary much in structure but consist typically of branching tubes which grow out in a region which, in an air-breathing insect, would be occupied by a spiracle. The atrium or spiracular chamber grows out and branches within the gills. Oxygen diffuses through the thin walls of the gills into the tracheae. Gills of this type are provided with hydrofuge hairs or processes so that if they are broken, water will not enter the tracheae. If the insect is out of water a broken tube can function as an open spiracle.

SPIRACLES

Various insects

Examine the following insects and note the number and arrangement of the spiracles.

1. *Acheta.* Spiracles are present on the mesothorax, metathorax and the first eight abdominal segments. This is the typical arrangement and insects with spiracles thus distributed are said to be *holopneustic.*

2. *Aedes, pupa.* A single pair of functional spiracles borne on the prothorax—*propneustic* type.

3. *Aedes, larva.* A single pair of posterior spiracles—*metapneustic* type.

Note that the immature stages of the mosquitoes are examples of aquatic insects which have open spiracles and come to the surface to breathe.

4. *Musca, larva.* One pair of spiracles on the prothorax, another at the posterior end—*amphipneustic* type.

5. *Protoparce, larva.* Spiracles on the prothorax and on eight abdominal segments—*peripneustic* type.

6. *Macronema* or other *Trichopteran larva.* No functional spiracles—*apneustic* (branchiopneustic) type.

Protoparce, larva

Remove a small portion of the integument surrounding a spiracle, bringing away a part of the underlying trachea with it. Boil in potassium hydroxide and examine in a drop of glycerine. Note that the spiracle is surrounded by a narrow sclerotized ring, the *peritreme.* Two opposing rows of fimbriated processes grow out from the peritreme, their free ends meeting in a straight line in the long axis of the *atrial aperture.* The branched hairs on these processes form an effective strainer which prevents particulate matter from entering the spiracle with the inspired air.

DRAWING: An external view of a spiracle.

Examine the inner surface under the high power of the dissecting microscope. Remove any remaining soft tissue and lift away carefully the tufts of tracheae which originate beneath the spiracle. Note that the atrial aperture is the opening into the shallow atrium or spiracular chamber. The *spiracular aperture* lies at the bottom of this chamber. Find the two sclerotic bars which form the closing mechanism of the spiracular aperture. One, the *bow,* is crescentic in form; the other, the *band,* is shorter, lies in the opposite wall of the atrium and bears at one end a projecting process known as the *lever.* The other end of the band is hinged to one end of the bow.

Having examined the position of these bars, dissect carefully a spiracle which has not been treated with potassium hydroxide and find a minute oblique muscle running from the lever to the free end of the bow. The contraction of this *occlusor* muscle draws the two sclerotized bars together thus closing the spiracular aperture. When the muscle relaxes, the bars spring back into place by their own elasticity or by the contraction of elastic fibers attached to the lever.

DRAWING: A diagrammatic representation of the closing mechanism.

172

THE TRACHEAE
Protoparce, larva

Cut the caterpillar along the mid-dorsal line and, transversely, along the back of the neck, and spread the insect in the dissecting tray. Remove anterior and posterior regions of the alimentary canal, leaving a short portion of the middle region in place. Find the positions of the spiracles.

Remove very carefully any muscles and fat that obscure the view of the tracheae leading from the prothoracic spiracle and find, attached to these tracheae, a small diffuse organ having the appearance of a string of white eggs or beads. This is the very important *prothoracic gland* (not a part of the respiratory system) which secretes the growth hormone. It runs longitudinally through the prothorax to the back of the head and transversely within the prothorax.

DRAWING: A prothoracic gland showing its relation to the tracheae.

Identify the other spiracles and note that from each spiracle a short tracheal trunk leads inward to one of a pair of *lateral tracheal trunks* which extend throughout the length of the abdomen and thorax and send branches into the head.

Find the following segmental branches given off from the lateral trunks. (1) A *ventral branch* or group of branches distributed to the organs and tissues in the ventral region. (2) A *dorsal branch* supplying the dorsal region. (3) A *visceral branch* supplying the digestive tract. Find also the segmental *ventral commissures* connecting the two lateral trunks.

DRAWING: An outline of the insect and a portion of the digestive tract. Fill in the principal tracheae exposed.

Apis mellifera, worker

Remove the dorsal wall of the thorax and abdomen from a newly killed bee. Remove the abdominal viscera carefully, observing their tracheal supply as they are being removed.

Find the abdominal *spiracles* and note that a short trunk from each enters the *lateral trunks* as in *Protoparce*, but that the lateral trunks here are enlarged to form relatively enormous *air sacs*. These are largest in the anterior segments and taper toward the posterior end. They will probably be collapsed and appear as thin white membranes but the student can judge

173

their size and appearance when distended by air. Cylindrical tracheae branch off from the sacs to supply the various organs.

Find the *ventral commissures* between the lateral trunks and note that those of the fourth to the seventh abdominal segment are also in part enlarged to form air sacs. The *dorsal branches* also are in part dilated to form sacs.

The lateral trunks pass as narrow tracheae through the petiole into the thorax where they are again enlarged to form air sacs. Dissect away the thoracic muscles sufficiently to expose these sacs, which need not be studied in detail.

Cut away the dorsal region of the head and note the presence of air sacs here also.

The bee is a strong-flying insect and needs a rich and constant supply of oxygen to its muscles. It is easy to understand how the release of pressure on its air sacs will cause the inrush of a large volume of tidal air into the respiratory system.

DRAWING: An outline of the abdomen showing the principal tracheae and air sacs.

TRACHEAL AND SPIRACULAR GILLS

Argia or other damsel fly nymph

Examine one of the leaf-like *anal gills* and note that the integument is thin so that the tracheae can be easily seen. Find the main trachea that traverses the length of the gill and the richly branched off-shoots from it.

DRAWING: A diagrammatic representation of the gill.

Simulium, pupa

This provides an example of spiracular gills. Find the large branching tubes given off from the prothorax. The detail of their structure will not be studied.

HISTOLOGY OF THE TRACHEAE

Melanoplus

Examine the prepared whole mounts of the trachea and find (1) the *epithelial layer,* a continuous layer of pavement epithelium, consisting of flat polygonal cells, which forms the outer layer of the trachea; (2) the *cuticular intima;* (3) the *taenidia* or spiral thickenings of the intima which give the cross-striated appearance to the tracheae.

DRAWING: A portion of the tracheal tube showing the features mentioned.

Acheta assimilis

Because of the flatness of the epithelium its cells do not show prominently in a cross section, but at ecdysis the intima is shed along with the cuticle of the body wall and at this time the actively secreting cells are taller. Examine a cross section of a moulting cricket and find the structures mentioned in the previous exercise. If cut at the right time the section will show the old intima separated from the cells and the new intima in process of formation.

DRAWING: A cross section of the trachea.

16 The Circulatory System and Associated Organs

GENERAL CONSIDERATIONS

There is in insects a single body fluid, the *blood* or *hemolymph,* which is not confined within closed tubes but flows through spaces in the head, trunk and appendages, bathing the tissues directly. These spaces or *sinuses* constitute the *hemocoele* or definitive body cavity. Coelomic cavities occur only in the embryo and are soon replaced by the hemocoele.

In addition to the sinuses there is a single tubular *dorsal vessel* through which the blood flows. This is probably the dorsal vessel of the annelidan ancestors and is all that remains of their complex blood system, though in some orthopteroid insects short segmental arteries, which may be vestiges of the parietal arteries, are given off from the vessel.

Small *pulsatile organs* or *accessory hearts,* frequently found in the path of the appendicular circulation, help to force the blood through the narrow channels of the appendages.

The dorsal vessel

The dorsal vessel (Figure 10), typically an unbranched tube, lies beneath the mid-dorsal line of the body wall. It is divided into a posterior *heart* and an anterior *aorta.*

The heart is usually restricted to the abdomen but in a few insects it extends into the thorax. It does not extend posteriorly beyond the ninth abdominal segment and is frequently reduced in extent and restricted to a few posterior segments. Paired segmental *ostia,* or valvular openings, in the lateral walls of the heart admit blood from the dorsal sinus into the cavity

176

THE CIRCULATORY SYSTEM AND ASSOCIATED ORGANS

of the heart. These close when the heart is contracted and the blood is forced along the channel of the heart and aorta. Intervalvular constrictions usually divide the heart into apparent segmental chambers, but internally the cavity of the heart is usually continuous, though in some insects, especially some aquatic species, the heart is divided internally into communicating chambers. These do not always correspond to the external divisions.

The heart is suspended from the dorsal integument by fine elastic fibers and is supported ventrally by the dorsal diaphragm.

The *aorta* extends from the anterior end of the heart into the head, terminating in an open mouth beneath or behind the brain. Its length depends largely on the extent of the heart but may be increased by bending or coiling. It is usually narrower than the heart but certain regions may be dilated.

The blood is kept circulating by the pulsations of the heart, sometimes aided by pulsations in the aorta and undulatory movements of the diaphragms. The blood coursing forward leaves the dorsal vessel through the mouth of the aorta, enters a sinus in the head and flows slowly back through the ventral sinus.

The walls of the dorsal vessel consist largely of circular muscle fibers. There is no intima but a connective tissue sheath is often present on the outside.

Sinuses and diaphragms

The trunk hemocoele is commonly divided into three sinuses by fenestrated septa or diaphragms. The heart lies in the *dorsal* or *pericardial sinus* which is partially separated from the remainder of the hemocoele by the *dorsal diaphragm*. This consists of segmental pairs of triangular *alary muscles,* enclosed between delicate connective tissue membranes. There is a pair of muscles for each segment through which the heart extends. The muscles are attached by their apexes to the lateral sides of the terga of the segments in which they lie. Their bases meet beneath the heart with which they are intimately connected. The septum, except in a few insects, is not attached to the body wall between the apexes of the muscles, therefore spaces are left between these points through which blood can pass from the perivisceral spaces into the dorsal sinus.

Many insects have a *ventral diaphragm* consisting of a delicate membrane containing strands of muscle fibers. It lies ventral to the digestive tract and, like the dorsal diaphragm, is attached only at two points in each segment. It cuts off a *ventral* or *perineural sinus* from a *middle* or *perivisceral sinus.*

Blood normally flows posteriorly in the perineural and perivisceral sinuses and anteriorly in the dorsal sinus. It can pass from one to another through

177

the fenestra in the diaphragms. Undulations of the diaphragms may help to keep the blood moving.

Pulsatile organs or accessory hearts are small muscular sacs which pulsate independently of the heart and may either force blood through an appendage by increasing the pressure on one side or aspirate blood from it by decreasing the pressure on the other side.

The blood or hemolymph

The blood consists of liquid *plasma* and formed elements, the blood cells or *hemocytes*. The composition of the plasma is less constant than that of vertebrates and in some respects differs widely from vertebrate plasma. Like the latter, however, it contains inorganic and organic substances in solution and transports food, hormones, waste products of metabolism and other substances. Respiratory pigments are absent except in a few chironomid larvae, the so-called blood worms, which have hemoglobin dissolved in the plasma.

The blood cells are for the most part mobile cells which may be regarded as the physiological equivalent of the white blood cells of vertebrates. There are no red blood cells. The hemocytes are more numerous than the white cells of vertebrates but far less numerous than the total cell count in this group. The actual number varies not only in different species but in the same species under different conditions. In many insects, numbers of these cells cling to the solid tissues and are not in constant circulation, which makes an accurate count difficult.

The classification of insect blood cells is difficult, workers on different insects having quite different views. This is due, in large part, to the wide variety of forms which the same type of cell may assume. The following are some of the principal types.

1. *Proleucocytes.* These are small, round or spindle-shaped cells with large nuclei and a small amount of basophilic cytoplasm. They are often seen in mitotic division and are believed to be the precursors of the other cell types, though these are said to multiply to produce other cells like themselves.

2. *Plasmatocytes or amoebocytes.* These are pleomorphic cells which may assume a great variety of shapes. They may be round, lenticular, fusiform or irregular with pseudopodium-like processes. The cytoplasm is more extensive than that of the proleucocytes. They are the most numerous of the blood cells and are the active phagocytes. They have the ability of uniting to form connective tissues in muscles and other organs or to form protective cysts around multicellular parasites which they thus immobilize.

3. *Granulocytes and spheroidocytes.* Blood cells have been described containing small granules or larger spheroidal inclusions. The nature and function of these are not always clear. Some may be degenerating cells, some trephocytes—i.e., cells secreting nutritive materials—others may be phagocytes with ingested particles. One type (adipoleucocytes) contains fat globules and may be wandering cells of the fat body.

4. *Oenocytoids.* These are round or oval cells with regular outline and homogeneous cytoplasm. They are not phagocytic and generally make their appearance in the blood during the moulting period. Dennell believes that they secrete the tyrosinase which functions in the hardening of the cuticle.

Tissues associated with the blood

THE FAT BODY *(corpus adiposum).* Extensive masses of fatty tissue are found, more or less regularly arranged, in the various spaces and sinuses surrounding the visceral and other organs. The fat body cells are derived from the mesoderm and are closely related to the blood cells. The tissue in most insects is in the form of fairly compact opaque sheets or strips, in others it is more diffuse, while in a few the cells float free in the blood. The cells are of two principal types, *trophocytes* and *urate cells.*

The trophocytes are the most numerous cells, often the only type present. They are food storage cells, synthesizing fats, glycogen and proteins for use in times of need such as periods of starvation, moulting or metamorphosis. The cells are at first small with homogeneous cytoplasm but as fat globules are secreted they become vacuolated, increase in size and the cell membranes tend to disappear.

Urate cells, containing uric acid crystals, are frequently found scattered among the trophocytes. In some insects they are excretory, removing uric acid from the blood, but in others the crystals seem to be formed *in situ* as an end product of metabolism within the cell itself. The crystals may be discharged from the cells and eliminated by the Malpighian tubules, or they may accumulate in the cells throughout the life of the insect.

ATHROCYTES. This term is suggested for several groups of cells, apparently identical in function, for which there is no collective term in use. They include *pericardial cells* associated with the heart or dorsal diaphragm, *garland cells,* strung between the salivary glands of muscoid larvae, and *nephrocytes,* found singly or in groups in the fat body or among other tissues. Apparently they supplement the work of the phagocytes in removing minute colloidal particles from the blood. In this respect they resemble the reticuloepithelial cells of vertebrates.

PHOTOGENIC OR LIGHT PRODUCING ORGANS. Bioluminescence occurs in many species of terrestrial insects belonging to widely separated orders and, in most species, it is associated with the fat body. In several species of Collembola and in some nematocerous larvae the fat body over most of its area gives off a continuous faint glow. In other insects, notably some Lampyridae and Elateridae, there are highly specialized photogenic organs, also derived from the fat body. These organs consist of a deep opaque layer of reflector cells containing urate crystals, a more superficial layer of light-producing glandular cells and, covering the organ, an area of transparent, unpigmented cuticle.

Probably in all species light production is the result of the oxidation of luciferin, catalyzed by the enzyme luciferase, a reaction which liberates a quantum of light and very little heat.

OENOCYTES. The oenocytes are large, round or oval cells with large nuclei and dense acidophilic cytoplasm. They originate from the ectoderm near the spiracles and in some insects occur as clusters of cells in this position, but they are often scattered at random among the cells of the fat body or other tissues. They are unicellular glands which show great secretory activity during the moulting period and Wigglesworth has obtained evidence that they secrete the lipoprotein of the epicuticle. Several other functions have been ascribed to them, but the evidence is inconclusive.

THE DORSAL VESSEL AND THE DIAPHRAGMS

Acheta assimilis

Cut through the abdominal pleural membranes and the thoracic pleura, discard the ventral wall, pin the remainder in the dissecting tray and remove the alimentary canal and reproductive organs.

The *dorsal vessel* should now be exposed as a delicate transparent tube in the mid-dorsal line, extending from the ninth abdominal segment through the thorax into the head. The abdominal portion is the *heart* which has a slightly greater diameter than the thoracic portion or *aorta*. Note that slight constrictions divide the heart into segmental "chambers." A pair of lateral valvular openings or *ostia* in each chamber permit the passage of blood into the heart. In the cricket the constrictions and ostia may be difficult to detect.

The heart extends from the ninth abdominal to the third thoracic segment and in each of these segments you will find a pair of triangular *alary muscles*. Note that the bases of these muscles are attached to the ventral side of the heart, while their apexes are attached near the posterolateral edges of the terga. Find the thin transparent membrane which holds the muscle fibers together and note that it is free from the body wall between the points of attachment of the muscles. The alary muscles and the membrane constitute the *dorsal diaphragm* which separates the dorsal or pericardial sinus, within which the heart lies, from the middle or perivisceral sinus surrounding the digestive tract.

Follow the course of the aorta through the thorax. Dissect away the dorsal portion of the head and note that the aorta terminates in an open mouth beneath the brain.

DRAWING: Outline of the insect showing the dorsal vessel and dorsal diaphragm.

Apis mellifera

Divide the abdomen into dorsal and ventral halves, leaving the head and thorax attached to the dorsal half. Pin both parts in the dissecting tray and remove the digestive tract.

Examine the dorsal portion of the abdomen. The modifications which have occurred in both the anterior and posterior regions have been accompanied by a reduction in the extent of the *heart* and *dorsal diaphragm,* which now extend only from the sixth segment to the third. Find the four pairs of *ostia,* which are more distinct here than in the cricket. Note that the heart narrows slightly between the ostia and is thus divided into four "chambers."

The heart narrows in the third abdominal segment to form the aorta which passes through the pedicil into the thorax. Dissect away the ventral regions of the thorax and expose the aorta which is coiled in the pedicil and propodaeum but straightens out in the thorax and terminates in the head beneath the brain.

Find, in the abdomen, the *alary muscles* which have essentially the same attachments as in *Acheta.* You should find distributed through the diaphragm a flocculent mass of translucent tissue formed by the *pericardial cells.*

DRAWING: Dorsal vessel and dorsal diaphragm.

Examine the ventral half of the abdomen and find the *ventral diaphragm,* a thin but firm transparent sheet of fine muscle fibers extending from the second to the fifth abdominal segment, having each of its lateral edges attached at four points at the lateral sides of the sterna. The sinus ventral to the diaphragm is the *ventral* or *perineural sinus,* within which the nerve cord lies. That part of the body cavity between the dorsal and ventral diaphragms, in which the digestive tract lies, is the *middle* or *perivisceral sinus*.

> **DRAWINGS:** 1. An outline of the abdomen showing the ventral diaphragm.
> 2. A diagrammatic cross section of the abdomen showing the positions of the heart, dorsal and ventral diaphragms, the digestive tract and the nerve cord.

THE HEMOCYTES
Melanoplus

Examine a stained blood smear of this or some other insect and find as many as possible of the hemocytes described earlier (p. 178). The amoebocytes and proleucocytes will probably be most numerous, but a few granulocytes or other types may be present.

> **DRAWING:** A group of hemocytes illustrating the different types found. Draw several amoebocytes.

THE FAT BODY

The fat body will have been seen in all of the specimens dissected. For a more detailed study of its distribution, the student, if he so desires, may dissect a caterpillar. The fat body of a cockroach should show the urate cells clearly.

Acheta assimilis

Study a slide showing a cross section of the abdomen and identify the fat body tissue distributed irregularly among the viscera but massed chiefly in the periphery mesal to the body wall muscles. It can be distinguished by the fact that it is very lightly stained and is arranged in irregular lobules, each containing a group of cells surrounded by a delicate noncellular membrane. The nuclei are small and more or less central in position. The cytoplasm appears as a fine, irregular network of granules with clear unstained meshes. The unstained areas are the fat globules.

The structure will vary according to the amount of stored food. When this is relatively small the cells are small and their boundaries well-defined. When food is abundant the cells are larger and their boundaries may be obscured.

DRAWING: A section of the fat body.

OENOCYTES

Acheta assimilis and Photinus sp.

Oenocytes may be easily distinguished in a cross section of the abdomen of *Acheta*. They occur singly or in small groups surrounded by fat body cells, chiefly in the peripheral regions. They stand out from the other cells by reason of their large size, the large granular nuclei and abundant homogeneous acidophilic cytoplasm.

Find similar cells in the section of *Photinus*. Here they are relatively very large and occur chiefly in the lateral masses of the fat body. It will be observed that when the oenocytes occur in groups they are not united to form an organ. Each is an individual unicellular gland.

DRAWING: A single oenocyte and a group of oenocytes.

PHOTOGENIC ORGANS

Photinus

Examine a cross section of the abdomen and find the photogenic organ which occupies the ventral region. The *reflector* will be found on the inner side of the organ. It consists of several layers of polygonal cells which, except for the nuclei, are unstained. These cells contain refringent granules of urates. The *glandular layer* lies ectad of the reflector. It also consists of several layers of cells but their cytoplasm takes a deep stain. The cells are arranged in vertical columns, and between the columns there are *tracheae* which send numerous branches to the cells. A rich supply of oxygen is needed for the active oxidation which takes place in these cells.

Note the thin *cuticular layer* on the outside, compare it with the cuticle on the dorsal side and note that, unlike the latter, it is not pigmented. It is in fact transparent.

DRAWING: A section through the photogenic organ.

183

17 The Reproductive System

GENERAL CONSIDERATIONS

Insects are unisexual but hermaphroditism sometimes occurs as an aberrant condition. Normal functional hermaphroditism has been described in at least one species, the coccid *Icerya purchasi*. The reproductive system includes both the external genitalia, which have been already discussed, and the internal genitalia which will be considered here. The latter consists of the gonads (ovaries or testes), the gonoducts and glandular and other structures associated with the system.

Origin

The germ cells have been shown in many insects to originate early in embryonic life as products of the cleavage of the zygote nucleus. As development proceeds, the primordial germ cells migrate to the dorsal region of the coelomic sacs in several of the abdominal segments. When the coelomic walls break down, two dorsal strands of mesodermal tissue, containing the germ cells, persist to form the genital ridges. From the posterior end of each ridge a solid strand of mesodermal cells, without germ cells, extends to the ventral region of the seventh segment in the female, the ninth or tenth in the male. The genital ridges develop into the gonads, the posterior strands into the mesodermal gonoducts (lateral oviducts or vasa deferentia).

The gonads may therefore be interpreted as remnants of the coelomic sacs and the mesodermal gonoducts as the persistent coelomoducts of the posterior segment contributing to the gonads.

The mesodermal cells of the genital ridge form the sheaths of the gonads as well as nutritive cells associated with the germ cells.

184

The reproductive system does not undergo metamorphosis. It develops in a straight line from the embryonic stage to the adult.

Female organs (Figures 10 and 11)

OVARIES. The ovaries are a pair of conspicuous organs lying in the dorsolateral regions of the abdomen (Figure 10), the size in any species varying according to the number of fully developed eggs which they contain. Each ovary consists of several or many tubules, known as *ovarioles,* within which the eggs develop. The ovarioles lie free in the hemocoele because the ovary is not enclosed in a sheath. Each ovariole terminates distally in a delicate *terminal filament* (Figure 11) and the filaments of each ovary form collectively a *suspensory ligament,* which anchors the ovary in the dorsal region of the thorax. The proximal region of the ovariole is a short slender duct, the *pedicil,* which communicates with the oviduct. The main body of the ovariole is the egg tube consisting of a proximal *vitellarium* and a distal *germarium.*

The germarium develops during embryonic life as a simple sac containing the primordial germ cells and groups of undifferentiated mesoderm cells. During postembryonic life the oogonia multiply and develop into primary oocytes. The first formed oocyte passes backward and a chamber is formed around it at the posterior end of the germarium. As other oocytes develop, similar chambers or *ovarian follicles* are formed between the germarium and the most recently formed follicle. Thus the oldest follicle is at the proximal end. The series of ovarian follicles, each containing an oocyte, constitutes the *vitellarium.*

In some insects the oogonia by repeated division give rise to two kinds of cells, one oocyte and several trophocytes or nurse cells. The nurse cells maintain protoplasmic connections with the oocyte. Ovarioles containing both nurse cells and oocytes are said to be "meroistic"; those containing no nurse cells are "panoistic." The nurse cells may pass back with the oocytes so that there is an alternation of oocytes and nurse cells in the vitellarium *(polytrophic ovarioles),* or they may remain in the germarium, each group connected with its oocyte by protoplasmic strands *(acrotrophic ovarioles).*

When an oocyte leaves the germarium it is accompanied by some of the indifferent mesoderm cells, which surround the oocyte and form an epithelial sheath. This *follicular epithelium* nourishes the oocytes in the panoistic ovariole, and in the meroistic ovariole probably takes over from the nurse cells when the latter degenerate. In either case the follicle cells secrete most of the yolk and the egg shell.

Oogenesis is not completed in the ovary; the mature egg is a primary

185

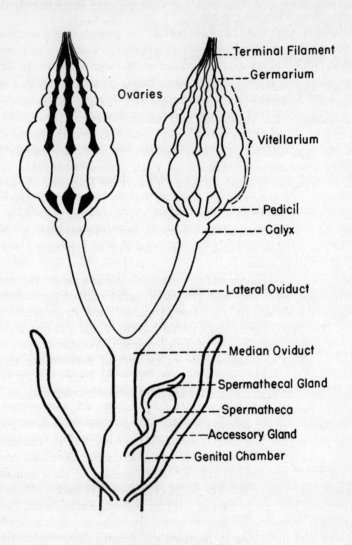

FIGURE 11. Female reproductive system.

oocyte and maturation divisions of the nucleus take place in the newly laid egg after the sperm has entered it.

OVIDUCTS AND GENITAL CHAMBER. The pedicils of the ovarioles open into the paired or lateral oviducts (Figure 11), usually into a somewhat enlarged portion of the oviducts known as the *calyx or ovisac,* in which one or more eggs may remain for some time before passing outward. The lateral oviducts are mesodermal in origin and, primitively, opened separately on the seventh abdominal sternum. This primitive condition persists in the Ephemerida but in other insects they open into a *median oviduct* which is formed by invagination of the integument and is therefore ectodermal in origin.

The median *gonopore,* or external genital opening, persists on the seventh sternum in Dermaptera but in other insects a secondary groove forms in the eighth sternum and is later cut off as a tube continuous with the median oviduct. A new genital opening, the *vulva,* is thus established at the posterior end of the eighth segment and the original gonopore is closed. This addition to the genital ducts receives the intromittent organ of the male and is known as the *genital chamber* or *copulatory pouch* (bursa copulatrix). It is typically a fairly wide tube but is often narrow, approximately the same width as the median oviduct of which it forms a continuation. When it takes this form it is usually called the *vagina.* In some insects the genital chamber continues still further back and opens in the ninth segment.

SPERMATHECA. In most insects a small sac, the *spermatheca* or seminal receptacle (Figure 11) opens into the bursa. At mating the spermatozoa make their way to the spermatheca where they may remain viable for a considerable time. Spermatozoa are ejected from the spermatheca as the egg passes through the genital chamber on its way outward. A spermatozoon enters the egg and stimulates it to complete its maturation divisions. Fertilization then takes place by the union of the male and female pronuclei, and development of the embryo begins at once.

The spermatheca originates as an ectodermal invagination, usually in the eighth segment. It is frequently provided with a gland which secretes the fluid surrounding the spermatozoa.

ACCESSORY GLANDS. Many insects have *accessory glands* opening into the posterior end of the genital chamber. These also are ectodermal, originating as invaginations of the venter, usually of the ninth segment. Their secretion is commonly used to attach the eggs to the substratum on which they are laid, hence they are sometimes called "colleterial glands," but they may have other functions.

Mesodermal glands are not common. In grasshoppers one such gland arises from the distal end of the calyx.

Male organs (Figure 12)

TESTES. The two testes occupy the same relative position as the ovaries. Unlike the ovaries, they are typically enclosed in a peritoneal sheath. Within the sheath the testis consists of a number of testicular follicles which correspond to the ovarioles of the female.

The apical region of each follicle is the *germarium* which contains the spermatogonia and indifferent mesodermal cells. It may contain also a large stellate *apical cell* which probably has a specialized nutritive function. According to Nelsen, spermatogonia in contact with this cell retain their primitive condition and do not transform into spermatocytes. They thus form a reservoir for the continuous production of spermatozoa.

Proximal to the germarium is the *zone of growth* where those spermatogonia that have lost contact with the apical cell multiply and increase in size to form primary spermatocytes. The spermatocytes derived from a single spermatogonium remain in contact and become surrounded by an epithelial cyst wall, derived from the mesodermal cells, which corresponds to the follicular epithelium of the female.

Next to the zone of growth is the *zone of maturation* where the maturation divisions take place. The most proximal region is the *zone of transformation* in which the spermatids transform into spermatozoa.

GENITAL DUCTS. Each testicular follicle discharges through a short, slender tubule, the *vas efferens,* into the *vas deferens* which is the homologue of the lateral oviduct of the female. Enlargements in the course of the vasa deferentia frequently form *seminal vesicles* for the storage of sperm. The vasa deferentia empty into the ectodermal ejaculatory duct, the origin of which was discussed earlier in connection with the external genitalia.

ACCESSORY GLANDS. Glands are normally associated with the male organs. They may be mesodermal in origin borne on the vasa deferentia or ectodermal, borne on the ejaculatory duct. They secrete a fluid which mixes with the spermatozoa. In some insects the fluid hardens to form a capsule, the *spermatophore,* which encloses a mass of spermatozoa.

GENITAL ORGANS OF THE FEMALE
Acheta assimilis

Remove the abdominal terga and pin the specimen in the dissecting tray. In a gravid female the dorsal and lateral regions of the abdominal cavity will be filled with yellow eggs within the ovarioles and the structure of the latter will be difficult to discern. Most of the eggs will be equal in size but the most anterior follicles will be smaller and should show a gradation in

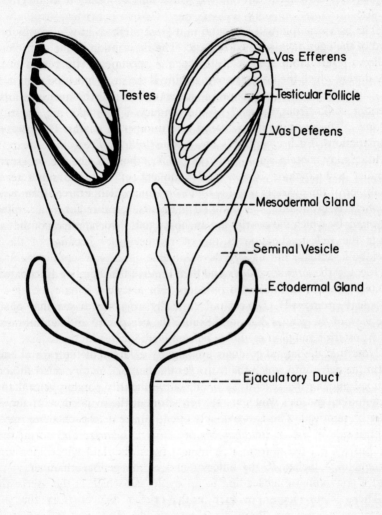

Testes

Vas Efferens

Testicular Follicle

Vas Deferens

Mesodermal Gland

Seminal Vesicle

Ectodermal Gland

Ejaculatory Duct

FIGURE 12. Male reproductive system.

size. If such a specimen is studied it should be supplemented by a nymph. The ovarioles here will be evident, but yolk deposition will not have started in the oocytes which will be small, white, and with only a slight gradation in size.

The best example will be found in a young female in which only one or two of the eggs have reached full size. The description of the ovarioles that follows refers more specifically to such a specimen. The period of adult life during which the oocytes are maturing is the preoviposition period. Note that the ovaries are not enclosed in a sheath and that the ovarioles arise by slender stalks from the end of the oviduct. The stalks are the tubular *pedicils*. The egg tube is composed of a number of chambers separated by constrictions. Each chamber is an *ovarian follicle*. The follicle nearest the oviduct may contain a full-grown egg. The other follicles are progressively smaller and contain younger and younger oocytes. The small terminal chamber of the ovariole is the *germarium* from which a thread-like *terminal filament* is given off. The terminal filaments together form a *suspensory ligament* by which the ovaries are anchored to the dorsal region of the insect. Note the rich tracheation of the ovary, necessary because of the high metabolic activity during egg development.

Identify the *lateral oviducts* and then remove the digestive tract carefully, taking care not to injure the oviducts. (In a gravid female the eggs also should be removed). Dissect out carefully any fatty tissue that obscures the view of the genital ducts and expose the nerve cord and ventral muscles. The posterior ganglion may now be removed.

Note that the lateral oviducts are slightly enlarged at their distal ends to form the *calyx* into which the ovarioles discharge. The oviducts run ventro-caudad and, in the seventh segment, curve mesally passing ventral to two longitudinal muscles which are the retractors of the ovipositor. The muscles may be removed. The two oviducts open, adjacent to each other, into the ventral side of the *genital chamber* or *bursa copulatrix*. The dorsal wall of the bursa is dilated to form a prominent pouch beneath which the oviducts terminate. Attached to the anterior end of the genital chamber you will find a convoluted duct leading to an ovoid sac which is the *spermatheca*.

There is no median oviduct in the cricket distinct from the genital chamber, neither are there accessory glands. The cricket lays its eggs individually in the soil and there is no need for the secretions of such glands.

Cut away the dorsal valvulae of the ovipositor and find the *vulva* between the bases of the first valvulae.

DRAWING: Dorsal view of the genital organs.

190

Melanoplus sp.

Remove the head and prothorax, cut off the wings and legs, slit the body wall along the mid-dorsal line and pin the opened specimen in the dissecting tray. Identify the two closely associated ovaries and the lateral oviducts, then remove the digestive tract. The statements made in the opening paragraph of the preceding exercise apply here also.

In *Melanoplus* the *ovarioles* are arranged linearly, arising in two rows from the dorsomesal region of a tube which is a continuation of the lateral oviduct and which constitutes the *calyx*. This is a primitive condition, as in nearly all insects the ovarioles originate thus in the ovary, but usually during the course of development the calyx shortens so that all the ovarioles arise at approximately the same level, as they do in the cricket.

Find the parts of the ovariole which are essentially similar to those in *Acheta*.

The anterior end of the calyx is produced to form a long convoluted tube. This is the *oviducal gland* which secretes the substance that glues the eggs together to form the characteristic egg pod. It is obviously mesodermal in origin and must not be confused with the accessory glands of other insects which are ectodermal and discharge into the genital chamber. Accessory glands are not developed in the grasshopper.

The calyxes continue behind the ovaries as the *lateral oviducts*. Near the posterior end of the seventh abdominal segment these enter the short common or *median oviduct* which opens into the *genital chamber*. The ovoid *spermatheca* lies dorsal to the median oviduct and partly obscures it from view. A coiled *spermathecal duct* leads from the spermatheca to the genital chamber posterior to the orifice of the oviduct.

> **DRAWING:** A dorsal view of the genital organs with the spermatheca displaced slightly to one side.

Dytiscus sp.

Remove the dorsal wall of the abdomen and dissect out the digestive tract.

The large ovaries, each consisting of numerous ovarioles, occupy most of the lateral regions of the abdominal cavity. Note that the follicles, or at least the distal ones which contain immature oocytes, alternate with smaller nurse chambers containing the nurse cells. At the proximal end where the oocytes are mature or nearly so, the nurse cells have been used up and are no longer present. The ovariole is polytrophic, unlike that of *Acheta* or *Melanoplus* which is panoistic.

191

Find the lateral oviducts and note that they empty into the median oviduct which in turn gives rise to the *bursa copulatrix,* a large and conspicuous curved chamber which continues posteriorly as a short *vagina.*

The *spermatheca* arises from the bursa near the junction of the latter with the median oviduct. It is in the form of a short tube folded on itself. It communicates with the bursa by means of a short *spermathecal duct.* The structure of the bursa and spermatheca varies somewhat in different species.

DRAWING: Dorsal view of the genital organs.

Danaus plexippus

Remove the integument of the right side of the abdomen, making the incision along the mid-dorsal line and somewhat to the right of the mid-ventral line. If the adipose tissue is abundant it must be removed very carefully, especially in the posterior region where there are delicate tubules.

A large brown sac-like organ will be quickly exposed at the level of the fourth or fifth segment. Clear it carefully of surrounding fat and note that its posterior end tapers to form a sclerotized tube which opens externally in the eighth segment. This is the *bursa copulatrix* which, in the higher Lepidoptera, opens independently of the vagina. Immediately in front of the tubular region the bursa gives off dorsally the convoluted tubular *seminal duct* which runs posteriorly to enter the median oviduct. The spermatozoa are deposited in the bursa and travel through the seminal duct to the vagina and into the spermatheca. Later they come in contact with the eggs as these pass outward. The course of the seminal duct will be followed later.

Dissect away the fat ventral to the bursa and find the right *ovary* which contains four *ovarioles.* The ovarioles of the nongravid female are long, very slender strands imbedded in the fat. In the gravid female each ovariole consists of a long string of follicles each containing a fully developed egg.

Find where the ovarioles connect with the *lateral oviduct* and trace the latter posteriorly. The two lateral oviducts enter the *median oviduct* which is a short tube that runs posteriorly to the right of the bursa and widens slightly to form the *vagina.* The vagina opens to the exterior on the ninth segment ventral to the anus.

Remove any fat surrounding the median oviduct and the vagina, taking care not to break the delicate tubules in this region. Find the seminal duct again and trace its course to the anterior end of the vagina. A second median tubule is given off from the vagina behind the seminal duct. This is the *spermatheca.* A third tubule, the common duct of the *accessory glands,* enters the vagina near its posterior end. This soon branches to form the two

192

glands, which are slender, convoluted tubules, each with a small bulb-like *reservoir* near its base.

DRAWING: A dissection of the reproductive organs from the right side.

Acheta assimilis

Examine a longitudinal section of the ovary of a young adult or fully grown nymph and find, if possible, a section which passes through a complete ovariole.

Find the *terminal filament* and note that it is cellular in structure, having small nuclei distributed throughout its length. The filament is continuous with the *ovariole sheath* which is epithelial with scattered nuclei. The sheath can be seen most distinctly in the region where the follicular epithelium is lacking but it can be traced as a thin membrane external to the follicle cells in the proximal region.

Identify the *germarium,* the narrow terminal chamber in which the *oogonia* can be seen as fairly large cells. Smaller *mesoderm* cells can be distinguished among them. Toward the proximal end of the germarium the oogonia begin to increase in size to form the *primary oocytes* and the development of these marks the beginning of the *vitellarium.* The distal oocytes are small and, owing to the way they are packed, they are quadrangular in outline. At first their breadth may exceed their length but they soon begin to lengthen and the older ones assume the typical oval form of the egg. Note the large centrally located nucleus or *germinal vesicle.*

The youngest oocytes are surrounded only by the ovariole sheath, while those somewhat older are partially surrounded by mesoderm cells which have passed back from the germarium and multiplied. In the oldest follicles the cells form a complete epithelial sheath around the oocyte and now constitute the *follicular epithelium.* In some sections the cells in the most proximal follicles may be quite tall. This is a sign of secretory activity. The epithelium elaborates nourishment for the oocytes, secretes the yolk and later secretes the shell.

Find a section which passes through a pedicil and note that the pedicil communicates with the calyx behind, but is shut off from the follicle in front. Communication is made with the follicle when the egg is fully developed and ready to pass outward.

DRAWING: Longitudinal section of an ovariole showing the structures mentioned.

Apis mellifera

Examine a section of the ovary which is of the polytrophic type. It is unlikely that the slides will show a complete longitudinal section of an ovariole, but one can be reconstructed by examining sections cut at different levels. The oocytes can be distinguished by the fact that they occur singly, the older ones surrounded by follicular epithelium, while the nurse cells are arranged in small groups and lack this epithelial sheath.

Sections of the oogonia and smaller oocytes will show a large rounded or oval nucleus containing a compact mass of deeply staining material near the center. Only a few sections of the larger oocytes will pass through the nucleus. The nuclei of the nurse cells or trophocytes are irregular in outline (a sign of secretory activity) and contain many small granules.

Sections passing through the germarium should show a compact mass of cells which may be sorted into two sizes. The larger cells are *oogonia*, the smaller *mesoderm* cells. Sections near the posterior end of the ovariole should show single *oocytes*, each associated with a group of *nurse cells* anterior to it.

Differentiation into follicles and nurse chambers begins at the distal or anterior end of the vitellarium where both are relatively small. Further back both have increased in size, the nurse chamber being larger than the follicle. Still farther back this size relationship is reversed, the follicles becoming progressively larger and the nurse chambers smaller as the nurse cells degenerate and the oocytes increase in size.

Find a section which passes longitudinally through at least one follicle and the nurse chamber in front of it. Note that the follicular sheath is not complete. A large pore at the distal end allows for close contact of the cytoplasm of the oocyte (ooplasm) and that of the nurse cells (trophoplasm).

DRAWING: A reconstructed ovariole.

Meloe angusticollis

Examine a longitudinal section of the ovary which is of the acrotrophic type, having all the nurse cells in the germarium. The ovary here consists of a number of short ovarioles arranged around a long oviduct into which they open by slender pedicils. Find a complete longitudinal section through an ovariole and note that there is a single large *oocyte* at the proximal end surrounded by *follicular epithelium*. There are one or two smaller oocytes distal to this and, beyond these, a number of closely packed *oogonia*. The distal region of the *germarium* is a large sausage-shaped chamber containing the groups of nurse cells. From each group *protoplasmic filaments* pass to an oocyte but these may be difficult to detect.

Because the oocytes must receive their nutriment from a distance through protoplasmic strands, an ovariole of this type is of necessity short, with few oocytes.

DRAWING: A section through an ovariole and a portion of the oviduct.

GENITAL ORGANS OF THE MALE
Acheta assimilis

Open the male in the manner directed for the female and identify the large white *testes* in the dorsal region. They may or may not be symmetrically arranged and in most specimens their anterior ends are in close contact. They are roughly ovate in shape with the apexes directed posteriorly, but their form is inconstant as a result of the pressure to which they may be subjected.

Push aside the coils of the intestine behind the testes and find the *vasa deferentia,* delicate tubules which leave the testes near their posterior end mesal to the apex. Remove the digestive tract taking care to leave the vasa intact. Ventral to the intestine there is a mass of coiled tubules, the *accessory glands,* borne on the anterior region of the median duct, which they hide completely. Note that the glands grouped in the middle of the dorsal area are somewhat smaller than the lateral groups. These smaller glands, according to Spann, secrete the inner and outer layers of the wall of the spermatophore, while the larger glands secrete the middle layer.

Remove the accessory glands carefully from one side of the median duct and trace the course of the vas deferens of that side. It runs to the ninth segment where it passes ventral to the large cercal nerve and then curves anteriorly. Before entering the ejaculatory duct the vas deferens enlarges and the enlarged region is thrown into close coils. This is the *seminal vesicle,* sometimes called the "epididymis." Beyond it the vas deferens narrows again and enters the median duct on the ventral side near the anterior end.

Examine that side of the median duct from which the glands have been removed and note that the end from which the glands arise is bilobate. The median duct is usually referred to as the "ejaculatory duct" and the glands arising from it might be thought to be ectodermal in origin, but it is not always possible to be certain where the mesodermal ducts end and the ectodermal duct begins in the absence of embryological and histological evidence. In the cricket, the bilobate anterior end of the median duct is

195

apparently formed by the union of the two ampullae of the mesodermal ducts and only the short wide portion of the tube posterior to the ampullae is the true *ejaculatory duct.* The glands are therefore mesodermal. The ejaculatory duct extends posteriorly to the wide *gonopore,* the opening into the phallus. Near the gonopore two small, round *ejaculatory vesicles* open into the duct. Dorsal to the duct at its posterior end there is a large oval body, the *dorsal pouch* or spermatophore sac of the phallus, within which the spermatophore is formed.

DRAWING: Dorsal view of the genitalia with the accessory glands removed from one side.

Examine a testis and note that, unlike the ovary, it is enclosed in a peritoneal sheath. Dissect part of the sheath away and trace the course of the *vas deferens* which extends within the testis to the anterior end. The testis within the sheath consists of a large number of tubular *testicular follicles.* The posterior end of each follicle is blind and free but the anterior end narrows to form a short, slender tube, the *vas efferens* which unites with the vas deferens.

DRAWING: A section of the testis showing the peritoneal sheath and the relation of several testicular follicles to the vas deferens.

Melanoplus sp.

Remove the head and thorax and open the specimen by cutting through the mid-dorsal line.

The two *testes* in the grasshoppers, and some other insects, are united to form a single dorsal organ, but each testis retains its individuality. The genital ridges in *Melanoplus* are suspended from the dorsal region by ribbonlike suspensory membranes. As development proceeds the two membranes unite and bind the testes together. The testes in the adult appear as a large spindle-shaped body dorsal to the digestive tract. Identify them and the *vasa deferentia* which leave the testes on the ventral side a short distance in front of the posterior end; then remove the digestive tract carefully.

The course of the vasa is essentially similar to that described in *Acheta.* The median duct is short and wide and gives rise to two groups of *accessory glands* which are much longer and less numerous than those of *Acheta.*

Dissect the testes and note that, although the two are bound together, their elements are easily separated. The long testicular follicles of each testis enter by slender *vasa efferentia* into its own vas deferens.

196

DRAWING: Dorsal view of the reproductive organs.

Tetraopes tetraophthalmus (milkweed cerambycid)

Cut off the wings and legs and remove the dorsal wall of the abdomen and metathorax. The hind-gut will be evident in the middle line, extending forward from the anus then looping back toward the posterior end. Push this gently to one side and find the large white *testes* which occupy most of the lateral and ventral regions of the abdominal cavity.

Find the large *penis* at the posterior end. From the dorsal view it is long, oval in form and the brown color of its sclerotized cuticle shows through the muscles on its wall. Push the intestine to the left and note that the dorsal side of the anterior end of the penis appears to be produced anteriorly as a wide tube which bends back on itself. This is the *endophallus,* and its extent within the body cavity, as well as the space occupied by the penis, depends on the extent to which the latter is retracted. In some specimens it may be completely protruded, in which case the everted endophallus appears as a long yellowish tubular extension from the end of the aedeagus.

Find the *ejaculatory duct* which enters the inner end of the endophallus. Do not confuse it with the Malpighian tubules which may be found in the same region and are similar in diameter. From its junction with the endophallus the duct curves to the left and runs posteroventrally. Its actual course will vary according to the extent to which the endophallus is extruded.

Having identified these structures remove the digestive tract carefully.

Find the ejaculatory duct again and follow it to a point just anterior to the last abdominal ganglion where it receives the *vasa deferentia.* It is very delicate and easily broken.

Examine the *testes* and note that each is divided into two parts therefore there are apparently four organs, two anterior and two posterior. The *follicles* of the anterior region will be seen radiating outward in all directions from a central point where they enter the *vas deferens.* The vas leaves the anterior testis as a straight tube and enters the posterior testis. Within this it is enlarged and convoluted and the follicles arise laterally along its length. The vasa leave the posterior ends of the testes and soon become slightly enlarged to form the *seminal vesicles.* A large tubular *accessory gland* arises from each vesicle. These are obviously mesodermal glands. Behind the glands the vasa decrease in diameter and soon enter the ejaculatory duct which runs posteriorly for a short distance, then bends to the right and follows an anterodorsal course to its junction with the endophallus.

DRAWING: Dorsal view of the genital organs with the penis (if retracted)

197

displaced posteriorly and to the right in order to show the structures described.

Dytiscus

Cut away the dorsal abdominal wall and remove the alimentary canal. The reproductive organs will be exposed as a mass of coiled and twisted tubules.

The two *testes* lie laterally in the posterior region of the abdominal cavity. Each testis with its *vas deferens* is in the form of a single long slender tubule which is closely coiled to form a compact, somewhat globular mass. This peculiar structure of the testis is characteristic of the Adephaga. Try to uncoil one testis and note that the single tubule of which it is composed is extremely slender and fragile in appearance, while the vas deferens into which it opens is somewhat stouter.

Find the *ejaculatory duct* which runs forward from the penis as a narrow median tube. Anteriorly it widens and forks to form two long and relatively wide blind tubes. These are ectodermal *accessory glands,* which extend a short distance anteriorly then bend on themselves to form two or three transverse coils. The vasa deferentia empty into the bases of these glands.

DRAWING: The reproductive organs showing those of one side in their normal position, those of the other side with their coils partially straightened out.

Apis mellifera

Remove the dorsal abdominal wall and expose the mass of whitish tissue beneath it. On each side of this mass you will find a long stout tube parallel to the sides of the abdomen. With the aid of a needle follow these tubes forward and note that they terminate in a slender, closely coiled tube, to the end of which a small thin, white or yellowish body is attached. This is the *testis* which could easily be mistaken for a piece of fat or connective tissue.

Remove the digestive tract carefully to expose the remainder of the reproductive system.

Examine the testis again and note its very small size and flattened condition. It may be triangular or, because of the pressure of adjacent structures, irregular in form. The testes reach their full size during the late pupal stage. At this time the spermatozoa mature and pass into the seminal vesicles and the testes begin to degenerate. It will be remembered that the drone has a very short life and if it mates, does so only once. There is no need for continuous production of spermatozoa by the testis.

The short coiled tube attached to the testis is the anterior region of the *vas deferens*. This is followed by a long, greatly enlarged glandular region, the *seminal vesicle*. The short terminal portions of the vasa are again narrow and enter a pair of large *accessory glands,* which are the largest and most conspicuous organs of the system. They are perhaps to be regarded as outgrowths of the proximal ends of the vasa, rather than as branches of the ejaculatory duct.

The *ejaculatory duct* is a long slender tube extending forward from the base of the accessory glands to enter the penis which, when at rest, is retracted within the abdomen. If the penis is extruded the duct will, of course, run in a posterior direction.

DRAWING: Dorsal view of the reproductive organs.

Acheta assimilis

Examine a whole mount and a longitudinal section of a testicular follicle and identify the various zones. The *germarium* is not unlike that of the female and the *spermatogonia* and smaller *mesoderm cells* should be readily identified. The *apical cell,* if present, may be difficult to distinguish.

Proximal to the germarium is the *zone of growth*. Here the spermatogonia have divided and the daughter cells increase in size, therefore the cells in the proximal region of the zone are larger than those in the distal region. The daughter spermatogonia, which increase in size to form the *primary spermatocytes,* do not separate completely from each other, therefore the spermatocytes in cross sections appear as circular cell aggregates, each individual cell forming a segment of the circle.

In the *zone of maturation* the spherical masses of spermatocytes are surrounded by an epithelial sheath, derived from the mesoderm cells, to form *sperm cysts*. In this zone the two maturation divisions take place and the nuclei of many of the cells may be seen in process of dividing. The most proximal sperm cysts contain spermatids and in the last zone, the *zone of transformation,* these transform into spermatozoa. The spermatozoa from each cyst remain massed together, their deeply stained heads arranged in a triangular formation with the paler tails forming a sinuous mass of fibers behind them.

DRAWING: A longitudinal section of the follicle.

199

18 The Nervous System and the Retrocerebral Incretory Glands

GENERAL CONSIDERATIONS

The central nervous system

The central nervous system originates early in embryonic life as a pair of ectodermal ridges, one on each side of the mid-ventral line. Segmental swellings which later develop into ganglia are formed in each ridge. Thus there is at first a pair of ganglia in each segment of the protocorm, but the two ganglia of each segment soon unite to form a single median ganglion. The ganglia of the segments behind the eighth abdominal always unite with that of the eighth, therefore there are never more than eight abdominal ganglia.

When the three gnathal segments are incorporated into the head, their ganglia unite to form the *subesophageal ganglion* (Figure 10) which lies in the ventral region of the head beneath the esophagus. This ganglion, the thoracic ganglia and the abdominal ganglia are all connected by longitudinal nerve cords or *connectives* to form the ventral chain (Figure 10). The subesophageal ganglion supplies nerves to the mouth appendages; the thoracic and abdominal ganglia each gives off two or more pairs of nerves to the organs in their respective segments.

The adults, and often the larvae, of most of the higher insects show varying degrees of cephalization and fusion of the trunk ganglia. As a result, the actual number of independent ganglionic masses varies, but each segmental component of a compound ganglion sends nerves only to the segment in which it originated.

The connectives, like the ganglia, originated in pairs. They may remain entirely separate or they may be united in part or in whole.

Those portions of the embryonic neural ridges which lie in the proto-

200

cephalon, in front and at the sides of the mouth, will develop into the brain. In the early stages only the ventral side of the embryo is developed, but as dorsal closure takes place, the two sets of rudiments are carried dorsally and meet and fuse above the pharynx to form the brain or *supraesophageal ganglion* which is connected with the ventral chain by a pair of *circumesophageal connectives,* one passing on each side of the pharynx or esophagus.

The *brain* (see Figure 10) consists of three pairs of lobes. The anterior and largest pair constitute the *protocerebrum;* behind this is a pair of antennal lobes, the *deutocerebrum.* These lobes are separated by some distance but their commissures lie within the substance of the brain. The third pair of lobes, forming the *tritocerebrum,* are more widely separated and their commissure (see Figure 14) is a free nerve cord passing ventral to the esophagus.

The optic ganglia develop independently of the eyes from the anterior end of the protocephalic neural ridges next to the protocerebrum. Some of their neurons send fibers to the retinal cells of the eyes and optic tract fibers pass from others to the protocerebral lobes. The nerves of the ocelli also originate in the protocerebrum. The deutocerebrum gives rise to the sensory and motor nerves of the antennae. The tritocerebrum gives rise to the labral nerve and the frontal ganglion connectives which connect the central and stomatogastric systems.

The metameric constitution of the brain is still a subject of dispute. Theories concerning it are bound up with those concerning the segmentation of the head. The deutocerebrum is usually regarded as the ganglion of an antennal segment, but there is strong evidence that both it and the protocerebrum originated, in the worm-like ancestors, as secondary condensations of nerve tissue associated with the sense organs of the prostomium. If this is so they are not to be regarded as belonging to the same series as the ventral chain. The tritocerebrum, on the other hand, is undoubtedly a segmental ganglion and is interpreted by most authorities as belonging to the second antennal segment, but this interpretation also has been questioned. It is certainly either the ganglion of the first true metamere of the head or else the simple prostomial ganglion, as found in the earthworm, to which the protocerebral and deutocerebral ganglia have been added to form the definitive brain.

The peripheral nervous system

The peripheral nervous system consists of the nerves which leave the central nervous system to supply the muscles, sense organs and other body structures. The optic and ocellar nerves are purely sensory. The antennal nerve may be mixed for a short distance at the base. The nerves of the ventral chain are all mixed, consisting of motor fibers which originate in the central nervous system and sensory fibers which originate in the periphery and run inward to the central system.

The stomatogastric or stomodaeal nervous system

The stomatogastric system consists typically of three small ganglia lying on the mid-dorsal line of the stomodaeum, and the nerves and connectives associated with them. The ganglia originate independently of the central nervous system as invaginations of the stomodaeal ectoderm. The *frontal ganglion* (Figure 10), lies anterior to the brain and dorsal to the mouth. According to Snodgrass, it always retains this position regardless of any changes in the structure of the head. It is joined to the tritocerebrum by a pair of arched nerve trunks, the *frontal ganglion connectives*. From its anterior border it sends nerves to the region of the mouth and from its posterior border it gives off a median *recurrent nerve* which runs along the pharynx to a point beneath or behind the posterior part of the brain where it enters the *hypocerebral ganglion* (Figure 10). This is not always developed as an independent ganglion. From the hypocerebral ganglion, a median *posterior recurrent* or *esophageal nerve* continues posteriorly and terminates in the *ingluvial* or *ventricular ganglion* which lies near the posterior end of the fore-gut. In Orthoptera there are two esophageal nerves and two ingluvial ganglia. The stomatogastric system innervates the fore-gut, the anterior region of the mid-gut and the aorta.

The incretory organs of the head (Figure 10)

Hormones essential to the processes of growth and metamorphosis are secreted by certain organs in the head which are either parts of the nervous system or intimately associated with it.

The brain contains a large number of *neurosecretory cells* (see Figure 14) whose secretion is necessary for growth. One of its principal functions is apparently to control the secretion of certain other glands.

Closely associated with the hypocerebral ganglion is a pair of small bodies known as the *corpora cardiaca* (Figure 10). They are partly nervous, partly epithelial in structure and, at least in some insects, originate from the same ectodermal invagination as the ganglion. They are connected by nerves to the secretory region of the brain and the brain hormone passes along these nerves to them.

202

On the sides of the esophagus, ventral to the corpora cardiaca and connected to them by nerves, there is another pair of small bodies, the *corpora allata* (Figure 10). These are wholly epithelial in structure and their secretion keeps the insect in the juvenile condition and prevents transformation to the adult instar.

Some insects have a *ventral gland* in the posterior region of the head cavity. This is the counterpart of the thoracic glands of other insects, which secrete the growth hormone.

The corpora cardiaca, the corpora allata and the ventral gland, when present, constitute the *retrocerebral endocrine system*.

Histology

THE NERVE CELL (Figure 13). The unit of structure in the nervous system is the nerve cell or *neuron*. The function of the neuron is to convey nerve impulses (a kind of electric current) from one region of the body to another, and to this end part of its cytoplasm is drawn out into long fibers. There are two kinds of fibers. The afferent fiber along which the nerve impulse travels toward the cell body is the *dendrite;* the efferent fiber, along which the impulse travels from the cell body to the point of

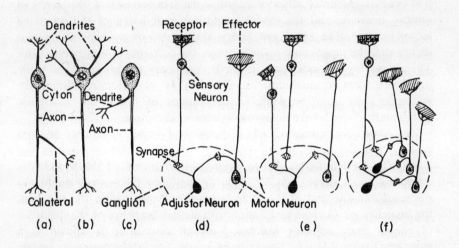

FIGURE 13. Neurons: (a) bipolar, (b) multipolar, (c) unipolar, (d) a simple nerve chain, (e) nerve impulses from different receptors converged on one effector, (f) nerve impulses from one receptor discharged on several effectors.

203

discharge, is the *axon* or *neurite*. There may be two or more dendrites but only a single axon which may give off branches known as "collaterals." The cell body containing the nucelus is the *cyton* or *perikaryon*. The neuron is staid to be *bipolar* if there is single dendrite independent of the axon (Figure 13, a), *multipolar* if there are more than one dendrite (Figure 13, b) and *unipolar* when the dendrite and axon leave the cyton by a common stem (Figure 13, c).

Functionally, the neurons are of three kinds (Figure 13, d). *Sensory neurons* are associated with the receptors or sense organs. Their cytons lie in the periphery and their axons pass inward through a nerve to the central nervous system. The cytons and dendrites of *motor neurons* lie within the ganglia and their axons pass out to the effectors which are chiefly muscles and glands. *Adjustor* or *intermediate neurons* lie wholly within the central system. They may be confined to a single ganglion or their axons may travel through the connectives to terminate in an anterior or posterior ganglion. They serve as intermediaries between sensory and motor neurons, acting like a switchboard to direct the nerve impulse along the right path.

The sensory neurons are bipolar or multipolar, the motor and adjustor neurons unipolar.

THE GANGLION. From what has just been said it is obvious that a ganglion consists chiefly of adjustor neurons, the terminations of the axons of sensory neurons, and the cytons, dendrites, and bases of the axons of motor neurons. The entire ganglion is surrounded by a very thin cellular membrane, the *neurilemma,* which covers the connectives and nerves also. The cytons for the most part lie in the periphery of the ganglion, while the fibers form a medullary mass known as a *neuropile*. Within the neuropile there may be denser condensations of fibers, the *glomeruli,* which mark places where numerous synapses take place.

The *connectives* consist chiefly of bundles of axons of adjustor neurons passing from one ganglion to another.

ACTION OF NEURONS. When a receptor is stimulated the stimulus is converted into a nerve impulse which travels along the sensory neuron to the ganglion. The end of the axon is branched and, within the ganglion, the branches are in close association with similar branches of the dendrites of one or more adjustor neurons. Such an association is known as a *synapse* (Figure 13, d). The impulse passes across the synapse, travels along the fibers of the adjustor neuron and then passes across a similar synapse between the adjustor and motor neurons. It then travels along the fibers of the motor neuron and is finally discharged on the effector, which makes the appropriate response—i.e., contraction in muscles, secretion in glands, etc. Such a response is known as a "simple reflex" and is the basis for most of the activities of the insect.

A nerve chain may consist of only three neurons (Figure 13, d) but is usually more complex. It is possible for impulses from several receptors to converge on a single motor neuron and follow a common path to an effector (Figure 13, e). The converse is also true. An impulse from a single receptor may be discharged on several motor neurons and evoke a response from several effectors (Figure 13, f).

THE BRAIN. (Figure 14). The structure of the brain is basically similar to that of a trunk ganglion but much more complex. The brain has a coordinating influence on the activities of the insect as a whole and there are several centers where numerous adjustor neurons make synapses directly or indirectly with nerve fibers from all of the sense organs and muscles of the head and with fibers from the trunk which reach the brain by way of the subesophageal ganglion and the circumesophageal connectives. The fiber tracts of the brain are therefore very complex.

A frontal section of the brain will show the neurilemma forming a sheath on the outside, numerous cytons in the periphery and a neuropile with denser association centers in the medullary region.

Some of the cytons in the dorsal portion of the interlobar region (pars intercerebralis) are usually larger than the others and stain differently. These are the *neurosecretory cells*.

Within the protocerebrum at least four association centers are to be found. The *protocerebral bridge* is a transverse condensation of fibers in the dorsal or posterior region forming a commissure between the two lobes. The *central body* also is an interlobar mass ventral to the protocerebral bridge. The *corpora pedunculata* or mushroom bodies are a pair of relatively large toadstool-shaped bodies, one in each lobe.

The corpus pedunculatum consists of an expanded *calyx* and a stalk or *peduncle*. Within the outer cavity of the calyx there is a large number of complex adjustor neurons known as *globuli cells*. The cytons of these cells are small with scanty cytoplasm and relatively large nuclei. Their greatly branched dendrites are found within the calyx where they make synapses with nerve fibers coming chiefly from the optic ganglia, the antennal ganglia and from the ventral chain through the subesophageal ganglion. The outgoing axons go chiefly to the central body, the antennal centers and the subesophageal ganglion. These fibers and the incoming ones make up the peduncles of the bodies.

The corpora pedunculata are the most important coordinating centers of the brain and, generally speaking, are best developed in those insects which show the more complex types of behavior.

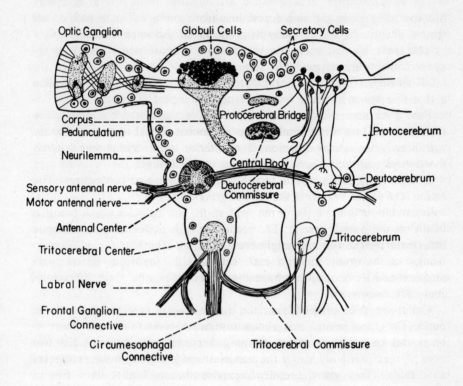

FIGURE 14. Structure of the brain and optic ganglion. Only a very few neurons and nerve tracts are shown.

THE GENERALIZED CENTRAL NERVOUS SYSTEM

Protoparce quinquemaculata, larva

Slit the body along the mid-dorsal line from the apex to the neck, and remove the integument carefully from the facial region of the head.

The *brain,* a small but conspicuous white bilobate body, lies above the apex of the frontoclypeus. The three pairs of lobes characteristic of the fully developed brain are not differentiated externally in the caterpillar and the nerves arise close together from the lateral angles.

Find four nerves originating from each of the two lobes and follow their course. Two stout trunks arise somewhat dorsal to the others and run in an anterolateral direction. The anterior one is the *antennal nerve,* the posterior the *optic nerve* which goes to the stemmata.

A third trunk arises ventral to the antennal nerve and forks close to the brain. The mesal branch is the *frontal ganglion connective.* It runs anteriorly, arching mesally to enter the median *frontal ganglion* which is a part of the stomatogastric system. The second branch is the *labral nerve* which innervates the labrum and neighboring muscles. The fourth pair of nerve trunks run ventrally, one on each side of the esophagus, to enter the anterior end of the subesophageal ganglion. These are the *circumesophageal connectives.*

Cut through the pharynx near the mouth, taking care not to break the connectives, and remove the alimentary canal. Note that the connectives enter the anterolateral angles of the *subesophageal ganglion* which can now be seen partly hidden by the tentorial bridge and the muscles attached to it. Dissect these away carefully to expose the ganglion. A short distance from the origin of the connectives in the brain you will find a transverse nerve cord which passes beneath the esophagus and unites with the two connectives. This is the *tritocerebral commissure,* sometimes called the "stomodaeal commissure," which unites the two halves of the tritocerebrum, the third lobe of the brain from which the connectives originate. It will be remembered that the ganglia of the ventral chain are primitively double, each pair being united by commissures. If the two ganglia of one segment moved dorsally, one on each side of the digestive tract, their commissure would remain ventral to the tract. The position of the tritocerebral commissure suggests therefore that the tritocerebral lobes were originally segmental ganglia of the ventral chain which have migrated dorsally and united with the prostomial elements of the brain.

The subesophageal ganglion, although apparently simple in structure, is formed by concrescence of the ganglia of the three gnathal segments.

Its nerves, therefore, supply the appendages of these segments and their muscles. Find the stout *mandibular nerves,* which originate from the anterolateral angles of the ganglion, and trace them to the mandibular muscles and the mandibles. Cut through the mandibular nerve of one side and tilt the ganglion upwards to expose two pairs of nerves given off from the ventral side. The anterior ones are the *maxillary,* the posterior the *labial nerves.* Follow the course of these nerves far enough to show their relation to the maxilla and labium.

A fourth pair of nerves, the *lateral* or *tegumentary nerves,* arise from the lateral borders of the ganglion and run to the neck region. It will be remembered that the neck belongs in part to the labial region. These nerves probably originate in the labial component of the ganglion.

Clear away the fatty tissue and expose the ganglia of the thorax and abdomen. Note that there is a ganglion in each of the three thoracic segments, but there are only seven abdominal ganglia because the eighth ganglion has migrated forward and united with the seventh. Apart from this the ganglia of the ventral chain have remained separate, each in the segment in which it originated. The short connectives between the subesophageal and first thoracic ganglion have remained separate. Those connecting the thoracic ganglia are united anteriorly but are widely separated posteriorly. The pairs of abdominal connectives are almost completely united but may be separate for a very short distance at their posterior ends.

Examine the third thoracic ganglion and the connectives anterior to it and find the three pairs of nerves given off from them. The posterior pair originates from the ganglion directly. Its first branch goes to the leg, the other branches innervate organs in the posterior region of the segment. Anterior to these another pair branches off from the connectives but has its roots in the ganglion. It innervates the anterior region of the segment. The third pair starts as a single *median nerve* at the fork of the connectives. It originates in the second thoracic ganglion, travels within the connective, then runs free for a short distance before it divides into two *transverse nerves* which run laterally near the anterior border of the segment and send branches to the respiratory organs. The median and transverse nerves are sometimes referred to as the *ventral sympathetic system.* Note that near their origins the transverse nerve and the connective nerve are united by a longitudinal branch and that beyond this there are other anastomosing branches.

Examine one of the anterior abdominal ganglia and note that, apart from the fact that the transverse nerves arise nearer to the ganglion and both of the other pairs arise directly from the ganglion, the distribution of the nerves is essentially similar to that of the thoracic nerves.

Examine the last abdominal ganglion and find the constriction between the ganglion of the seventh segment and that of the eighth which has united with it. Note that the nerves of the former are distributed to the seventh segment only, while those of the eighth ganglion, which is itself compounded of the ganglia of the eighth, ninth and tenth segments, run posteriorly and are distributed to these three segments.

DRAWING: The central nervous system showing the ganglia and the principal nerve trunks. Details of minor branches need not be shown.

CONCENTRATION OF THE TRUNK GANGLIA
Dytiscus sp.

Remove the dorsal wall of the thorax and abdomen, then remove the digestive tract and uncover· the ventral cord. Note that the abdominal ganglia have all migrated anteriorly and lie in the metathorax within the trough formed by the large sternal apophyses. There are four of these ganglia so closely united that their connectives have virtually disappeared. The posterior one is larger than the others and is obviously a compound ganglion. Note that the nerves pass successively farther back in the abdomen, each pair going to the segment in which its ganglionic component originated.

Remove any muscular tissue in front of the abdominal ganglia, cut through and remove the apophyses of each thoracic segment. Find the two long connectives joining the abdominal to the metathoracic ganglion. The latter lies behind the second apophyses and is joined to the mesothoracic ganglion by connectives so short that the two ganglia almost form a single mass. A pair of fairly long connectives join the mesothoracic to the prothoracic ganglion.

DRAWING: Ganglia of thorax and abdomen with the stumps of their nerves.

GANGLIA AND INCRETORY GLANDS OF THE HEAD; STOMATOGASTRIC SYSTEM
Melanoplus or other acridid

Remove the head and pin it under water with the facial aspect upward. Pass the pins obliquely through the genal regions. The brain lies in the region between the compound eyes, therefore the integument must be removed very carefully in this region. Remove the frons and vertex, making the incisions just mesal to the bases of the antennae. While doing this, pass the point of the scalpel or needle beneath the lenses of the ocelli in order to detach the ocellar nerves from the integument. Remove carefully any muscles or other tissues that obstruct a clear view of the brain. Do not disturb the fore-gut.

The conspicuous white, lobed brain should now be exposed. Manipulate the antennae to find their nerves and note the part of the brain to which they are attached. The antennae and the area of integument immediately surrounding them may now be removed, leaving the stumps of the antennal nerves attached to the brain. Find the following structures in the brain.

The protocerebrum consists of a pair of large lobes which form the dorsal and largest region of the brain. A slender nerve, terminating in a small ganglionic enlargement, arises from the apex of each lobe and a similar nerve from the median line. These are the *ocellar nerves* which respectively supply the lateral and median ocelli.

The optic ganglia are attached to the lateral side of each protocerebral lobe. Cut away a portion of the cuticle around the eye to expose the ganglion which is as large or larger than the brain, broad beneath the eye and tapering to a narrow stalk where it joins the brain.

The *deutocerebrum* lies ventral to the protocerebrum on the anterolateral sides of the brain. It consists of two separated rounded antennal lobes each of which gives rise to an *antennal nerve*. The nerve soon divides into a *sensory branch,* supplying the sense organs of the antenna, and a *motor branch* supplying the antennal muscles.

The tritocerebrum consists of two small, widely separated, conical lobes straddling the pharynx and lying ventral and somewhat posterior to the antennal lobes. Each lobe gives rise to two nerve trunks. The anterior and smaller trunk runs ventrally (toward the mouth region) and soon divides into two branches as in *Protoparce.* Follow the arched *frontal ganglion connectives* to the median *frontal ganglion* dorsal to the mouth. The other branch is the *labral nerve* and it supplies the region of the labrum and clypeus.

The posterior and larger trunks given off from the tritocerebral lobes are the *circumesophageal connectives.* They pass ventrally, one on either side of the stomodaeum, to join the subesophageal ganglion. Do not follow their course at this time.

DRAWING: Anterior view of the brain and its nerves, including the optic and frontal ganglia.

Remove most of the brain, leaving the stumps of the tritocerebral lobes with the circumesophageal connectives attached. Find the *recurrent nerve* which runs from the posterior margin of the frontal ganglion along the mid-dorsal line of the pharynx and enters a second median enlargement, the *hypocerebral ganglion,* just behind the brain. At this point there are three closely united bodies. The *hypocerebral ganglion,* which is part of the stomatogastric system, forms the bottom of a shallow trough, the sides of which are formed by two elongated bodies, the *corpora cardiaca.* These are attached to the sides of the ganglion and project dorsally. A slender nerve will be found attached to the anterior end of each corpus cardiacum. This has its origin on the posterior side of the protocerebrum. On the sides of the esophagus, ventral to the corpora cardiaca, there is another pair of small bodies, the *corpora allata.* A short nerve attaches each of these bodies to the corpus cardiacum of the same side.

The corpora cardiaca and corpora allata are incretory glands whose hormones influence the course of growth and metamorphosis. The cardiacal nerve which originates from the protocerebrum is apparently formed from dendrites of the neurosecretory cells of the brain, and it has been shown that the brain hormone can pass along these fibers to the corpora cardiaca. Thus the incretory glands of the head are all closely associated.

The relations of these organs may be further checked by a lateral dissection. Remove the abdomen of another specimen, cut along the mid-dorsal and mid-ventral lines of the thorax and neck and remove the left body wall, leaving the fore-gut intact. Expose the brain and pharynx by removing the muscles, tentorium and any other structures that obscure the view. Find the corpus cardiacum and corpus allatum again and trace the origin of the cardiacal nerve from the protocerebrum.

Note that a pair of *posterior recurrent nerves* or *esophageal nerves* originate from the hypocerebral ganglion and run posteriorly along the sides of the fore-gut to terminate near the posterior end of the latter in a pair of *ingluvial* or *ventricular ganglia* which send nerves to the posterior region of the fore-gut and the anterior region of the mid-gut.

The recurrent nerves and the frontal, hypocerebral and ingluvial ganglia with the nerves given off from them constitute the stomatogastric or stomodaeal nervous system.

Follow the circumesophageal commissures around the pharynx, dissecting carefully to expose the *subesophageal ganglion.* Find the *tritocerebral commissure* which, as in *Protoparce,* passes ventral to the pharynx. The stout *mandibular nerves* will be found at the anterior end of the ganglion near its junction with the commissures. The *maxillary nerves* arise near the middle of the ganglion and the *labial nerves* posterior to them. Identify these nerves by tracing them to the muscles or mouthparts which they innervate.

> **DRAWINGS:** 1. Lateral aspect of the dissected head showing the brain and subesophageal ganglion.
> 2. A dorsal view, reconstructed from the two dissections, showing the fore-gut, the stromogastric system and the incretory glands.

Musca domestica or other muscoid larva

Slit the body wall from end to end along the mid-dorsal line and spread in the dissecting tray. Flood briefly with methylene blue or other suitable dye.

The larval head is largely in the embryonic condition and invaginated within the thorax; therefore, the brain and related organs lie within the thorax. Cut through the viscera at the fourth or fifth body segment and remove the posterior portion. There may be considerable visceral fat in the anterior region and two large salivary glands in the lateral regions. Dissect these away carefully until the nervous system is disclosed. This consists of three lobes, a pair of spherical lobes and a median ovate lobe posterior and ventral to them. The paired lobes are the *brain* and the median lobe the greatly concentrated *ventral cord*. The two are closely joined, separated only by the passage through which the slender esophagus passes. The brain may appear to consist of four lobes but the apparent anterior lobes are part of the frontal sac, the invaginated portion of the head rudiments.

Find the terminal portion of the *aorta* which passes between the lobes of the brain dorsal to the esophagus. Just in front of the brain the aorta is surrounded by a slender ring-like organ which receives on each side a branch from a rather prominent trachea. The organ is the *ring gland* or Weismann's gland which is formed by the fusion of the hypocerebral ganglion and the retrocerebral incretory glands. It has been shown that the dorsal portion of the gland is formed from the corpora allata, the ventral portion by the hypocerebral ganglion and the corpora cardiaca and that the lateral portions are probably the homologue of the prothoracic glands. It has been demonstrated experimentally that the secretions of the ring gland play a very important role in influencing the course of growth and metamorphosis.

> **DRAWING:** A dorsal view showing the ganglia, the anterior end of the aorta and the ring gland.

HISTOLOGY OF THE BRAIN AND OPTIC GANGLIA

Melanoplus or other acridid

Examine slides showing frontal sections through the brain. No one ideal section will be found, therefore it will be necessary to examine several serial sections.

Note first that the general structure of the brain is similar to that of other ganglia. On the outside you will find a thin cellular membrane, the *neurilemma,* which surrounds the brain, optic ganglia and nerves. In the peripheral *region,* internal to the neurilemma, there are large numbers of cytons. The medullary region consists almost entirely of fibers forming a neuropile, within which there are denser condensations of fibers, the *glomeruli* or association centers.

THE PROTOCEREBRUM. A deep median groove divides the protocerebrum into right and left lobes, but the term *protocerebral lobes* is sometimes used only for the lateral portions of the lobes while the median portions are known as the *interlobar region (pars intercerebralis).* In the dorsal periphery of this region you should find some large cytons which may be more deeply stained than the others. These are the *neurosecretory cells.*

Find the mushroom-shaped *corpora pedunculata,* one in each lobe. Note the concave *calyx* and the stalk or *peduncle.* The outer cavity of the calyx contains large numbers of *globuli cells,* small cytons with large nuclei and scanty cytoplasm.

Two median glomeruli lie in the interlobar region. The *protocerebral bridge (pons cerebralis)* is in the form of a thin curved plate extending transversely. The *central body (corpus centralis)* is situated ventral to the pons and contains several glomeruli.

THE DEUTOCEREBRUM. Sections through the deutocerebrum, which is ventral to the protocerebrum, show in each lobe a clearly defined *antennal center.* Within each center there are several small glomeruli arranged around a looser central neuropile. Find a section which passes through the *antennal nerve* and note that the fibers of the nerve have their origin in the center. The two centers are widely separated but are connected by a mass of transverse fibers forming the *deutocerebral commissure.*

THE TRITOCEREBRUM. The two lobes are widely separated. In each there is a small central neuropile from which the fibers of the nerves, commissure and connectives originate.

THE OPTIC GANGLION. Each ganglion is triangular in section, wide beneath the eye and narrow at its junction with the brain. Find the pigmented basement membrane of the eye and the numerous short *postretinal fibers* which pass through it to the first neuropile of the ganglion. This is the *periopticon* or *ganglionic plate (lamina ganglionaris).* From the periopticon, chiasmatic fibers pass to the second neuropile. These crossing fibers are known as the *external chiasma* and the neuropile as the *epiopticon* or the *external medullary plate (medulla externa).* Proximal to the epiopticon, other fibers, the *internal chiasma,* connect it with a third neuropile, the *opticon* or *internal medullary plate (medulla interna).* From the opticon, fibers constituting the *optic tract* pass to the important association centers of the brain, especially to the corpora pedunculata. Some commissural fibers pass from one optic ganglion to the other. It should be possible to trace some of the fiber tracts in the brain.

Find the *neurilemma* and the peripheral *cytons.* The cytons send their axons into the neuropiles where they make synapses with the postretinal fibers and with one another.

DRAWING: The brain and one optic ganglion showing in the one drawing as many as possible of the structures mentioned.

19 The Sense Organs

GENERAL CONSIDERATIONS

There is a great variety of sense organs in insects and only a few examples will be discussed and studied here. Most sensilla, apart from the eyes, were primitively associated with setae, therefore the cuticular component of these organs is usually a seta, a modified seta or sometimes, apparently, a flattened or dome-shaped plate in the position formerly occupied by a seta. In such organs the cells associated with the seta are usually present and, in addition, one or more sensory neurons whose cytons lie among or beneath the epidermal cells. From the cytons a specialized dendritic process goes to the cuticular component of the sensillum and the axon travels through a nerve to the central nervous system.

When the cuticular component is in the form of a seta the sensillum is said to be *trichoid*. When it is in the form of a cone projecting from the surface, the organ is a *sensillum basiconicum*. If the cone is sunk in a cavity beneath the surface, it is a *sensillum coeloconicum,* and if it is sunk so deep that it communicates with the surface by a tubular canal the organ is known as a *sensillum ampullaceum*. Some sensilla lack a seta-like component but have instead a dome-shaped or a flattened plate. These are known as *sensilla campaniformia* and *sensilla placodea* respectively.

There are other sensilla which have a cell complex similar to that of a seta but have no specialized cuticular component, though some of them which function as auditory organs may have an adjacent area of the cuticle modified to form a tympanic membrane. These are known as *sensilla scolopophora* or *chordotonal organs.*

215

Names based on cuticular structure were first used because the functions of some of these organs were uncertain and because sensilla with similar external appearance may have different functions.

Generally speaking, if the cuticular portion is thick-walled and there is a single nerve cell, the sensillum responds to mechanical stimuli. If it is thin-walled and there is a group of nerve cells it responds to chemical stimuli.

The *eyes* are of three kinds, compound eyes, ocelli and stemmata. The last are found only in holometabolous larvae and are the precursors of the compound eyes. The ocelli and stemmata are known as simple eyes because they have a single lens system and a single retinal system. They vary widely in structure.

Compound eyes are all built on the same general plan. They consist of a varying number of *ommatidia* or individual visual elements. Each ommatidium has the following structure. (1) The *dioptric* or lens system consists of a cuticular lens and, underlying this, a transparent group of cells or cell secretions known as the *cone*. (2) The *receptive system* consists of a group of six to eight elongated cells, arranged in a column. They constitute the *retinula* and each cell gives off a postretinal fiber to the optic ganglion. The light is focused on these cells, each of which has a specialized sensitive region known as the *rhabdom*. (3) The *pigmentary system* consists of groups of pigmented cells which isolate the ommatidium from its neighbors. Each ommatidium sees a small portion of the field and collectively they form a direct mosaic image; therefore, the larger and more convex the eye the wider is the field of vision, and the greater the number of ommatidia in a given area the more distinct is the image.

A MECHANICAL RECEPTOR

Acheta assimilis (section of cercus)

A section through any thick-walled seta of any insect will be suitable for this exercise.

Note that the seta is thick-walled and has the typical structure described earlier. Among the epithelial cells at one side of the base of the seta you will find a large, oval *sense cell*. From the distal end a short *sense rod,* containing the dendrite, extends to the base of the seta with which it makes contact. The *axon* is given off from the opposite end of the cell and travels through a nerve to the central nervous system.

It may be necessary to examine two or more sections to find all of the structures of the sense cell.

DRAWING: The seta with underlying epithelial and sense cells.

A CHEMICAL RECEPTOR

Apis mellifera (antenna)

Examine the surface of the antenna under the highest power of the dissecting microscope and note the very large number of clear oval areas. These are *sensilla placodea* or pore plates. There are some 3000 on each antenna of the worker. In addition to the plate organs there are numerous tall cones or pegs (sensilla basiconica), which are also thin-walled, and ordinary setae similar to that just examined. The thin-walled sensilla are olfactory organs.

Examine longitudinal and cross sections of the antenna and find satisfactory sections through some of the plates. Note that the plate is very thin compared with the surrounding cuticle. Underlying the entire plate you should find a large cell known as the *cap cell*. At a lower level there is another club-shaped cell whose narrow end penetrates the cap cell and terminates against the plate. This is the *enveloping cell*. It will be noted that the arrangement of these cells is exactly like that of the tormogen and trichogen of a seta.

Beneath the enveloping cell there is a thick cluster of *sense cells*. There are so many sensilla that it is difficult to isolate the sense cells of the individual sensillum, but by examining several sections, it should be possible to ascertain the arrangement of these cells.

The *distal processes* of the sense cells are arranged in a bundle which penetrates into the enveloping cell and makes connection with a slender *terminal strand* which continues distally through the cell to make contact with the plate.

The proximal processes, or axons, of the sense cells are also arranged in a bundle which travels to the central nervous system.

The cellular elements of the sensilla basiconica are arranged in the same way as those of the plate organs.

DRAWING: Reconstruction of a single sensillum.

THE COMPOUND EYE

Acheta assimilis

Sections showing all details of the compound eye are difficult to make

217

and may not be easily obtainable. Examine the slides available and find as many as possible of the following structures.

Each ommatidium has at its outer surface a small area of the cuticle modified to form the cuticular lens. Immediately beneath this there is a translucent cone-shaped body, the *crystalline cone*. Ental to the cone there is a column of elongated cells. These are the sensory cells which collectively form the *retinula*. They extend inward to the pigmented *basement membrane* of the eye and each gives off from its inner end a *postretinal fiber* which travels to the optic ganglion. If a cross section is available it will show that the retinula consists of six or seven cells arranged around what appears to be a central rod. This is the *rhabdom,* the sensitive region of the retinula, to which each cell contributes.

The longitudinal section should show three pairs of pigment cells on each side of the retinula. There are two pairs lateral to the cone. The outer ones are the *iris pigment cells,* the inner ones the *corneal cells.* An elongated *retinal pigment cell* lies on either side of the retinula. The two groups of pigment cells overlap and surround the ommatidium so that each ommatidium is completely light-insulated from its neighbors.

DRAWING: A section of an ommatidium showing as many as possible of the structures mentioned.

Bibliography

The entries listed here contain topical bibliographies which the student should consult as a guide for further reading.

BUTT, F. H. 1957. The role of the premandibular or intercalary segment in head segmentation of insects and other arthropods. *Trans. Amer. Ent. Soc.*, **83**:1-30.

COMSTOCK, J. H. 1918. The wings of insects. Ithaca, Comstock Publishing Co.

COMSTOCK, J. H. and J. G. NEEDHAM, 1898-1899. The wings of insects, *Amer. Nat.*, **32** and **33** (23 articles).

DENNELL, R. 1947. A study of an insect cuticle: The formation of the puparium of *Sarcophaga falculata Pand.* (Diptera). *Proc. Roy. Soc. (London)*, **B134**:79-110.

DuPORTE, E. M. 1956. The median facial sclerite in larval and adult Lepidoptera. *Proc. Roy. Ent. Soc. (London)*, **A31**:109-116.

DuPORTE, E. M. 1957. The comparative morphology of the insect head. *Annual Rev. Ent.*, **2**:55-70.

DuPORTE, E. M. and R. S. BIGELOW. 1953. The clypeus and epistomal suture in Hymenoptera. *Can. J. Zool.*, **31**:20-29.

FERRIS, G. F. 1940. The myth of the thoracic sclerites of insects. *Microentomology* **5**:87-90.

FERRIS, G. F. 1942. Some observations on the head of insects. *Microentomology*, **7**:25-62.

FERRIS, G. F. 1943. The basic material of the insect cranium. *Microentomology*, **8**:8-24.

FRAENKEL, G. and K. M. RUDALL. 1947. The structure of insect cuticle. *Proc. Roy. Soc. (London)*, **B134**:111-143.

GUSTAFSON, J. F. 1950. The origin and evolution of the genitalia in insects. *Microentomology*, **15**:35-67.

HANSTRÖM, B. 1928. Vergleichende Anatomie des Nervensystems der wirbellosen Tiere. Berlin, Julius Springer.

HINTON, H. E. 1947. The dorsal cranial areas of caterpillars. *Ann. Mag. Nat. Hist.*, (II) **14**:843-852 (1947).

HINTON, H. E. 1947. The gills of some aquatic beetle pupae (Coleoptera: Psephenidae). *Proc. Roy. Ent. Soc. (London)*, **A22**:52-60. Spiracular gills.

HINTON, H. E. 1955. On the structure, function and distribution of the prolegs of the Panorpoidea, with a criticism of the Berlese-Imms theory. *Trans. Roy. Ent. (London)*, **106**:445-556.

IMMS, A. D. 1957. A general textbook of entomology. 9th ed., revised by O. W. Richards and R. G. Davies. London, Methuen.

KOIDSUMI, K. 1957. Antifungal action of cuticular lipids in insects. *J. Insect Physiol.,* 1:40-51.

MICHENER, C. D. 1944. A comparative study of the appendages of the eighth and ninth abdominal segments of insects. *Ann. Ent. Soc. Amer.,* 37:336-351.

NELSEN, O. E. 1931. Life cycle, sex determination and testes development in *Melanoplus differentialis* (Acrididae, Orthoptera). *J. Morph. and Physiol.,* 51:467-525.

PRYOR, M. G. M. 1946. On the hardening of the cuticle of insects. *Proc. Roy. Soc. (London),* B128:393-497.

QUADRI, M. A. H. 1940. On the development of the genitalia and their ducts of orthopteroid insects. *Trans. Roy. Ent. Soc. (London),* 90:121-175.

RICHARDS, A. G. 1951. The integument of arthropods. Minneapolis, Univ. Minn. Press.

SNODGRASS, R. E. 1927. Morphology and mechanism of the insect thorax. *Smithsonian Misc. Collections,* 80(1):1-108.

SNODGRASS, R. E. 1928. Morphology and evolution of the insect head and its appendages. *Smithsonian Misc. Collections,* 81(3):1-158.

SNODGRASS, R. E. 1931. Morphology of the insect abdomen. Part I, General structure of the abdomen and its appendages. *Smithsonian Misc. Collections,* 85(6):1-128.

SNODGRASS, R. E. 1933. Morphology of the insect abdomen. Part II, The genital ducts and the ovipositor. *Smithsonian Misc. Collections,* 89(8):1-148.

SNODGRASS, R. E. 1935. Principles of insect morphology. New York, McGraw-Hill Book Company, Inc.

SNODGRASS, R. E. 1957. A revised interpretation of the external reproductive organs of male insects. *Smithsonian Misc. Collections,* 135(6):1-60.

SPANN, L. 1934. Studies on the reproductive system of *Gryllus assimilis Fabr. Trans. Kansas Acad. Sci.,* 37:299-340.

WIGGLESWORTH, V. B. 1951. The principles of insect physiology. 5th ed. London, Methuen.

Index

Acheta
  abdomen, 23
  circulatory system, 180
  digestive system, 159
  fat body, 182
  female reproductive organs, 188
  head, 100, 107
  integument, 146
  male reproductive organs, 195
  mouthparts, 122, 125, 127, 129
  muscles of abdomen, 28
  muscles of leg, 72
  salivary glands, 161
  thorax, 35, 38, 41, 49
Acroneuria
  abdomen of nymph, 26
  thorax, 35, 46
Acrosternite, 13
Acrotergite, 12
Aedeagus, 83
Alimentary canal
  histology of, 162
  origin of, 150
Anasa, abdomen of, 27
Anisolabis
  head, 103, 111
  labium, 131
  male genitalia, 85
Antecosta, 12
Antenna, 117
Apis
  abdomen, 27
  antenna, 119
  circulatory system, 181
  epipharynx, 124
  head, 105, 109
  legs, 72
  male reproductive organs, 198
  mouthparts, 133
  ovary, 194
  respiratory system, 173
Apodeme, 12
Arthropodin, 144

Athrocytes, 179
Axillaries, 58

Basalar plates, 41
Basicoxite, 67
Basisternite, 46
Benacus, legs of, 70
Bibio, pretarsus of, 69
Blaberus
  coxa, 68
  male genitalia, 86
Brain, 201
  histology of, 205
  metameric constitution of, 201

*C*alosoma, abdomen of larva, 22
Calyx
  of corpora pedunculata, 205
  of ovary, 187
Cantharis, head of, 113
Chauliognathus, head of, 113
Chitin, 144
Cicindela
  mandible, 127
  maxilla, 128
Clypeus, 97
Conjunctiva, 9
Conocephalus, ovipositor of, 77
Contractile vesicle, 64
Corpora allata, 203
Corpora cardiaca, 202
Corydalis, larva
  abdominal appendages, 65
  segments, 8
Coxopodite, 64
Coxosternites, 22, 46
Cuticle, 144
  tanning of, 145
Cuticulin, 144

Danaus
  female reproductive system, 192
  mouthparts, 135

221

Dorsal diaphragm, 177
Dorsal vessel, 176
Dytiscus
  anal glands, 162
  digestive tract, 161
  female reproductive organs, 191
  foreleg, 72
  head, 112
  labium, 131
  male reproductive organs, 198
  nervous system, 209

Ectophallus, 83
Ejaculatory ducts, 82, 83
Endophallus, 84
Epidermis, 145
Epimeron, 41
Epipharynx, 120
Epipleurites, 41
Episternum, 41
Eristalis, pretarsus of, 69
Esophagus, 151
Euschistus, abdomen of, 27
Eusternum, 46
Eyes, compound, 116
  structure of, 217

Fat body, 179
Frenulum, 61
Frons, 97
Frontoclypeus, 95
Frontoparietal region, 93
Furcasternite, 46

Gena, 95.
Gonapophyses, 75
Gryllotalpa, foreleg of, 71
Gula, 111
Gyrinus
  hindleg, 70
  male reproductive organs, 88

Halteres, 53
Hamuli, 61
Harpagones, 85
Harpalus
  head, 113
  labium, 131
Head
  metameric constitution, 99

orientation, 93
structure, 93
Hemocytes, 178
Hemocoele, 176
Hemolymph, 178
Heterojapyx, abdominal appendages
  of, 64
Hexagenia
  male genitalia, 85
  wing articulation, 58
Hypandrium, 25
Hypopharynx, 121
Hypostoma, 98
Hypostomal bridge, 109, 110

Intergnathal cavity, 125, 151
Intervalvula, 79

Jugum, 58, 61

Labium, 121
Labrum, 120
Leptinotarsa, head of, 104

Magicicada
  female genitalia, 80
  male genitalia, 90
Malpighian tubules, 154
Mandibles, 121, 125
Mantis
  foreleg, 70
  head, 104
Maxilla, 121, 127
Mediosternite, 44
Mediotergite, 22
Melanoplus
  abdomen, 25
  brain, 210, 213
  external anatomy, 14
  female reproductive organs, 191
  incretory glands, 211
  male reproductive organs, 196
  stomatogastric nervous system, 211
  subesophageal ganglion, 211
  trachea, histology of, 174
Meloe
  mandible, 126
  maxilla, 129
Meron, 52, 68

Mesenteron, 153
  histology of, 163
Mesonotum, 33
Metanotum, 33
Morphology, definition of, 1
Musca
  abdomen, 26
  mouthparts, 138
  ring gland of larva, 212
Muscles
  of abdominal wall, 28
  alary, 177
  of cibarium, 155
  of labium, 130
  of labrum, 123
  of leg, 72
  of mandible, 126
  of maxilla, 128
  of pharynx, 155
  of thorax, 37

Necrophorus, head of, 113
Nervous system, origin of, 200
Nesomachilis, abdominal appendages
  of, 64
Neuron, 203
Notaulices, 51

Occipital foramen, 98
Occiput, 98
Oenocytes, 180
Optic ganglion, 201
  histology of, 213
Ostia, 176
Ovipositor, 75

Panorpa, coxa of, 68
Paragnetina, thorax of, 35, 36, 46
Paramere, 83, 84
Parietals, 95
Passalus, foreleg of, 71
Pediculus, foreleg of, 70
Penis, 82
Pericardial sinus, 177
Perineural sinus, 177
Periphallic structures, 84
Peritrophic membrane, 153
Perivisceral sinus, 177

Phallobase, 83
Phallomere, 83
Phallotreme, 83
Phallus, 82
Pharynx, 151
Photinus
  oenocytes, 183
  photogenic organ, 183
Photogenic organs, 179
Phragmata, 34
Phyllophaga
  head, 111
  labium, 132
  mandible, 126
  maxilla, 129
Planta
  of pretarsus, 67
  of proleg, 66
Pleural apophysis, 41
Pleural coxal process, 41
Pleural ridge, 41
Pleural wing process, 41
Pleuron, 39
Pleurostoma, 95
Postalar bridge, 37
Postcoxal bridge, 41
Postgena, 98
Postscutellum, 34
Precoxal bridge, 41
Precoxale, 41
Prescutum, 34
Proctodaeum, 153
  histology of, 167
Pronotum, 33
Propodaeum, 28
Prothoracic gland, 173
Protoparce, larva
  cibarium, 156
  digestive tract, 156
  head, 106, 108
  labial glands, 158
  Malpighian tubules, 158
  nervous system, 207
  primary segmentation, 11
  prolegs, 65
  spiracle, 172
Pseudovipositor, 27
Pteralia, 58
Pterothorax, 9

Reproductive system, origin of, 184
Ring gland, 212
Romalea
  abdomen, 25
  external anatomy, 14
  hypopharynx, 124
  labium, 130
  leg, 66, 69
  thorax, 35, 42, 44
  wing articulation, 59

Salivary glands, 154
Sclerite, 9
Scutellum, 34
Scutum, 34
Segmentation
  primary, 11
  secondary, 11
Sense organs, classification of, 215
Seta
  glandular, 149
  structure of, 148
Sialis, abdominal appendages of, 66
Siphona, mouthparts of, 139
Spina, 46
Spinasternite, 46
Spiracles, 169, 171
Spiracular gills, 171
Sternacosta, 46
Sternal apophyses, 43, 46
Sternum, 44
Stomodaeum, 151
  histology of, 162
Stylus, 64
Subalar plates, 41
Subcoxa, 64
Subgenital plate, 24
Suture
  antecostal, 12
  basicostal, 67
  clypeogenal, 97
  coronal, 95
  defined, 9
  epistomal, 98
  frontal, 95
  frontoclypeal, 95
  frontogenal, 95
  gular, 112
  hypostomal, 98

  laterofacial, 97
  laterosternal, 46
  mid-cranial, 95
  occipital, 98
  pleural, 41
  pleurosternal, 43
  prescutal, 34
  postoccipital, 98
  scuto-scutellar, 34
  sternacostal, 46
  subgenal, 95

Tabanus, mouthparts of, 136
Tagmata, 8
Telopodite, 64
Tentorium, 113
Tergum, 33
Theca, 84
Thermobia
  abdominal appendages, 65
  ovipositor, 76
  penis, 84
Tibicen
  male genitalia, 92
  mouthparts, 140
Tipulidae, thorax of, 50
Trachea, 170
Tracheal gills, 171
Tracheoles, 170
Trophocytes
  of fat body, 179
  of ovary, 185

Urate cells, 179
Urogomphi, 22

Valvifer, 76
Valvula, 76
Ventral diaphragm, 177
Ventrosternite, 22, 44
Vertex, 95
Volsella, 90

Wings
  articulation, 58
  modifications, 60
  topography, 56
  venation, 56